The Bee, the Beetle and the Money Bug

Adhil Shetty is chief executive officer and co-founder of bankbazaar. com. With 50 million customers, BankBazaar is India's largest fintech co-branded credit card issuer and free credit score platform. Adhil has championed digitized finance and paperless lending, which help Indians in the farthest reaches of the country access credit in a contactless manner.

Adhil is one of the most widely read columnists in India. His takes on personal finance are carried regularly in well-known publications, such as *Mint, The Economic Times, Business Standard, Financial Express* and *Moneycontrol.* He is also co-chair of the FICCI Fintech Committee

A Chennai native, Adhil graduated with a masters from Columbia University, New York. He returned to India to launch BankBazaar with Rati Shetty and Arjun Shetty. He lives in Mumbai with his wife and daughter. His passions outside digital finance are cooking and watching foreign films. You can find him on LinkedIn and Twitter (@adhilshetty).

A.R. Hemant is head of communications at BankBazaar. A journalist by training, Hemant has worked with and written for *Hindustan Times,* NDTV, *India Today* and Yahoo! India before finding his calling in consumer finance. Hemant loves crunching numbers, something he has carried from his days as a cricket reporter into his current job, where he tries to make sense of mortgage rates and deposit returns.

When not overwhelming friends and family with personal finance minutiae, he can be found working for the welfare of community dogs or tweeting cricket stats. An alumnus of the Indian Institute of Mass Communication, New Delhi, Hemant has lived in six different states across the country. For now, he has home in Bengaluru with his wife and their pug Baburao. You can find him on LinkedIn and Twitter (@arhemant).

'Adhil's book is a primer that ticks every box! I first met Adhil when he had just returned to India and shared a bright idea of what is now BankBazaar. This book, in a way, incorporates his learnings in his journey at BankBazaar. It's easy to read with hardly any long boring paragraphs. It takes you from Maslow's Hierarchy Pyramid to their own 5S Pyramid (Save, Secure, Savour, Strengthen, Serenity) and then to a Systematic Kindness Plan (or the act of giving back). The book is enjoyable and educative!'

K.V. Kamath
Chairman, National Bank for Infrastructure and Development,
Former Chairman, Infosys and ICICI Bank, and
Padma Bhushan Awardee

'I mentioned Adhil's engagement with digital KYC policy in my own book. Amidst the pandemic, India made giant strides on this front with contactless video KYC. Adhil is passionate about democratized digital access to credit and personal finance for very Indian. He is playing an important role in enabling customers to understand and access the right financial product.'

Nandan Nilekani
Chairman and Co-founder, Infosys,
Founding Chairman, UIDAI (Aadhaar), and Padma Bhushan Awardee

'Adhil Shetty and bankbazaar.com were very early birds in what is now a valuation game in the Indian fintech space. Shetty did the heavy lifting of identifying and then convincing the early adapters to go online for various bank-related services, such as home loans and credit cards. I am delighted that the insights from this journey are now hard-coded in the offline world in the form of this book, which is not promising overnight wealth or multi-bagger stock tips, but a feet-on-the-ground way to be in control of your finances. Another great step forward in India's financial literacy journey.'

Monika Halan
Adjunct Professor, NISM,
and Author of *Let's Talk Money*

'Writing a book on personal finance has never been an easy task. I am glad that the author duo of bankbazaar.com, Adhil Shetty and

A.R. Hemant, have come forward and taken this responsibility. In the current times when financial frauds have increased, small customers and retail investors need to be even more vigilant, and this book is a guiding light to that. In the past couple of years, BankBazaar has excelled as a leading voice in the personal finance space, particularly in banking. The organization has been helping the masses take the right decision on banking-related issues. As a business news editor, I have collaborated with the author duo many times on various topics, be it policy rate change, loans, deposits, and so on. Whenever I have worked with them, seldom have I not been impressed by their understanding and knowledge of the subject. It gives me immense pleasure to see this book, whose readers, I believe, will be able to manage their personal finances better. This book will be a North Star for bankers and citizens alike.'

Skand Vivek Dhar
Senior Editor, Jagran New Media

'Adhil Shetty brought about a revolution in India's personal finance space when he established BankBazaar. He made comparison of loans, credit cards, deposits and many other banking products possible, all in a single place, and enabled customers to make informed choices. If information is power, Shetty has truly empowered India's consumers. The understanding of credit scores and credit reports has also exploded by leaps and bounds due to Adhil's work.'

Neil Borate
Deputy Editor, *Mint*

'Throughout my journey of two decades in personal finance journalism, my biggest observation has been this: no matter how educated people get, many remain financially illiterate throughout their lives. But there is a lesson, given by a family member when I was a kid, that I ought to remember: even a scientist has to maintain a bank account.

Personal finance is an important skill to have; we need to learn how to manage our money and how to make our money work for us. Unfortunately, our school curriculum still doesn't include personal finance as a mandatory subject. Until that happens, books such as *The Bee, the Beetle and the Money Bug* must be read.

Shetty has been a personal finance veteran and has written a number of columns across publications educating people about how to best manage their money. Just like many of his columns, the book doesn't give you the next big investment idea. It rather tells you how to get an understanding of your money box. The next big investment idea may not do you much good, but understanding how your money behaves will give you better control of it, how to better earn it, how to better invest it and how to better spend it. Do read the book.'

Kayezad E. Adajania
Editor, Personal Finance, Moneycontrol

'I remember Adhil Shetty from more than a decade ago when BankBazaar and I were relatively new in our individual pursuits. Over the years, the platform spearheaded by him has shaped into a data mine that is valued by personal finance journalists across the spectrum for its neutrality and accuracy.

Importantly, his views on everything regarding banking have always been insightful, balanced and customer-facing. Not surprisingly then, excerpts from his upcoming book promise that it is not going to be one of those get-rich-quick guides, but a dependable repository of financial wisdom.'

Nidhi Sinha
Editor, *Outlook Money*

'Adhil Shetty has been writing for *The Telegraph*'s personal finance section and the Union Budget special edition for almost a decade now. His articles have covered the whole gamut of personal finance issues—small savings, insurance, credit cards, mutual funds and home loans to just name a few. In his crisp writing style, Adhil has offered sound advice and analysis for *The Telegraph*'s readers without sounding didactic. The topics of discussion are always relevant and interesting. His articles are a joy to read because of his lucid writing style, in-depth research and understanding of the subject. Writing on technical topics for the lay reader is no mean task. Adhil has kept our readers engaged for almost a decade by coming up with fresh ideas every other week. A book on personal finance by Adhil is something to look forward to. We wish him all the best in his endeavour.'

Sucheta Mallick
Senior Assistant Editor, *The Telegraph*

The Bee,
the Beetle
and the
Money Bug

The bankbazaar GUIDE
to the FINANCIAL WILD

ADHIL SHETTY
with A.R. HEMANT

RUPA

First published by
Rupa Publications India Pvt. Ltd 2023
7/16, Ansari Road, Daryaganj
New Delhi 110002

Sales Centres:

Allahabad Bengaluru Chennai
Hyderabad Jaipur Kathmandu
Kolkata Mumbai

P-ISBN: 978-93-5520-825-5
E-ISBN: 978-93-5520-826-2

First impression 2023

10 9 8 7 6 5 4 3 2 1

The moral right of the authors has been asserted.

CONTENTS

INTRODUCTION

It isn't normal to know what we want.
It is a rare and difficult psychological achievement.

—Abraham Maslow

THE GREAT RESET

A spikey virus came alive in the wet markets of Wuhan. Life as we knew it came to a screeching halt.

With the pandemic receding in 2022, India has been making a strong comeback after witnessing some tough quarters. This book will start by taking stock of the difficulties we have been through so far. And while we begin on a somber note, I promise you that the book will end on an optimistic one.

Our recent difficulties helped frame the need for a book such as this. Globally, socio-economic uncertainties still remain. The pandemic certainly jolted us. The loss of life, income and monetary savings is yet to be fully accounted for. Uncertainties have brought with them economic hardships.

In India, the Centre for Monitoring Indian Economy said that 97 per cent Indians got poorer in terms of income in 2021. Unemployment, a lesser concern compared to the colossal death toll, soared to nearly 15 per cent in the second wave of the pandemic in India.[1] According to the World Bank, the global economy hadn't witnessed such a drop, of 3.3 per cent, since the Second World War.[2]

Emerging economies had it worse. What hurt others hurt India much more. Pew Research Center estimates that during the pandemic, around 75 million Indians fell into poverty—that is, their daily income was $2 or less.[3] The Indian middle class, those earning $10–20 a day, reduced by 32 million people.[4]

A crisis of this magnitude has exposed our vulnerabilities. Our collective resolve was needed to get over this crisis. The virus attacked not just our health but also our financial stability.

Consider the steep costs of treatment. Many swapped family gold and property for medicines, a hospital bed, or a few hours of oxygen supply. It was not a price high enough. Lives were still lost.

Survivors were not spared either. First-time investors venturing into the stock markets in 2019 took a hammering they will not forget. As the pandemic spread in the early days of 2020, years of stock market gains were wiped out. Young graduates waiting to start their careers got stuck at home. Their savings ran thin. Credit was not easily available to them. Jobs were hard to find.

The retired have been left to re-evaluate their financial plans. Globally, over the long term, interest rates have declined. This threatens the fixed income earnings of the elderly.[5] Now, they must face the double whammy of inflation spikes. Mid-career professionals and families with young children must juggle multiple financial priorities. They have spiking household expenses and loan payments, but incomes are not growing as fast as they should.

Those without health insurance were the worst-off. Hospitalization costs have never been cheap. Extreme choices had to be made. Imagine this: if everyone in your family is sick and you do not have insurance, do you pay to save a spouse, a child or a parent?

What is an individual to do in such dire straits? There are no easy answers to such questions.

There are only...

Controllables and Uncontrollables

Never let the future disturb you. You will meet it,
if you have to, with the same weapons of reason
which today arm you against the present.

—Marcus Aurelius, Roman emperor
and stoic philosopher

When systems fail and the odds seem bleak, individuals learn to stand up for themselves. But it is not enough to react to chaos. You must expect it and prepare for it. To prepare your finances for good times and bad, you need information. Knowledge is, thus, your greatest friend. It is a great strength to be able to make informed decisions inside the swirl of chaos. Decisions will have favourable or unfavourable outcomes. But when made in an informed manner, they are more likely to be favourable.

If you have picked up this book, it is because you seek information. You want to know how to make better financial decisions for desirable life outcomes. It could be regarding your child's education, buying a home or becoming financially independent. This book aims to provide you not only with the awareness required to control your 'controllables' but also prepare you for the 'uncontrollables'.

You cannot stop a contagion. You cannot expect the stock market to act rationally. You may even try in vain to tell dictators not to start costly wars that heighten inflation. These are examples of uncontrollable variables. They bring chaos.

Chaotic situations, such as the Covid-19 pandemic, are the worst-case, once-in-a-century scenarios. There is life outside such hopelessness. That life is full of possibilities and positive outcomes. We must strive towards that life, aligning our financial choices with it.

If your decisions and reactions are informed, you have better chances of reaching your preferred future—not just in terms of your finances but also life. With planning and a little bit of luck, you will get better at creating positive outcomes for yourself. That will put you on the path to Serenity.

What's in This Book for You?

Since 2008, I have been the CEO of BankBazaar. The company is now India's largest co-brand credit platform and online provider of free credit score services.

In the same period, I have also been a contributor to the personal finance sections of some of India's best-known publications, such as *Mint, The Economic Times, The Times of India, Dainik Bhaskar* and *Outlook Money.*

I have had a chance to track, study and deeply understand the challenges faced by Indian households in managing their money. My job has also given me a ringside view of both the regulatory evolution supporting the growth of financial services and the systemic problems that prevent people from managing their money better.

Be it selling financial products through BankBazaar or writing on issues of personal finance, my aim is to help consumers make the best possible financial decisions for themselves.

Being able to take those good decisions is easier said than

done. Financial literature is often steeped in obfuscation and jargon. This does not help in a country with low rates of financial literacy. So we aim to simplify financial literature, take the jargon out and make it easier for people to understand money. They will apply the information to critical decisions and experience better life outcomes.

This book will be an attempt to distil my learnings on personal finance into an easy-to-read page-turner. I hope that it improves a layperson's understanding of money management, giving them greater control over the controllables in their lives.

Who will find this book useful?

A huge chunk of BankBazaar's visitors fall within the age bracket of 22–35 years. Firstly, there are the young people who have just begun their working lives. They need handholding when it comes to making financial decisions. They fall in the 22–27 age bracket. We call them Early Jobbers. They may have a salary account and aspirations to fulfil, but they do not have experience with money management.

Then there is the 28–35 age group. This bunch has already taken a loan, made an investment or have financial responsibilities towards their families. We call them Moneymooners. They are more financially informed than Early Jobbers. They broadly know what they want to do with their money. But they, too, need validation for and refinement in their financial plans.

These two cohorts visit BankBazaar in the millions. They compare and buy the products we sell. They read the articles and see the videos we produce on subjects as diverse as credit card charges, government saving schemes or interest rates.

The learning has not been one-way. We, too, have learnt from them. We have learnt of their financial problems, their financial constraints and what gets in the way of their aspirations. Through our writings, we have aimed to quench their thirst for simplified financial content. We have done it for years. And now, with this book, we bring our learnings to you.

If you are not an Early Jobber or a Moneymooner, you may simply be a person looking for a foot in the door. The wild world of personal finance might be calling out to you, but you do not know where or how to start. You might even be hesitant or procrastinating. You might be in need of a push. My hope is that this book provides you a nudge in the right direction.

The 5S Pyramid

In 1943, American psychologist Abraham Maslow proposed a hierarchy of human needs. In his paper, titled A Theory of Human Motivation[6], Maslow imagined human needs layered like a pyramid.

'[...] the appearance of one need usually rests on the prior satisfaction of another, more pre-potent need,' he wrote.[7] Man is a perpetually wanting animal, he explained. His higher needs can be met only after the base ones are satisfied.

Maslow classified human needs as physiological well-being, safety, love, esteem and self-actualization. At the base of Maslow's hierarchy lie physiological needs. These can be the absolute basic needs critical to survival: nutrition, water, clothes, sleep or sex. Maslow explains that physiological needs, such as food, take precedence when all other needs in the upper tiers of the hierarchy remain unmet. Everything else is pushed into the background. 'For the man who is extremely and dangerously hungry, no other interests exist but food,' he wrote.[8]

Next come safety needs. These are connected to physical safety, health and financial security. 'The peaceful, smoothly running, "good" society ordinarily makes its members feel safe enough from wild animals, extremes of temperature, criminals, assault and murder, tyranny, etc.,' Maslow wrote.[9]

He suggested that hunger and safety are lesser needs in the modern world. 'The healthy, normal, fortunate adult in our culture is largely satisfied in his safety needs,' he said.[10] If you have stepped out to buy groceries at the local supermarket, there is next to no chance of you being mauled by a lion.

But more discerning readers may be able to infer that some of the securities mentioned above are now at risk. It should be noted that risks evolve with time and, thus, we must prepare for them. For example, a twenty-first-century Indian is at a much greater risk from extreme temperatures, but at a lower risk from malaria in comparison to a nineteenth-century Indian for whom the opposite may be true.

HIERARCHY OF NEEDS
Abraham Maslow

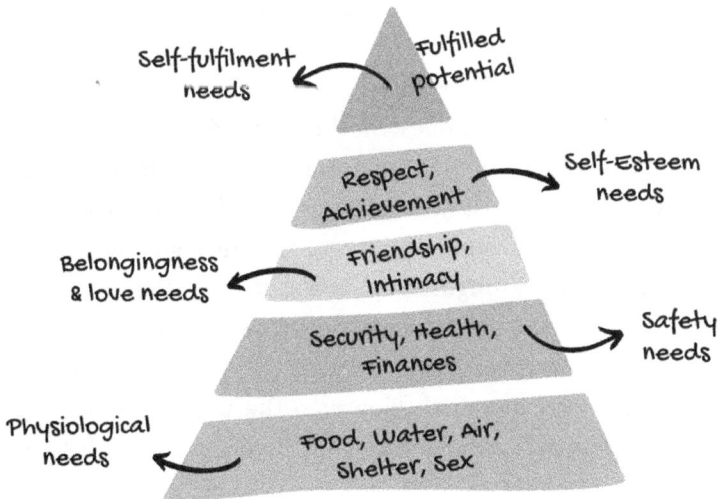

After these comes the need for love: friendship, intimacy, relationships and people to share your life with. Then, there are needs related to esteem: confidence in oneself, getting respect from others and establishing achievements.

Lastly, there's the need for self-actualization, which is fulfilling one's potential and finding happiness. 'A musician must make music, an artist must paint, a poet must write, if he is to be ultimately happy. What a man can be, he must be,' wrote Maslow.[11]

At BankBazaar, we were inspired to create our own hierarchy of financial needs of every household. We called it the 5S Pyramid. Like the simplified Maslow's hierarchy, the 5S Pyramid has five layers: Save, Secure, Savour, Strengthen and Serenity. This explains its name.

Starting with the all-important base of the pyramid, which is about savings, the book will talk about building your finances from the ground up.

It will help you secure your finances with insurance, savour your money and life in a guilt-free manner, strengthen yourself by building assets and achieve peace of mind—Serenity—when it is time for you to let go of your worries.

The 5S Pyramid mimics Maslow's hierarchy. Savings are the building blocks of your financial life. Without them, the rest is not possible. Insurance secures your finances. Savouring is about responsibly enjoying your life with your loved ones. The fourth layer, strengthening, is about investing and home ownership. It provides you with a sense of achievement in your financial life. And finally, Serenity is about the fulfilment of your financial potential. However, the path to Serenity is not straightforward. The vagaries of life often get in the way.

THE 5S PYRAMID
BankBazaar

Serenity ← Credit score, Debt-free assets, Retirement

Home, Assets, Investments → Strengthen

Savour ← Credit card, Personal loan, BNPL

Insurance: Health, Term, Vehicle, Property → Secure

Save ← Savings, Fixed deposits, Liquid mutual funds

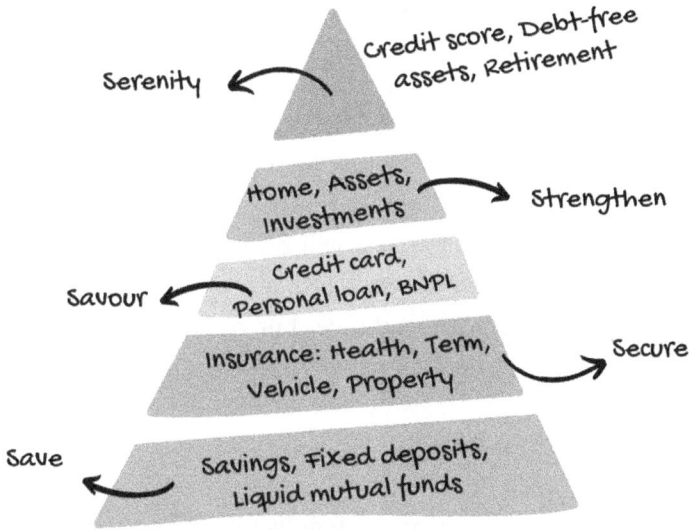

For example, let us take the simple matter of a savings account. Ordinarily, it should be a no brainer to park your funds in a bank account instead of stuffing them under your mattress. Right? Unfortunately, in these last few years, Indian depositors have had the rude shock of seeing their banks being put under moratorium by the Reserve Bank of India (RBI).

A moratorium is a temporary pause on a particular activity. In this case, it was a pause on depositors being able to withdraw money from their bank accounts. It was for a good reason: to preserve the bank's health.

The moratoria were necessary to prevent large-scale withdrawals by panicky depositors, which could have destabilized those banks. But the moratoria also made it difficult for depositors to access their funds for critical needs, such as education, medical treatments or weddings.

Therefore, it is not enough to have a 'fill it, shut it, forget it' approach to a savings account. It is also important to be aware of risks, such as the deteriorating financial health of one's bank.

What are these risks, and how can you identify and reduce them? How safe is your bank? How can you optimize the safety of your money and not lose guaranteed returns? Where should you draw the line on bank deposits? These are some of the savings-related issues that we will dive deep into.

From there, we will work our way upwards, simplifying other complex topics: insurance, borrowing, investing, asset building, home ownership and retirement planning.

What This Book Will Not Do

The aim of this book is not to help you become rich in a year.

It does not aim to tell you which upcoming company could give you 1,000 per cent returns on a stock investment. It also will not tell you the best insurance policy or mutual fund (MF) you could buy today. It would be beyond the scope of this book to make such fantastic claims.

If you are a layperson, reading this book will tell you about the bare minimum you need to achieve with your money. This book will help you structure your finances. It will help you understand goal-setting, risks and rewards, and mistakes to avoid.

In the end, this book will also delve deep into the things that you need to figure out for yourself—like your financial legacy, giving back to society or which of your heirs get your assets after you.

This knowledge, I hope, will empower you enough to answer the unanswered questions yourself. And then, you will be able to take rewarding investment decisions, find financial security and stability, and achieve Serenity.

In short, the point of this exercise is financial literacy. And so much more needs to be done towards achieving this goal.

India is currently home to about 20 per cent of the world's population. In 2015, a global survey by Standard & Poor suggested that barely 24 per cent of India's adult population is financially literate.[12] This was well below the global average of 33 per cent or the much higher 52 per cent in the European Union.[13]

Another study by the National Centre for Financial Education in 2019 arrived at somewhat the same conclusion: India had around 80 per cent literacy, but financial literacy languished at a lowly 27 per cent.[14]

For a country to realize its full economic potential, the management of its resources is important. For most Indian families, money is a meagre resource. Managing it well will unlock upward social mobility. But that cannot precede financial literacy. It must happen first. It must happen now.

With this book, we are about to undertake a journey into the financial wild. It is only fitting that we draw cues from Mother Nature.

From the honey-gathering worker bee, we learn diligence and consistency when we save money.

From an ironclad beetle, with its unbreakable exterior, we learn to protect our finances.

From the bowerbird, we learn to express ourselves and savour life.

If this book helps you become more aware of your finances and nudges you towards Serenity, its objective would be fulfilled.

Now, let us move ahead to lay the base of our 5S Pyramid.

I

SAVINGS AND THE BUILDING BLOCKS OF YOUR FINANCIAL LIFE

THE BEE

Saving up is a challenge. Just ask a worker bee.

A dozen worker bees would have to work their entire lives to make a teaspoon of honey, which is barely enough to sweeten a cup of tea. It is hard work to find, collect, transport and process nectar till the time it becomes the yellow sticky thing you have with breakfast.

The worker bee's lifespan, which could range from a few weeks to a few months, is spent making food. It locates flowers and sucks out the nectar using its long tongue. It has two stomachs—with one being used for storing and transporting nectar. To fill that, it has to visit over a thousand flowers—a heavy burden indeed.

The bee is not just making food to ensure the survival of its colony through harsh and bloomless winters, it is also cross-pollinating crops, powering a multi-trillion dollar global agricultural industry and ensuring human survival.

The bee sometimes carries as much cargo as its body weight. The enzymes in its stomach help turn the nectar into honey. Once back at the colony, it pumps out the nectar through its mouth into the mouth of a receiver bee, which adds its enzymes and vomits the semi-processed honey into an empty hive cell. But the nectar is still thin. Much still needs to be done. The bee then flaps its wings about 12,000 times a minute to fan and thicken the nectar. Finally, it secretes wax from its abdomen to cover the cell to protect this food, which offers sweet nutrition to help sustain its demanding work life.

A bee's life reminds us of the little things that lay the foundation of life on Earth. Here is a lesson in personal finance. Bees tell us about the enormous challenges as well as the fitting rewards of saving up.

It is not easy to save money, but save you must. Savings are the building blocks of your finances; the very thing that would one day make it possible for you to buy a home, take that vacation you always wanted, educate your children or retire on your terms. And just like the bee, you must give it all you have.

Why Save?

Savings make the base of our 5S Pyramid. They enable your ascent to the peak of the pyramid—Serenity.

Opening a savings account with a bank or post office is the first step in the process of financial growth and the fulfilment of one's aspirations. All other financial progress stems from here: taking a loan, buying insurance, using your preferred payment app or investing for wealth creation. Just like the satisfaction of one's physiological needs forms the basis in Maslow's hierarchy, having a savings account is the crux of the 5S Pyramid.

If you are reading this book, it is likely that you already own one or multiple savings accounts. Therefore, you already know about its basic benefits. As per a World Bank report, 80 per cent of Indian adults owned a savings account as of 2017[1], compared to 53 per cent in 2014.[2]

The number may have improved in later years, thanks to the deepening internet and cell phone penetration, and financial awareness. These have enabled digital account openings at a grand scale.

THE 5S PYRAMID
BankBazaar

Serenity ← Credit score, Debt-free assets, Retirement

Home, Assets, Investments → Strengthen

Savour ← Credit card, Personal loan, BNPL

Insurance: Health, Term, Vehicle, Property → Secure

Save ← Savings, Fixed deposits, Liquid mutual funds → You're here

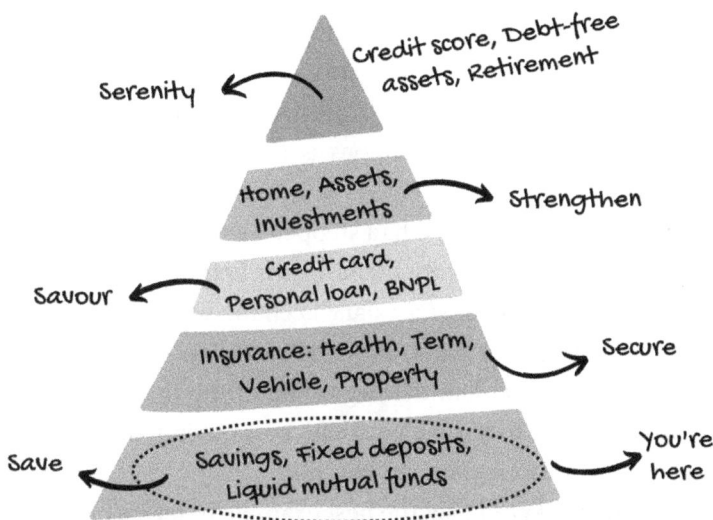

But saving is not merely about ensuring a bank balance. There is much more to it. It is a skill, an art, a science and, above all, a constant challenge.

Therefore, over the next few chapters, with the help of case studies, stories and anecdotes, we are going to look at ways that will help you save in a smarter way and help you move from the base of the 5S Pyramid to its peak.

My First Savings Account

My career started with Cisco Systems in 2001. I worked in Bengaluru. I used to cycle to work. My home was on Rest House Road and my workplace on Richmond Road. I would ride my bicycle through Cubbon Park to get to work. The office was in the then quiet Bengaluru, near the hockey stadium.

One day, my boss saw me riding to work. She asked me if I had trouble paying for transport. She even generously offered to give me a raise if my income was not enough. I assured her that my biking was for non-financial reasons, that I enjoyed cycling and it was good for health. Besides, anyone who has taken a walk through Cubbon Park will tell you that being in its oxygenated and leafy confines is one of the great joys of living in Bengaluru.

This was the first time I had stepped away from my parents' home in Chennai. It was after landing my first job that I opened my first savings account: a salary account with HSBC Bank. The first money that came into that account was my salary from Cisco. This marked the beginning of my many firsts: my first income, my first rent payment and buying the first gift using my own money for my parents.

Looking back, did I set the best example in terms of saving? Probably not. I enjoyed a good life in that period between 2001 and 2003. I managed to save only a little and ended up spending nearly everything I had earned. In retrospect, at the very least, I should have started a savings plan. Now, I always recommend that people save at least 20 per cent of their disposable income.

I am today convinced that that adage is true: being rich is not how much money you have, but spending less than you earn.

The Importance of Savings

Bank savings constitute a large chunk of household savings in this country. The RBI said in June 2020 that currency and bank deposits formed nearly 70 per cent of India's household financial assets.[3] The central bank describes these assets as 'bank deposits, debt securities, MFs, insurance, pension funds and small savings'. Of this, commercial bank deposits constitute a whopping 52.6 per cent. Currency holdings are at 13.4 per cent. Deposits with cooperative banks form another 3.8 per cent. These bring the value tied to bank deposits and cash holdings to 69.8 per cent of household assets.[4]

Indians are over-dependent on their humble savings account. It, therefore, becomes much more important to use it smartly. It is not enough for a bee to create honey. It should also be able to enjoy it.

Savings, when managed smartly, leads to liquidity, which can be used in times of need, insurance against economic risks, better return on investment and timely repayment of debts. Above all, smart savings leads to the achievement of our objective: reaching the apex of our 5S Pyramid, which is Serenity.

How Much Should You Save?

Alpana, an Early Jobber, lost her job as an accountant in Chennai when her company downsized in the aftermath of the 2019 economic slowdown. Many of her peers also lost their jobs. The situation, however, did not perturb Alpana. She has always followed a simple rule of thumb: she saves up to at least six times her monthly income as a fixed deposit (FD) with the bank she has her salary account in.

Alpana calls this money her emergency fund. She had started saving up as soon as she had started working. She concluded that to be financially independent, it is not enough to have a job and an income stream. She knew she also needed money in her account to be truly secure.

When she lost her job, she did not have to return to her hometown, like some of her co-workers. She continued staying in Chennai. Thanks to her savings, she could continue paying rent and meet her other necessary expenses, such as food, healthcare, utilities and transportation. After a three-month wait, she landed a new job. The savings, thus, ensured that Alpana could avoid the setback of being pushed back to her hometown from where a professional comeback could have been difficult.

Table 1

Emergency Funds and How Long It Takes to Create It				
Monthly Take-Home Income	20 Per Cent Savings	Emergency Fund Size		
		3 x Income	6 x Income	9 x Income
₹25,000	₹5,000	₹75,000	₹150,000	₹225,000
₹35,000	₹7,000	₹105,000	₹210,000	₹315,000
₹50,000	₹10,000	₹150,000	₹300,000	₹450,000
₹75,000	₹15,000	₹225,000	₹450,000	₹675,000
₹100,000	₹20,000	₹300,000	₹600,000	₹900,000
Time Needed To Create Fund*		~15 months	~28 months	~41 months

*Using a recurring deposit returning 5.5 per cent. Income tax as applicable. Time required will be lower with a higher interest rate and lower with a lower rate.

It brings us to the two most important questions about savings. One: have you created an emergency fund? Two: how much savings do you consider enough?

The first is a simple yes-or-no question. An emergency fund is your rainy-day purse. If you have not created your emergency fund, waste no time. Get started on it right away.

Emergencies can arrive in any form and hurt your everyday finances. For example, in India, expensive hospitalizations push

7 per cent of the population below the poverty line every year.[5]

You might lose your job or business. There might be an urgent need for travel. Your plumbing repair might cost you dearly. It is best to anticipate and prepare for such contingencies.

The second question is more difficult to answer. There is no one-size-fits-all answer. You must find one that suits your unique situation.

In this book, we are going to examine answers to many questions like these. The answers require calculations. Sometimes, the answer is arrived at by extensive number crunching. At other times, we find the answer through a rule of thumb, which is an oversimplified solution to the problem.

For instance, we say that the rule of thumb for an ideal emergency fund is that it should be three to six times your monthly income. This can help you tide over a wide variety of emergencies. But if the risks involved are higher, the emergency fund needs to be bigger. For example, you might have a health condition that requires frequent medical intervention that is not covered by your health insurance.

Note that your progress to savings, which are three to six times your monthly income, will take time. You can start by setting aside at least 20 per cent of your monthly take-home pay as compulsory savings at the beginning of every month. If you have high disposable income, aim to save a higher per centage.

The emergency fund is the most basic form of saving. It is also necessary not to confuse it with other forms of savings, such as those for retirement, achieving life goals like buying a house, or for children's education and marriage.

Each objective for saving is unique. Each objective requires its own approach for fulfilment. Mixing up your objectives may make it difficult for you to achieve any of them.

Saving Too Little and Saving Too Much

Manoj, 25, works at a leading start-up in Gurgaon. It is his first job. He earns ₹42,000 a month. His significant expenses every month include rent, takeaways, transportation and entertainment. He has no savings so far. Recently, he came down to his last thousand bucks as he entered the last week of the month. It made sustenance tricky. He had to borrow from his parents to make ends meet till his next pay cheque reached his bank. He needs to review his priorities to avoid experiencing acute financial stress again. He needs to save proactively and cut down on non-essential spending.

Let us compare Manoj to Lenny, 26. He is in his second job at a firm in Noida, earning ₹75,000 per month.

Lenny's finances are sorted. He eats home-cooked meals, rides a scooter to work and spends lightly on entertainment. He lives in a shared accommodation and splits rent with his co-workers. He now has more than ₹450,000 saved in his salary account. These are passive savings. He made no attempt to save this sum proactively. The savings accumulated because he lives frugally and spends much less than he earns. Each month, he saves close to ₹40,000. The money stays in his account, unspent.

Lenny is in a better place to manage his liquidity needs in comparison to Manoj. Lenny keeps the money in his account because he believes he could need it any moment. To him, this is the easiest way to access his funds. Unfortunately, such financial behaviour, too, is problematic.

American rapper Snoop Dogg once said, 'If you stop at general math, you are only going to make general math money.' A large, unspent balance at the month end is good, but still a problem. It reveals that Lenny's money does not get proactively managed. He is earning a much lower rate of return than he ought to on his savings. On the other hand, Manoj's problem is that he is not saving at all.

A savings account will typically pay you interest at the rate of 3–4 per cent per annum. As a crude example, ₹1,000 saved for a year at 4 per cent will give you ₹40 as interest, which is a very low return. Therefore, you should move surplus liquidity into savings and investment instruments that can provide better returns.

Now, here is how Manoj and Lenny have decided to remedy their respective problems.

Manoj has started saving ₹8,000 at the beginning of every month before he spends a single rupee. While it continued to stretch his finances, he now has the option of dipping into his savings instead of borrowing from his parents or using his credit card.

On the other hand, Lenny has started keeping only ₹50,000 as surplus funds in his salary account. He has moved the rest of his savings into an FD that gives him 6 per cent interest. He is, therefore, earning 50 per cent higher than the 4 per cent his savings account provides. He has also decided to divert his future savings towards more attractive investments, like MFs and a provident fund (PF), where his returns could be much higher than 6 per cent.

Where Should You Save Your Money?

Let us take stock of ongoing challenges in the banking industry.

Your bank deposits are like a loan to the bank—the bank pays you an interest on the loan. Your deposit is the raw material of the lending industry. Banks attract deposits in various forms, such as salary accounts or current accounts. They then use the funds to create lending products, such as loans and credit cards.

You earn 3–6 per cent interest on your deposits. Banks earn interest on their loans, typically starting at 7–8 per cent. This difference in interest rates keeps banks in business.

Therefore, for you as a lender to your bank, it is important that the bank repays you on time—which is whenever you need your money. This is possible when the bank's own borrowers repay their loans on time.

If those borrowers are unable to repay their dues, their loans turn 'bad'. Then, the bank finds it harder to pay back your deposit. The larger its bad loans, the tougher it is for a bank to repay its depositors. A bad loan is one against which dues are unpaid for 90 days. It gets classified as a non-performing asset (NPA). Unfortunately, India has had an NPA problem in the recent past.

Loans are assets for the bank. Deposits are liabilities.

In December 2019, the RBI said that commercial banks in India had a gross NPA ratio of 9.1 per cent.[6] It means that for every ₹100 loaned out by commercial banks in India, ₹9.1 had turned bad.

With the economic disruption caused by the Covid-19 pandemic, this ratio was expected to deteriorate to the double digits again. Thankfully, it went in the other direction. The RBI reported in March 2022 that the gross NPA ratio had improved to 5.9 per cent, the lowest it had been since March 2015.[7]

That said, India fares poorly on this metric globally. A 2019 survey of the 11 largest emerging economies showed that India ranked last on this metric.[8] In comparison, China was at 1.8 per cent, Brazil was at 3.1 per cent and Mexico at 2.1 per cent, as per 2019-Q2 numbers.

But what does it mean to you, the depositor? Let us understand the problem through a recent example.

In 2020, it was reported that a cooperative bank had given

73 per cent of all its loans fraudulently to a single troubled corporate entity, which later defaulted on its dues.[9] In case of a default, a borrower is unable to repay a loan within the stipulated time frame as mentioned in the loan agreement.

The money had gone out from the bank. It was not coming back because the borrower was in deep trouble. When depositors of the bank found out, they attempted a bank run. In a bank run, a large per centage of a bank's depositors try to withdraw their money. They do so as they are anxious about the bank's ability to repay their deposits.

Sensing the bank's collapse, the RBI had stepped in and restricted withdrawals from the bank. Initially, depositors could withdraw a pittance of ₹1,000. Eventually, the RBI raised the limit to ₹10,000 and later to ₹1 lakh. This allowed 84 per cent of the depositors to get their money out.[10] But it left the remaining 16 per cent depositors, who held large deposits at the bank, in the lurch. Neither could they access their money, nor could they make a deposit insurance claim that would have allowed them to recover some of their money.

A bank with large NPAs poses risks to its depositors, who may not be able to get their money out. But there are checks and balances in the banking system to provide security to depositors to some degree. For example, the Deposit Insurance and Credit Guarantee Corporation (DICGC), an RBI subsidiary, provides insurance for deposits up to ₹5 lakh per depositor per bank.[11] The DICGC ensures that the depositor's money—both principal and interest—stays safe to the extent of ₹5 lakh, be it with commercial or cooperative banks.

Such insurance coverage kicked in when the RBI cancelled a bank's licence and its liquidation started. Within this, a company's assets are sold—or liquidated—to raise funds to pay off the people it owes money to.

The requirement of licence cancellation created a grey area in which banks' licences were not being cancelled, but they were being put under indefinitely long moratoria, barring depositors from withdrawing their funds.

In 2021, this shortcoming was finally addressed. Finance Minister Nirmala Sitharaman announced in her 2021 Union Budget speech that the insurance coverage would be extended to cases where banks are temporarily unable to repay depositors. 'I shall be moving amendments to the DICGC Act, 1961 in this Session itself to streamline the provisions, so that if a bank is temporarily unable to fulfil its obligations, the depositors of such a bank can get easy and time-bound access to their deposits to the extent of the deposit insurance cover,' the finance minister said in her speech.[12]

However, the upper limit of ₹5 lakh still applies. Anything over and above for the depositor is at risk.

This brings us back to the big question: where is it safe for you to keep your money? Would it be safe in a piggy bank? Under your mattress? With your parents?

The answer is simple. Despite the risks—real or perceived—your money is safest in the custody of a large, stable bank. It is your best bet. Large Indian banks have an excellent track record in managing depositor's money. No large Indian bank has failed since India's independence. I use the word 'large' to differentiate between well-capitalized banks that have excellent corporate governance, quality customer service and relatively low levels of NPAs and smaller banks that do not.

There were eight banks for which the DICGC settled deposit insurance claims in 2020–21.[13] All eight were cooperatives. As per the RBI's notices, their earning potential was badly hurt and their ability to manage depositor funds had come under doubt.

Banking-related risks need to be understood and managed. Let us take a deeper look at how to manage these risks.

Diversify Your Savings

We have established that a large bank is the best place to keep your money. Consider your bank a temporary parking spot for your income. It should hold the cash you need for your immediate wants and needs. These could be cash for your rent, EMIs, groceries, utilities, and so on. The rest of your savings should ideally sit in an FD or an investment account, where it will earn a higher rate of return.

Diversity in savings and investment is necessary. We will cover diversification of investments in 'Strengthen', the chapter on investments. For now, let us focus on diversification of savings.

Depending on the type of flowers and trees in a beehive's vicinity, the flavour of the honey varies in colour, texture and taste. Similarly, different kinds of savings provide you with different advantages, such as diversified rates of return, more points of access to your money and higher safety of your capital.

Let us understand this with an example.

Shravan has one account each in a government, private and a local cooperative bank. He receives his salary in the government bank account. He uses this account to park his cash for immediate needs. This account pays him interest at the rate of 3 per cent.

He transfers surplus funds into the private bank account. From there, he gets 6 per cent interest on a recurring deposit (RD), which he uses for creating his emergency fund.

Shravan also opened an FD of ₹1 lakh with the cooperative bank, which was giving him an unusually high return of

7 per cent. However, he understood that a high exposure to this bank may not be in his best interest. Lately, there have been news reports of rising NPAs there.

These three accounts helped Shravan ensure that:

1. His capital remains safe with two large banks.
2. He gets better average returns by splitting his money in multiple accounts as per his risk tolerance.
3. He creates multiple points of access to his money, and if there is any problem with one bank, he can approach the other two.
4. He keeps his deposits below the deposit insurance limit of ₹5 lakh in the cooperative bank. If that bank goes under, his money would stay protected.

Tools That Help You Save

Savings Accounts

The Indian banking ecosystem is diverse. It provides you many options in terms of where you can hold your money. As far as savings accounts are concerned, you can choose from government banks, private banks, small finance banks, cooperative banks and even the humble post office.

I often get asked by family members about which of these is their best option. I always respond with my own version of the adage from *Spiderman*: with low risk comes low return. The deposit interest rates at large government banks are the lowest. Government savings—both banks and postal savings— are perceived to carry the least risk. Same goes for large private banks.

Across the market, we typically see that the deposit interest rates at large banks, which are perceived to be safe, tend to be mostly, but not always, lower than their smaller peers. Interestingly, even the public sector postal savings tend to offer higher interest returns than private banks.

Further, the returns offered by private banks are lower than those given by small finance banks, an RBI-designated category of local banks. These, too, are private banks. But they have very small market shares and considered riskier than the large private banks.

It is advisable to park the bulk of your savings with large, stable banks and go for a carefully calibrated exposure when it comes to smaller banks.

How much exposure to small banks is safe? As mentioned before, if a small bank happens to go belly-up, your deposits up to ₹5 lakh can be claimed through deposit insurance. You however, might not be able to recover the rest.

Today, thanks to changes in regulations, you can open a savings account from the comfort of your house. Banks have enabled digital account openings, which allow you to authenticate yourself using Aadhaar and Permanent Account Number (PAN).[14]

Your PAN is your tax identity and is mandatory for several financial tasks such as opening a bank account, making investments, taking a loan and filing taxes.

The authentication process, also known as the Know Your Customer (KYC) process, is critical to account openings from a regulatory standpoint. KYC establishes that the person opening an account is indeed who he says he is.

The RBI has done some stellar policy work during the pandemic, due to which customers today can use video KYC to complete the process of opening their bank account. Earlier, you were required to meet a bank officer at the branch or at home for opening an account. Now, the officer validates your identity remotely over a video call.

I must congratulate the officials at the RBI for creating such a forward-looking policy that is now in action at every bank in India, enabling paperless digital account openings of customers through their cell phones.

Considering pandemic-related difficulties, the RBI is going to treat digital KYC as full KYC.[15]

Fixed and Recurring Deposits

As per the RBI's quarterly estimates report for June 2020, deposits at commercial and cooperative banks form about 56 per cent of household financial assets.[16] They are the bedrock of the 5S Pyramid. They stabilize your household finances and help you prepare for achieving your other goals as specified in the pyramid: Secure, Savour, Strengthen and Serenity.

FDs, also known as term or time deposits, are a fixed-interest loan to a bank or post office. Its term may range from seven days to a decade. A savings tool offering moderately higher returns than a savings account, the humble FD is loved for its assured returns and capital safety.

A one-time deposit is an FD, while an RD requires you to make a fixed monthly contribution for six months to 10 years. When created at the same bank, FDs and RDs offer the same returns. While an RD is ideal for creating your emergency fund, an FD is ideal for holding it. During an urgent need, you can liquidate either. You will only lose a portion of your interest for the premature liquidation. FDs can be availed in several variants.

One is the tax-saving FD with five-year lock-ins that helps you save income tax under Section 80C of the Income Tax Act.

The other is the sweep-in FD facility. Here, your bank automatically transfers surplus funds over a defined limit into an FD, where you will earn higher returns. This is a great tool for lazy savers. The bank can be instructed to automatically do the savings on their behalf.

You can open and operate an FD or RD with your bank through netbanking or the mobile application of your bank. In case of post office deposits, you will have to visit your nearest post office with your documents.

Interestingly, we have the concept of FDs for senior citizens, too. These typically earn 25 to 50 basis points more than regular FDs. One basis point is one-hundredth of a per centage. This makes them a safe and attractive option for senior citizens, who prefer capital safety and guaranteed returns.

This is interesting because not all forms of savings and investments have a senior citizen variant. You do not get a senior citizen MF or a senior citizen stock investment plan, for example.

However, young people—and I consider myself in that category, being in my 40s—need to avoid making the mistake of investing only through FDs. This is because they yield low post-tax returns. Therefore, a 7 per cent FD returns only 4.9 per cent if your highest marginal income tax rate is 30 per cent. In a later chapter, 'Strengthen', we will look at why low returns will not help you create wealth.

FDs and RDs are good for capital safety and moderate returns. But they are terrible for long-term investment owing to their low returns. In summary, use bank deposits for savings and not investments.

Liquid MFs

Being a smart saver is about gouging out an extra per centage or two in interest without taking undue risks. There are many ways to do this. Liquid Mutual Funds (LMFs) are one of them.

The MF marketplace is vast and colourful. It has tonnes of options for just about any financial objective—even savings. We will take a deeper look at it in 'Strengthen'.

First and foremost arises the question, 'What is a mutual fund?' It is money pooled by several investors and managed by a fund manager who decides which financial securities to buy, hold or sell. These are difficult decisions for a layperson to make. They are, therefore, best left in the hands of a professional money manager.

MFs can be bought from online distributors, banks, offline agents or even directly from the MF house's website. For getting started with an MF investment, all you need is an operational KYC-compliant bank account. Every MF has a theme. When you buy any MF, you are essentially buying a collection of securities selected as per the fund's theme.

Equity funds buy stocks in high-performing companies. Debt funds invest in the government and corporate bond markets. Liquid funds invest in money market instruments—highly liquid debt instruments, such as treasury bills issued by the Government of India.

LMFs have the reputation of sometimes providing marginally higher returns than bank deposits. In the past, we have seen this difference to be as much as 100 to 200 basis points. In the decade gone by, LMFs had often returned 7–9 per cent per annum.

The pandemic years have not been great for LMFs and their returns are now comparable to those of a savings account, offering 3–5 per cent. However, interest rates have started rising in 2022, and so the LMF returns will go up.

Understand the first difference between an FD and an MF. While an FD advertises a fixed return that you will earn at the end of the term, an MF does not. It is composed of market securities, whose values fluctuate daily and, therefore, cannot guarantee returns. An FD advertises forward returns. An MF can only advertise its backward returns, and backward returns do not guarantee forward returns.

For example, an FD guarantees you will earn 6 per cent over the next year. It is a fixed, assured return. But an MF cannot guarantee a return. Its performance depends on market conditions and the fund manager's abilities. It can only advertise returns earned in the past. For example, an LMF may say it earned 9 per cent in 2013. But past returns do not guarantee that the same LMF will earn 9 per cent again in 2022.

Notwithstanding this, LMFs are considered among the least risky MFs. This is because the securities they are composed of are stable, offering guaranteed returns and liquidity. LMFs typically contain liquid debts that mature in a short period of time—91 days or less. The short maturity makes them immune to risks that can cause volatility in other debt MFs that carry bonds with longer maturity durations of years or even decades.

Let us simplify the above paragraph further. Plotted on a graph, an LMF's growth would appear as an almost straight line. This represents stability, steady growth and extremely low chances of suffering losses.

On the other hand, a long-term debt fund, whose returns will fluctuate basis interest rate movements in the financial markets, will plot somewhat like a roller coaster ride.

Graph 1

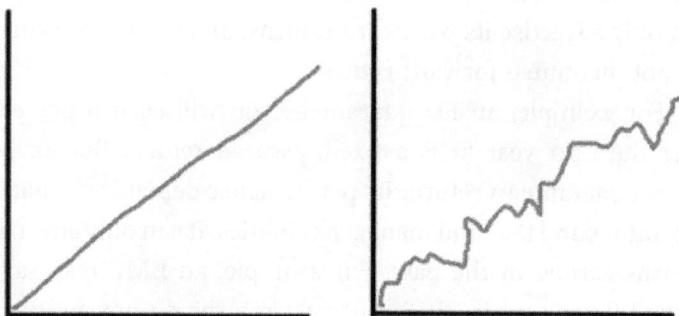

While the left graph shows what the growth trajectory of most liquid funds looks like, the right one shows that of a long-term debt fund, which is more volatile.

There might be the rare occasion when LMFs may not perform to expectations. While picking an LMF, do look at its past performance, the fund manager's credentials and the quality of securities it is composed of. You may want to refer to its fund rating. There are several MF research websites that analyse funds on various parameters, such as performance, risks and costs. These websites also assign star ratings to funds, which help investors assess their quality.

Like any other MF, you can buy an LMF directly from any fund house's website using a compliant bank account. Alternatively, you could buy them from one of the many online aggregators that recommend MF schemes suited to your needs.

How I Save

I have three layers to my savings.

1. I have two savings accounts, with one in a private bank that pays a higher interest rate.

2. When I have surplus liquidity and if I do not want to spend it that month, I move it to a liquid fund. I dip into this fund only when I need money for making any payments. The liquid fund is also my emergency fund. I am, however, yet to get to the six-month level. I am working my way towards it.

3. My longer-term savings are tied to Nifty and Sensex index funds. I put the money there and forget about it. Why do I do this? There is much more to come on index funds in 'Strengthen'. So stay the course, dear reader.

Mind the Taxes

Savings help you earn interest.

Interest is income.

Income attracts taxes.

Where taxes need to be paid, taxes need to be saved. Such are the complexities of taxation. Some forms of income attract lower taxes than others. Some income is tax-free. Some income is fully taxable. Other incomes fall between these two extremes.

An LMF investment held for three years and returning 6 per cent per annum may attract lower taxes than an FD also returning 6 per cent over three years.

When Usman, a software engineer in Bengaluru, came to understand the layered nature of taxation, he decided to split up his savings into bank accounts, FDs and LMFs. This diversified not just his rates of return on savings but also the rates of taxation on those returns. Usman feels this set-up allows him to legally avoid, lower or delay taxes on all three forms of savings. Here is how it helps him.

Usman keeps money for his immediate needs in a savings

account, which pays 4 per cent. Under Section 80TTA of the Income Tax Act, 1961, interest earned on savings accounts (all banks and postal savings combined) is tax-free up to ₹10,000 in a financial year. In India, a financial year starts from 1 April and ends on 31 March of the next calendar year. Since Usman's savings balance is moderate to low, he comfortably stays under the ₹10,000 mark and thus avoids paying taxes on savings interest.

Next, he keeps his emergency fund in a bank FD that pays him 6 per cent. His interest earnings are taxed as per his slab.

If he were a senior citizen, he could have earned ₹50,000 tax-free as interest from FDs and RDs every year under Section 80TTB of the Income Tax Act, 1961. But he is 35 years old and within the 30 per cent tax slab. The interest he earns on his deposits will be taxed at 30 per cent. Therefore, the 6 per cent FD, in reality, pays out 4.2 per cent—just about the same as his bank account. These returns are inadequate.

The tax on FDs cannot be avoided. Usman will have to pay the tax even if he decides against redeeming the FD the same year. To avoid the tax hit, he decided to move a part of his FD into an LMF. Unlike the FD, the LMF allowed him to pay taxes only on redemption, which may be within the same year or in the next three years or never. The LMF has been generating an average of 6.5 per cent per annum over the last few years. As and when Usman decides to redeem his LMFs, he will have to pay taxes on his gains. But that day may be far in the future.

In essence, this set-up increases his overall returns from savings and reduces his taxes without making him take high risks or restricting access to his funds.

Table 2

Returns on ₹10 Lakh, Saved in Different Instruments, Without Withdrawals			
	Option 1: Just Savings Account	Option 2: 10 Per Cent Savings, 90 Per Cent FD	
Amount	₹1,000,000	₹100,000	₹900,000
Interest Rate (in per cent)	4.0	4.0	6.0
Interest	₹40,000	₹4,000	₹54,000
Tax-Free Returns	₹10,000	₹4,000	₹0
Taxable Returns	₹30,000	₹0	₹54,000
Tax @ 30 Per Cent	₹9,000	₹0	₹16,200
Post-Tax Returns	₹31,000	₹4,000	₹37,800
Effective Rate of Return (in per cent)	3.1	4.0	4.2
Net Savings	₹31,000	₹41,800	
Final Returns on Total Savings (in per cent)	3.1	4.2	
Particulars	Option 3: 10 Per Cent Savings, 50 Per Cent FD, 40 Per Cent LMF		
Amount	₹100,000	₹500,000	₹400,000
Interest Rate/Annual Growth Rate* (in per cent)	4.0	6.0	6.5
Returns*	₹4,000	₹30,000	₹26,000
Tax-Free Returns	₹4,000	₹0	₹0
Taxable Returns*	₹0	₹30,000	₹26,000
Tax @30 per cent	₹0	₹9,000	–
One-Year Returns Without Liquidation*	₹4,000	₹21,000	₹26,000

Effective Rate of Return (in per cent)	4.0	4.2	6.5
Net Savings	₹51,000		
Final Returns on Whole Savings (in per cent)	5.1		

The rates of return are for illustrative purposes only. Actual rates may vary. LMF returns are not guaranteed and may not necessarily be higher than FD returns or savings returns; actual returns depend on market factors. MF returns are taxable only on redemption. Returns on fixed deposits are annualized for simplification; actual returns may be influenced by frequency of compounding as per the bank's policies.

Laddering for Better Returns

How long should your FD tenure be? It can be seven days to a decade. But what will be the best for you?

The lowest interest rates are offered on the shortest tenures: seven days to nine months. The highest rates are offered on the longest tenures: typically, three years and upwards.

Getting the best returns in a low-interest-rate scenario poses a challenge for an intrepid money manager. In a low-rate scenario, you should avoid locking into a long tenure. What if you locked into a 5.5 per cent deposit for five years and then the rate went up to 7.5 per cent a year later? You would miss out. Similarly, if you had a 7.5 per cent deposit for five years, which is nearing maturity, you may be able to renew it only at 5.5 per cent. Your renewal will be at discount. This is bad for you.

On the other hand, in a high-rate scenario, you would want to lock into a high rate for the long term. Doing so will protect you from falling rates. Either way, how do you decide what is good enough?

The answer may lie in hedging your deposit tenures. Nanda, a corporate communications professional from Bengaluru, uses a method called laddering with her deposits. It gives her better average returns, which is better than the bare minimum returns. Laddering needs her to create multiple deposits of different tenures rather than locking into one tenure with a single deposit. This keeps her from the need to time the rate cycle. This way, she is getting the best of any situation.

So for example, Nanda has ₹5 lakh in her savings. She could make a single deposit with it. But she will have to lock into one tenure at one rate. This would mean low returns. However, with laddering, Nanda splits the money into five deposits at different rates. Each deposit will renew at different intervals of one, two, three, four and five years. Doing so ensures better average returns. For example, the one-year deposit will return 4.5 per cent. The two- and three-year deposits will return 5 per cent. And the others will return 5.7 per cent.

With the ladder, one deposit will mature each year. She can put it to its intended use, such as paying for her daughter's school fees. She could also choose to renew the deposit at the prevalent rate, which would hopefully be higher. She has, however, locked into an 8 per cent RD for 10 years. This is often as good as deposit rates can get.

When the rates are high, go for longer tenures with your deposits. When they are low, ladder them and wait for higher returns.

Start Early

Time is critical—probably more critical than the rate of return you earn on your savings. Time compounds even the smallest returns, turning them into a fortune as you go along.

'Compound interest is the eighth wonder of the world,' goes a quote attributed to Albert Einstein. 'He who understands it, earns it; he who doesn't, pays it.'

Let us say you wanted to save ₹1 crore in a time period of 20 years. If you invested ₹10,000 every month for the next two decades and earned an average annual return of 12 per cent, you would hit your goal. But if you saved the same money for only 10 years, you would end up with just around ₹23 lakh. If you kept at it for 30 years, you would save ₹3.52 crore.

This is the power of compounded returns and is the most important lesson that you will need to learn in money management. We will take a deeper dive into it in 'Strengthen'.

The Importance of Budgeting

Sylvia is an Early Jobber and works as a pharma marketing executive. She decided to pursue education in the United Kingdom. She made it her top-most priority. She needed to get her finances straight to achieve it. It was not easy. To achieve her goal, she needed ₹20 lakh. It required her to take a two-pronged approach: saving more and spending less. For this, she learnt how to budget.

A domestic budget is a financial map. It allows you to see where your money is and where it needs to go. Expenses can be essential or discretionary. You can survive without discretionary spends. But essential expenses are vital to your life. For example, paying rent or your loan EMIs are essential. Eating out or taking a holiday abroad are discretionary expenses. Efficient saving is about tightening essential spends and cutting down on discretionary ones, wherever possible.

Sylvia tried to save 20 per cent of her take-home pay every month. Not satisfied with the results, she upped her savings to 25 per cent. To accommodate the savings, she analysed where her money was going. She went through her bank and credit card statements. She used a money manager app to track her expenses using SMS transaction alerts. She identified areas where she could tighten her finances. Eating out? Cut it down. That streaming subscription she did not need? Cancelled it. Rent taking up a lot of her income? She shifted to a smaller accommodation.

Using the budget, she identified her financial priorities and ensured they were adequately financed. Saving for college, paying rent, utilities, transport and groceries took up 80 per cent of her income. She used the other 20 per cent for discretionary spends. Well, we should also be able to enjoy our income.

Sylvia was gradually able to increase her savings to 30 per cent. This allowed her to hit her goal in two years. Bonus earnings and doles from her parents also helped.

The Power of Automation

Vikas, an Indore-based trader and a Moneymooner, struggled to keep track of his payments and frequently missed his due dates. He had three late credit card payments in 2020. He had made two late electricity payments. Another time, he had forgotten to maintain funds in his bank account and missed a car loan payment instalment. He had to pay penalties for all the late payments.

If you are paying late, the matter cannot be straightened by simply completing the payment. You will have to bear the consequences too.

Because of the late credit card and loan payments, Vikas' credit score had fallen from 808 to 715. He was no longer eligible for the lowest interest rates on the home loan he was considering. For now, Vikas will have to pay far more— potentially lakhs of rupees for the same loan.

Your credit score is a measure of your ability to repay your past loans. A lower score—anything under 750—implies you have had troubles paying your loans on time. This reduces your credit-worthiness in the eyes of lenders. Let us understand why it hurts your finances to pay a higher interest rate on your loan as a result of your poor credit score.

Assume you are to take a home loan of ₹50 lakh for 20 years at an interest rate of 7 per cent. On this loan, you will pay a total interest of ₹43.03 lakh. So you have borrowed ₹50 lakh, but need to repay ₹93.03 lakh over the next 20 years.

But if your credit score was poor and you took the same loan at 8.5 per cent, the interest on it would be ₹54.13 lakh. That is an additional ₹11.10 lakh.

If Vikas were to take the more expensive loan, this additional interest would be the real cost of his late payments, not the few thousand rupees he is coughing up in penalties and credit card interest. This cost could potentially hurt his long-term finances, lower his disposable income and impact his ability to save.

To rectify this, Vikas has now automated his payments. His utility payments, EMIs and credit card payments are now automatically deducted from his bank account through the bill payment facility. He also automated his savings, parking 20 per cent of his take-home pay in an RD.

He, thus, worked on improving his savings and nullifying negative savings. Since he has started making timely payments, he has been able to keep high-interest debt at bay, ensuring they do not eat into his savings. This will also help him gradually improve his credit score.

Make Smart Substitutions

Shankar took a cab to work every day. The rides cost him ₹200 per trip, totalling over ₹2,000 per week or nearly ₹9,000 a month. Not only was this proving to be costly for Shankar, it was also often inconvenient. Surge pricing cost him even more. Peak-hour delays often left him stranded at work. He took a personal cab instead of shared rides. He preferred the privacy. He could get the same privacy if he simply owned a vehicle. It would be much more convenient and cost roughly the same.

Shankar did the math. He dipped into his savings, took a loan of ₹4 lakh and bought a car for his daily commutes. The monthly loan payment over six years would be just over ₹7,000. He rationalized that despite the overheads from petrol, maintenance and insurance, he is more comfortable owning a vehicle. He was no longer at the mercy of cab drivers during peak hours, and could also listen to his favourite podcasts and music on his commute.

Substitutions come in many forms. They help control costs without making any compromise on quality of life. I can attest to that.

After my charmed existence in Bengaluru, I went to the United States. I attended a graduate programme at Columbia University. As a student, my earning capacity was all but gone. I had to tighten my expenses.

The one year in college was challenging. I had little income. But I helped myself by taking on campus jobs—even the ones I was overqualified for. I once worked in the mail room of the distance education school on campus. My job was sticking labels on packages. I also worked as a research assistant and staff assistant. The jobs yielded small incomes that contributed towards my living and tuition expenses.

I continued to be careful about my expenses. To cut corners, I started cooking for myself at home. Similar to my habit of biking, this, too, was healthier and cost-effective. Cooking also helped me bond with college mates. They would come over to share meals. I continue to cook for myself. As of today, I can cook mutton biryani, Mangalorean chicken curry, Spanish omelette and pasta.

Substitutions allow you to find ways to live your life without wrecking your bank balance: home-cooked meals instead of food deliveries; online streaming versus a visit to the local multiplex; taking the bus versus ordering a ride; buying reusable used goods instead of brand new ones.

Find the substitutions that work for you. Save your money.

Paying for a Farmhouse with a Paperclip

Deals help you save money. There is always one to help you achieve your financial goals.

Have you heard of the story of the man who traded a paperclip for a house?[17] That is exactly what a Canadian named Kyle MacDonald did between July 2005 and July 2006.

In July 2005, Kyle dropped a post on Craigslist, the famous classified ads website. In his ad, Kyle said he wanted to barter a paperclip with a bigger, better item. His post read:

> This red paperclip is currently sitting on my desk next to my computer. I want to trade this paperclip with you for something bigger or better, maybe a pen, a spoon, or perhaps a boot... I'm going to make a continuous chain of 'up trades' until I get a house. Or an island. Or a house on an island. You get the idea.[18]

Kyle managed to trade the red paperclip for a wooden fish pen. A few days later, he traded the pen for a hand-sculpted doorknob. Shortly afterwards, he traded the doorknob for a Coleman stove.

You see where this is going?

In November, he traded the stove for a Honda generator.

So far, so good. Then, his genius plan hit a speed breaker as he briefly lost the generator's possession. He hunted it down and traded it for a beer keg, a neon Budweiser sign and an I.O.U. for a keg refill—an 'instant party'.[19] Next month, he traded the 'instant party' for a snowmobile. His project to up-trade the paperclip to a house started gathering media attention. He soon traded the snowmobile for a trip for two to Yahk, Canada.

Kyle then sold one spot on the trip for a box truck, and the box truck for a recording contract with a music label. He traded the contract with an aspiring singer who offered to pay him a year's rent in Phoenix, Arizona. He then traded the rent-free year for one afternoon with rock music legend Alice Cooper, and that afternoon for a motorized snow globe branded by Kiss, the famous rock band. In June 2006, Kyle traded the snow globe for a role in a movie to be made by Hollywood actor and director Corbin Bernsen who wanted to add to his vast collection of snow globes.

Barely a month later, Kyle traded the movie role with the town council of Kipling, Saskatchewan, which provided him a two-storied 1,100 square foot farmhouse.

The key takeaway from this fun project was that there is a world beyond how corporations want you to spend your money—by influencing you through messages that constantly tell you to buy the things you think you need, but in reality do not.

The world is full of interesting deals. Look for them. Bargain hard. After all, this is about getting the most out of your hard-earned money.

The One-Week Rule

Alternatives to this are called the one-day rule and the one-month rule.

It is especially useful for impulsive spenders who struggle with savings—often, these are people who suffer from FOMO (fear of missing out).

Basically, the rule works this way. Some shiny new thing has caught your fancy. You really want to buy it. But you do not know whether making the purchase would be a financially wise decision. Therefore, you should wait for a week (or a day or a month, depending on which rule you choose to go with).

If, by the end of that period, you are still convinced you need to make this purchase, go for it. But it may so happen that the break may give you pause to think about your actions and whether there are better uses for the money.

Turn your FOMO into JOMO—the joy of missing out. You might save yourself from wasteful expenditure.

Step Up Your Savings Game

With time, age and work experience, your income will rise. Do not save at 40 like you did at 25. Make your higher disposable income work for you.

If you are saving 10 per cent of your income now, work towards hitting 20 per cent and from there, 30 per cent. Stepping up your savings will help you hit your financial goals faster.

Amitabh, a financial analyst and a Moneymooner, has been stepping up his savings in line with his income rise each year. When he was 30, he started saving ₹5,000 a month in an investment scheme that returned an average of 12 per cent per annum. If and when continued for 30 years, this scheme would give him a corpus of ₹1.76 crore. Amitabh understands that he needs to invest more with time.

So he stepped up his monthly contributions by 10 per cent

each year—₹5,000 in the first, ₹5,500 in the second, ₹6,050 in the third, and so on.

By the time he would reach the thirtieth year, his monthly contribution would theoretically be ₹79,315. This sounds like a lot now. But when the time comes, inflation would have done its part to reduce this large sum into a pittance that would not pinch Amitabh's pocket. This plan would return a whopping ₹4.41 crore in 30 years, and he would not have to stretch himself for getting there.

There are other ways to exceed your goals. You could use windfalls, periodic incomes and bonuses to boost your savings. Your emergency fund needs topping up periodically to match your latest income and lifestyle. You also need to top it if you have dipped into it recently.

Don't Forget to Enjoy Your Money

Nasima, an Early Jobber, has a refreshing take on managing her money. The Hyderabad-based dentist prioritizes savings and investments. But she avoids doing so at the cost of enjoying her life.

Each month, Nasima sets aside 10 per cent of her income to experience something new or something she had wanted to for quite some time. This could be a fine-dining experience, a concert, a spa treatment, a dinner with her friends, a weekend getaway or anything that brings her joy and comfort.

Nasima strictly enforces the 10 per cent rule because she understands that unchecked discretionary spending could slow down her savings and investments, which would, in turn, slow down the achievement of her other goals: buying a house and planning a trip to Dubai.

I share in Nasima's aspirations. I love to travel with my

family. I self-finance my trips. Holidays can be a major expense for my family. My approach is to start saving three to six months ahead of a planned trip. I divert money from my salary into my liquid fund. I dip into the fund when I am ready to travel.

The bee must work all its life to find, collect and process honey. But it also must find the time to enjoy the sugary treats.

II

SECURE: PROTECTING YOURSELF AGAINST LIFE'S VAGARIES

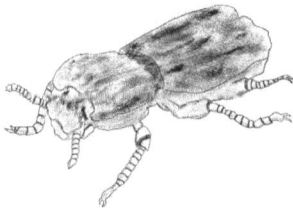

THE IRON BEETLE

The diabolical ironclad beetle is an amazing insect. It can scuttle away scot-free from any external trauma, such as being stomped upon or even being run over by a car. It has the hardest of all arthropod exoskeletons—if an entomologist needs to study it, they will have to drill through its tough shell.

Iron beetles are tiny creatures, measuring about an inch. They are found largely in the woods of USA and Mexico. They live under tree barks, feeding off the fungus on damp wood. They are called the 'the ironman' of the beetle world. They appear to be encased in an intricate armour, which gives them their name. They are fascinating to look at, almost like a piece of iron art. In Mexico, in Mayan tradition, they are sold as living brooches and called makech. They are encrusted with gems and attached to chains.

Their bodies are a bioengineering marvel. Scientists believe the beetle's elytra—the outer wing case—fit snugly like a jigsaw. It gives the beetle its unbreakable quality by distributing stress across the length of its body.

The iron beetle teaches us that trauma can arrive in any shape or form. As money managers, we need to prepare our finances for extreme events that can throw us on our backs. There are many ways to do this. We would prefer to own enormous amounts of cash to deal with our problems. But a simpler and more accessible way is to own insurance coverage. In most cases, insurance does not cost much and will steel you against life's curveballs. And while life may still find a way to throw you on your back, getting back on your feet will be much easier if you have insurance.

THE 5S PYRAMID
BankBazaar

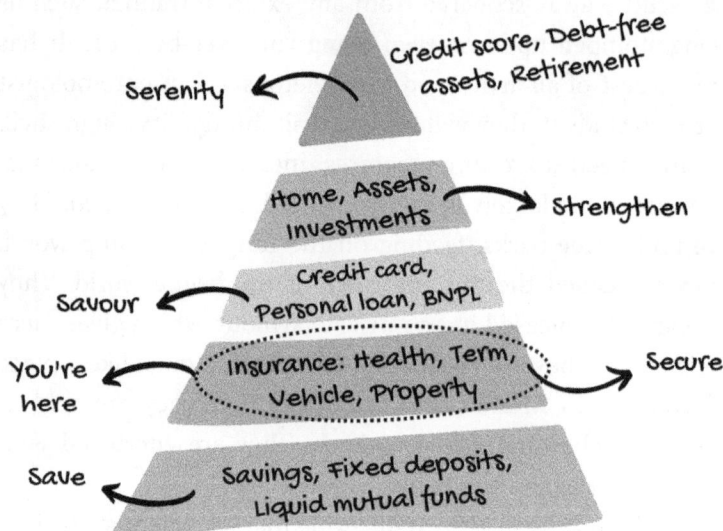

Serenity ← Credit score, Debt-free assets, Retirement

Home, Assets, Investments → Strengthen

Savour ← Credit card, Personal loan, BNPL

You're here ← Insurance: Health, Term, Vehicle, Property → Secure

Save ← Savings, Fixed deposits, Liquid mutual funds

The Need for Insurance

You have savings and investments. You do not want them to be washed away by the unexpected arrival of the four Ds: death, disease, disability and disasters. You need to protect your hard-earned wealth against these events.

Insurance, or forms thereof, has existed for ages across cultures. To cite an example, an early form of insurance known as bottomry contract existed in Babylon in as early as 4000–3000 BC.[1] Bottomry was a maritime contract. It was created to safeguard the business interests of merchants undertaking long and rough sea voyages. The ship owner, as per the contract, took a loan and pledged his cargo ship as collateral. If the ship returned from its voyage, the lender got his money back with interest. If the ship sunk or returned impaired, the lender lost his money.

In today's time, we have modern-day insurance policies that help us when the seas of life get rough. Despite having savings in your bank, one major crisis could bankrupt you. So you need insurance to protect yourself from that crisis.

For example, through health insurance, you can cover costly hospitalization. Through life insurance, your family members can replace your income and comfortably continue living their lives. Through automobile insurance, you can cover damages caused in accidents. Through home insurance, you can cover damages caused to the structure and contents of your house in case of a mishap.

Like the iron beetle's tough armour, insurance protects us from dire straits. Insurance, in most cases, is economical. Everyone should have it. But everyone does not have it.

India's Low Insurance Penetration

The Covid-19 pandemic highlighted the importance of insurance and why you cannot ignore it. The pandemic had countless cases of entire families being hospitalized. As per media reports, many of these families did not have health coverage necessary to protect their savings.

In a survey conducted between 2017 and 2018, the National Sample Survey Office sampled 113,823 urban and rural households.[2] The findings indicate that a whopping 85.9 per cent of the rural and 80.9 per cent of the urban population did not have health insurance.[3] The survey reported that out-of-pocket expenses for a single hospitalization in private hospitals cost ₹15,937 in rural areas and up to ₹22,031 in urban areas.[4] Bear in mind, India's per capita income is less than a lakh.[5]

According to government data, the average Indian earned ₹94,270 in 2019–20 and ₹85,110 in 2020–21.[6] This indicates that hospitalization costs are damaging to an average Indian household. Around 79.5 per cent of the rural population paid their hospital bills independently.[7] They had to sell assets such as gold and property. Another 13.4 per cent borrowed.[8] In urban areas, 83.7 per cent of the families paid out of their savings, with 8.5 per cent relying on loans.[9] Using insurance is a rarity.

From 2018, this situation improved marginally with the arrival of the Pradhan Mantri Jan Arogya Yojana (PM-JAY). The central government health insurance scheme aims to cover hospitalization costs for the poorest 70 crore Indians. The scheme covers their families for up to ₹5 lakh a year.

According to statistics from NITI Aayog, the central government policy think tank, another 25 crore Indians are covered under various social and group health insurance schemes, such as those provided by their employers.[10] The rest—nearly 30 per cent of the population, almost equal to the European Union—have no coverage.[11]

A hospitalization is an impediment to an average Indian family's aspirations. After a family member undergoes hospitalization, it becomes tougher to fulfil aspirations, such as owning property, attaining higher education or having a retirement on one's own terms.

Our purpose is to achieve Serenity—the top tier of the 5S

Pyramid. And for many Indians, hospitalization is one of the biggest impediments to Serenity.

Crowdfunding platforms in India host campaigns to finance people's mounting hospital bills. Cancer treatment formed a large chunk of the funding requests.[12] In 2020 and 2021, crowdfunding was frequently done to help those battling the virus. One often sees people campaigning to raise lakhs of rupees but falling short.

The pandemic has caused great uncertainty about life and health. If you have not bought insurance still, when will you?

Not Enough Life Insurance Either

The annual report published by the Insurance Regulatory and Development Authority (IRDA) makes for a sober reading. The 2020–21 report highlights that India has an insurance penetration of 4.2 per cent and insurance density of $78.[13]

Insurance penetration is calculated as insurance premium in terms of a per centage of the country's Gross Domestic Product (GDP), which is the value of the sum of goods and services produced in a year. Insurance density is calculated as premium as a ratio of population.

India fares poorly on these parameters, lagging behind developed nations. For instance, the global insurance penetration is 7.4 per cent, with USA and Canada leading the world at 11.8 per cent.[14] Global insurance density is at $809.[15] USA and Canada lead again at $7,270.[16]

It is clear that buying insurance is not a priority for a vast majority. This is a huge problem. The next problem is that of a low persistency ratio—the per centage of people who continue with their coverage beyond the first year.

For example, in 2018–19, the Life Insurance Corporation of

India had a thirteenth month persistency ratio of 66 per cent.[17] This means that if 100 people had bought life insurance, only 66 renewed it the year after. The thirteenth month persistency ratio of 24 life insurance providers ranged from 53.49 per cent to 83.55 per cent.[18] This shines a light upon a worrying situation: not only is there low insurance penetration in India, the policies bought are being abandoned quickly.

The sixty-first month persistency ratios are even more troubling. For IRDA's 24 life insurance providers, the ratio varies from 53 per cent to 22.61 per cent, with an unweighted average of 38.22 per cent.[19]

I am not an exception to this statistic. When I started working, I purchased a life insurance policy following my father's recommendation. I do not remember whether it was a term plan or traditional insurance. Sadly, I let the policy lapse.

The low persistency demonstrates that too many Indians do not have a life insurance. In hindsight, I understand this is financially risky behaviour for people with dependents and liabilities. In case of their untimely death, the dependents will bear the brunt of the loss of income. That would make it harder for them to face liabilities such as loans.

A health or life insurance policy is typically a long-term relationship with the insurance provider. Your attempt should be to secure your coverage at low costs while you are young and healthy. Buying them at a ripe age is much more difficult due to the higher costs as well as the conditions placed upon your medical fitness.

Not owning insurance, abandoning existing coverage or leaving your purchase decision to a later stage of life are some of the risks you should avoid. The ironclad beetle does not let go of its shell and neither should you.

How Insurance Works

James Surowiecki, an American journalist and author of the 2004 book, *The Wisdom of Crowds*, sums up the purpose of insurance: 'Life insurance became popular only when insurance companies stopped emphasizing it as a good investment and sold it instead as a symbolic commitment by fathers to the future well-being of their families.'

Insurance came into existence to moderate future uncertainties, and were designed to help protect your loved ones and prized possessions if you became victims of unfortunate circumstances. The insurance product model works on the principle of collecting individual sums of money based on risk, pooling them together and reinvesting them in interest-generating assets.

When you buy an insurance policy, you purchase it as a cover for a particular event for a certain time frame for a specific sum, and make regular payments called premiums. If what you insure against ends up happening, you file for a claim. With regards to health insurance, cashless claims can be made or one can also seek reimbursements for the payments already made. Hospitals falling within the insurance provider's network will carry out cashless transactions. If the hospital is outside the network, you will have to claim reimbursements.

The insurance company will cover your financial loss from the money pool accumulated from all the policyholders' premiums. This is mostly the case, with some exceptions, and depends on the type of policy you choose. In simple terms, insurance is a risk management tool to safeguard yourself and your family against possible financial risk, just like the ironclad beetle's shell protects it against predators.

Health Insurance and Why Everyone Needs It

Most of humanity is likely to be affected by major or minor health problems, periodic disease outbreaks, accidents or other ailments that might lead to the need of extensive treatment or hospitalization. Yet, many dither on buying health insurance.

Make no mistake: owning health coverage should be assigned the highest priority—at par with buying food and paying rent.

Roti, Kapda Aur Makaan was an iconic 1974 Bollywood film about the bare necessities of every Indian—food, clothing and shelter. In the 2020s India, roti and kapda are largely fulfilled necessities. What would be the title of a modern remake of the movie? *Makaan, Data, Naukri Aur Healthcare*, perhaps?

Healthcare is not just a matter of insurance. It is also a hotly debated political issue around the world. Who deserves healthcare, how much should the coverage be and whether the government must pay for it are some of the questions that evoke starkly divided responses.

In most countries, exchequer-funded healthcare is a reality. In developed countries, such as the Nordic nations, healthcare is top-class and globally renowned. In less developed places, it is limited. Therefore, individuals and organizations must pay for the private healthcare they can afford.

Let us come back to the ground realities in India. There are several government-sponsored healthcare schemes that cover your medical and hospitalization costs to a degree.

Subsidized healthcare at government-funded hospitals and clinics exist in most states. For example, in Delhi, healthcare services can be accessed for free through the state government-funded mohalla clinics.[20] An additional layer of protection may also be availed through employer-provided group insurance.

The overarching problem is that India spends poorly on healthcare. As per the government's Economic Survey report, the central and state governments' budgeted expenditure on healthcare climbed to 2.1 per cent of the GDP in 2021–22.[21] The year when the pandemic struck, the expenditure had risen sharply from the previous year's 1.3 per cent.[22] The government's stated aim is to get to 2.5 per cent by 2025.[23]

As per World Bank data from 2018, India spent 2.95 per cent of the GDP on healthcare.[24] Of that, nearly 70 per cent was private expenditure—people spending on healthcare out of their own pockets.[25] The rest came from government. The same year, China reportedly spent 5.17 per cent of its GDP on healthcare.[26] USA, infamous for its exploitative and privatized healthcare, spent 16.69 per cent, and France, rated No. 1 on healthcare by many studies, spent 11.19 per cent.[27]

It is clear: India must catch up in terms of healthcare. We must spend more on it and work on improving insurance penetration.

Employer- or government-provided group coverage is often inadequate. It may be a one-size-fits-all cover that could be too small for your individual needs. Whether it is the government or your employer, they are all trying to balance the costs of insurance with their revenues.

This brings us to the point of it all: as an Indian, these statistics compel you to buy your personal health insurance, a retail policy that you should choose as per your paying capacity and unique health risks.

For example, your employer might be providing you a cover of ₹2 lakh. But after assessing the costs of treatment of a critical illness, like cancer, in your location, you find that you will require at least ₹10–15 lakh. Since your employer is not covering you to that extent, it makes sense for you to buy a personal health policy from the market.

Like the ironclad beetle's exterior, health insurance is the shell that protects your domestic economy from financial trauma. If you did not have coverage, you will have to use your savings, ask for help from family or friends or rely on the mercy of strangers to crowdfund your treatment.

How Much Health Coverage Is Enough?

Health insurance is a basic need. But how much of it do you need? There are various cues you could take to determine the optimal level of coverage for you and your family.

The first cue is your own immediate environment. Understanding your family's medical history helps. Past hospitalization costs or costs of treatment of critical illnesses can give you a basic idea of the coverage you will need.

Secondly, consider where you are. For instance, if you are in a small city with a reliable network of local hospitals, the expenses incurred may be lower. However, if you have to travel to a big city to avail specialized treatment, your costs could escalate. Look at what a room in your preferred hospital costs. Get a policy that allows you to access that room without difficulty, whenever you need it.

Third, consider medical inflation. As per a 2018 report, medical inflation in India happens at twice the rate of overall inflation.[28] So if the inflation rate is 6 per cent in a year, medical inflation would be 12 per cent. To simplify this, a treatment that cost ₹5 lakh last year will cost ₹5.60 lakh this year. Therefore, your coverage should also factor in inflation and be adequate for the immediate future.

Lastly, consider a couple of rules of thumb. You can get a cover equal to 100 per cent of your annual income. In most cases, this coverage should cost you between 0.5 per cent and 2 per cent of your annual income. You could go higher and own a cover that is 200 per cent or more of your annual income. The price will be higher, but the choice is yours.

Table 3

Costs of Basic Health Policies from Top Insurance Providers			
Policy Name	Annual Premium at Age 26	Annual Premium at Age 36	Annual Premium at Age 46
Star Health - Medi Classic - Individual - Basic	₹7,074	₹7,993	₹11,831
HDFC ERGO - My: Health Suraksha	₹7,642	₹9,027	₹11,665
The New India Assurance - Mediclaim Policy*	₹6,044	₹6,408	₹10,631
National Insurance - Mediclaim Policy - Individual Plan	₹7,653	₹8,588	₹12,399
Oriental Insurance - Individual Mediclaim Policy*	₹6,899	₹8,885	₹15,361

Costs of basic health coverage from top-five insurance providers as per gross health (retail) premium collected in FY 2020–21 (as per industry performance report (provisional and unaudited) in FY 2020–21). Data pertains to individual health insurance cover of ₹5 lakh for 30-year-old male individuals residing in Bengaluru and is correct as of 31 May 2021. Data is indicative. Actual premium may vary from the data mentioned in the table depending on health condition of insured and other factors.
*Without third-party administrator charges.

These are good data points to kick-start your hunt for the ideal cover.

For example, if you are 30 years old and have an annual income of ₹10 lakh, an equal-sized health policy's premium may range between ₹5,000–₹20,000. The key is to neither under-insure nor over-insure. If you under-insure, you can be vulnerable in the face of a sudden and costly hospitalization. If you over-insure, you may be diverting money away from high-priority goals such as investing in your retirement.

You should buy the optimal coverage now and enhance it every few years to account for inflation and your financial responsibilities as per the stage of life you are at. For instance, if you are young, single, healthy and without dependents, consider a basic cover of at least ₹5 lakh. As you get married, have children and earn a higher income, buy additional coverage for the additional health risks you would have.

Life will attempt to crush you every now and then. But like the ironclad beetle, be uncrushable.

Is Your Insurance Premium High?

Health insurance premiums vary according to criteria like age, medical history, tobacco and alcohol habits, the city you live in, and so on.

Age matters. The higher your age, the costlier your coverage. If you have pre-existing health conditions such as diabetes your premiums will be higher. Youth, which goes with good health, should be used to your benefit. Lock in your health coverage at a low cost when young. This will save you money when you get older.

Zonal classifications of cities play a part. Zone 1 (Delhi and Mumbai) have costlier healthcare, and insurance premiums there will be higher compared to Zone 2 (most Tier 1 cities, such as Chennai and Bengaluru) and Zone 3 (the rest).[29]

Secondly, premiums are influenced by the benefits that policies offer. For example, a policy with a high hospital room rent will cost more than another policy with a low cap on rent.

The greater the benefits, the higher the costs. For example, a basic, no-frills policy will only cover hospital treatment. A more inclusive premium policy may also cover domiciliary treatments, i.e. treatments at home.

The questions to consider will be these: what do you want and how much can you afford?

How to Inflation-Proof Your Health Coverage

Anuja has a health cover of ₹10 lakh and she pays an annual premium of around ₹8,000 for it. This is her basic coverage. The 25-year-old copywriter is wise enough to know that this coverage will be inadequate in a few years due to medical inflation. She is going to need additional coverage at a later age. To safeguard herself against future health costs, she decides to increase her coverage by 400 per cent. She buys additional coverage of ₹40 lakh.

You would have assumed that she paid another ₹32,000 for the additional coverage. But she did not. Anuja merely bought a super top-up plan, which was even more economical. The additional coverage has an annual premium of just ₹800.[30] How did that happen?

Your basic policy can be used the moment you need to make an eligible claim. However, a top-up policy is activated only after you have paid the deductible. What is a deductible?[31] It is the amount you pay—either out of your pocket or through your basic insurance coverage—before the top-up insurance starts to cover you.

For example, you have a basic cover of ₹10 lakh. You also have a top-up policy of ₹40 lakh with a deductible of ₹10 lakh.

Your hospitalization bill is ₹15 lakh. Of this, ₹10 lakh—the deductible—will be paid by your first policy. The rest will be covered by your top-up. Your top-up policy will be called into action only after you have paid your deductible. And because the chances of that happening are low, your top-up coverage is cheap in comparison to your basic coverage.

It is now common to get top-up coverage even up to ₹95 lakh without burning a hole in your pocket. Assuming you have a good basic coverage, a large top-up, which can be a top-up or a super top-up plan, will cost you a fraction of what a base policy costs. A basic cover boosted by a super top-up allows you to maintain adequate coverage, beat medical inflation and comfortably pay off just about any hospital bill—much like the ironclad beetle's layered exoskeleton which makes it indestructible.

Top-Up versus Super Top-Up Health Insurance

Gulab is a Delhi-based Wealth Warrior (what we call those above 35). Wealth Warriors are not necessarily as digitally savvy as Early Jobbers or Moneymooners, but their higher purchasing power makes them a significant target for high-end goods and services, especially those meant for families and children.

Gulab had bought a ₹5-lakh health insurance policy after the first few years of his career as an architect. He felt the coverage might be inadequate after getting his third pay hike and decided to buy a top-up of ₹10 lakh. It turned out to be a good decision, as, after a few years, Gulab needed to undergo an emergency surgery and his hospitalization expenses came to ₹7 lakh. His base coverage paid ₹5 lakh and the rest came from his top-up. As a result, he faced no financial strain and did not have to dip into his savings and investments.

Table 4

Health Insurance Policies: What They Normally Cover			
In-patient hospitalization with room rent, subject to defined caps	Costs of surgery, intensive care, tests, scans, consultation, medical treatment	Pre- and post-hospitalization medical expenses up to a fixed number of days	Ambulance coverage up to a defined limit
Medicinal supplies, surgeries, doctor and surgeon's fees	Annual health check-ups	Daycare treatment up to defined limits	

But let us examine what else might have happened—and this is going to require your full attention to understand how top-up plans work.

If Gulab had to undergo two different treatments for the same health problem, where one treatment would have cost him ₹3 lakh and the other ₹4 lakh in the same year, he would not have been allowed to use the top-up. This is so because neither treatment crossed the ₹5-lakh limit, which is the minimum a treatment should cost before the top-up plan gets activated.

This would have meant that he would have had to pay the second instalment of ₹4 lakh entirely out of his own pocket because similar treatments in the same policy year are not likely to be covered by a basic policy. Even if similar treatments were covered in the same year, the policy would cover just ₹2 lakh for the second treatment (because the maximum sum assured is ₹5 lakh) and Gulab would have had to pay the rest.

If you do not wish to have such a limitation, a super top-up is ideal. You can use a super top-up for multiple treatments where the collective expense exceeds the primary insurance policy's deductible threshold.

Now, there are also high-value coverages widely available that combine basic coverage with top-ups. Called one-crore covers, they provide you a rounded, large-sized cover that would inflation-proof you for the immediate future. For example, the first ₹5 lakh is your basic coverage and the other ₹95 lakh would be your top-up. This combination allows you to buy a large cover at low costs.

But keep in mind that this coverage is subject to various caps and limits. Even though you have insured yourself for ₹1 crore, terms and conditions will apply, and the actual coverage for your usage might be much lower.

What to Buy When Buying Health Coverage

An iron beetle's armour interlocks smoothly like a jigsaw. Similarly, the various benefits of health insurance also need to fit together to make for a cohesive policy with comprehensive protection.

We have looked at the ideal coverage size (also known as the sum assured) and the various ways to calculate it. Now, let us get a deeper understanding of common health insurance features and add-ons.

When Sajith's father underwent prolonged cancer treatment, he relied on his employer-provided health insurance to cover the costs. The treatment used up most of the sum assured within the policy. It left little coverage for Sajith, a Wealth Warrior, and his wife. They also did not own a personal health cover. They were now at financial risk if another health crisis were to strike the family.

Table 5

Health Insurance: Typical Exclusions and Waiting Periods				
All treatments excluding accidents in the initial waiting period of 30 days	Specified treatments, pre-existing diseases and critical illnesses normally not covered up to 48 months	Deductible and co-pay amount will have to be paid by policy holder as agreed upon.	Dental, cosmetic treatments, genetic disorders, contraceptives, routine eye care, sexually transmitted diseases	Ailment caused by drug abuse, acts of self-harm or participation in dangerous activities

Sajith had to act quickly to secure coverage. He had seen how costly a critical illness was and how important adequate coverage was. He decided to buy a fully loaded, comprehensive cover for himself and his wife. He wanted to spare no expense. He logged on to an insurance policy aggregator and started evaluating options. He had the choice of buying individual policies for each of them. Instead, he streamlined his costs by buying a family floater plan.

A floater policy covers multiple members of a family by providing them shared benefits. Where two individual policies would have cost Sajith around ₹12,000 each, a floater cost him only ₹15,000.

Speaking for myself, my floater plan is important to me—it covers my wife and daughter. Though I do have my corporate cover, I want to ensure that I have my personal coverage in place once I retire. My floater coverage is of ₹50 lakh. It was ₹20 lakh when I had got married. I increased it after the birth of our daughter.

Coming back to Sajith, he wanted the best possible coverage. The policy he picked was from an insurance company with a

95 per cent claim settlement ratio (CSR). It had comparatively low waiting periods for the coverage of pre-existing diseases—just two years as opposed to the three or four years that other policies imposed.

Table 6

Health Insurance: Typical Riders and Add-Ons				
Critical illness cover that pays out a lump sum upon the diagnosis of a listed illness. Also available as stand-alone policies	Personal accident cover that covers death or disability caused by an accident	Room-rent waiver removes or raises limits on daily hospital-room charges	Daily cash rider provides petty cash to cover non-medical expenses or loss of income during hospitalization	Maternity add-on covers hospital and medical expenses during childbirth

His pre-hospitalization expenses for three months and post-hospitalization expenses for six months will also be covered. The policy will also cover eye treatments, dental treatment, maternity, one annual health check-up and give a no-claim bonus that increases his sum assured by 10 per cent for every year he makes no claim.

Most importantly, the policy provides a restoration benefit. This covers him against multiple hospitalizations within the same year. If his sum assured was used up in one hospitalization and he required a second the same year, the sum assured would be fully replenished because of the restoration benefit.

With this policy, there will not be a limit on his room rent, which means he will be free to choose a private air-conditioned room at any hospital. There is no co-pay, meaning that 100 per cent of his future hospitalizations will be covered by the insurer and he will not have to pay a mandatory per centage of the costs.

Knowing Your Exclusions

When you buy health insurance, take a good look at what the policy excludes. Exclusions are pre-defined situations that the policy will not compensate you for. While some are permanent, others are temporary in the form of waiting periods.

Exclusions are not standardized. They vary from one policy to another. Generally, the more you pay for your coverage, the fewer your exclusions tend to be.

For example, maternity benefits—the hospitalization costs incurred during childbirth—are typically not covered by basic policies, but can be by policies with premium benefits. Hospitalizations followed by diseases that pre-existed before the policy term will not be covered for two to four years in most cases. Cosmetic surgeries and treatment, including dental treatments, are not covered. Self-harm, participation in dangerous activities, suicide attempts or the treatment of HIV-related complications are some of the commonly excluded items.

With an evolving society comes greater sensitivity to exclusions. Nobody should be left behind. For example, now, mental health coverage is provided by many insurers.[32]

Remember that it is in your best interest to read the policy offer document carefully before signing the dotted line. Look out for any clause or phrase that might impact your ability to use your coverage.

Riders and Add-ons

As the names suggest, riders and add-ons improve the functionality of your health insurance policy. They can address special needs, giving you a rounded coverage. To avail them, you will have to pay a price over and above the basic premium. The IRDA has capped the charges at 30 per cent of the basic premiums for such additions.[33]

If your insurance policy has a cap on room rent, you can opt for a room-rent waiver with a higher cap or preferably a room-rent waiver with no upper limit at all. It allows you a breather, as it is true that room rents can rise exponentially with time.

Not all health insurance policies provide maternity cover. Early Jobbers, Kavitha and Gokul, opted for a maternity rider when they took their insurance policy. They were newly married and were planning to start a family. They felt more secure with a maternity rider. Some policies cover newborns as well in your family floater plan.

In case you are worried regarding critical illnesses such as cancer, a critical illness rider can also be an option for you. It covers you against a pre-defined list of life-threatening diseases by paying out a fixed one-time sum assured regardless of the actual hospitalization costs.

Riders and add-ons are cheap additions to your policy and help you get more out of it. However, buy only those that help you with your needs. For example, if you are a bachelor, you do not need a maternity add-on.

There is a critical difference between regular health insurance and a critical illness insurance plan. Critical illness plans can be bought as riders or as stand-alone policies with fixed benefits. However, they are not substitutes to regular health insurance, which will cover you in a wider range of scenarios. In pre-defined conditions, a critical illness plan will pay out once and terminate. You cannot use or renew the same policy again. It can provide padding to your basic and top-up coverage by covering non-medical costs and replacing lost income. It cannot, however, replace your basic and top-up coverage.

Planning Coverage for Your Parents?

My parents were smart enough to buy policies when they were young. They can now confidently pay for their healthcare.

I know of cases where family elders have agreed to pay as much as ₹1 lakh as premium. Yet, they were denied new health policies because they were above 60 and had pre-existing conditions, such as diabetes and hypertension. I can understand why health insurance companies do this. They do not want to sell to people with pre-existing conditions, as the claims could end up being large. They might also be apprehensive about people buying coverage after coming to know they need to make a large claim.

Covering one's parents can be tricky. Insurance awareness in earlier generations was comparatively lower. So often, the only coverage the elderly have today is the one offered within their children's office policies.

The other way to cover your parents is through family floater plans. Floater plans can include your family members: your spouse, children, dependent parents, and in some cases, your in-laws as well. However, it is widely recommended to cover the elderly separately and not include them in your own plan.

Krishnaraj, a 30-year-old civil engineer in Coimbatore, wanted to cover himself, his 28-year-old wife and his 59-year-old father. He bought one policy for ₹10 lakh for himself and his wife, and another for ₹10 lakh for his father. He did this even though he was being quoted a slightly lower price for covering all three in the same policy.

Covering his father separately was necessary because his healthcare needs were different from the couple's. With advancing age, his father is more likely to be in need of the coverage. If that were to happen and if the three were covered within the same policy, it would have left the couple less to use in case they, too, underwent a health crisis.

For example, let us say the father required a hospitalization that cost ₹11 lakh. This would leave no coverage for the couple in the same year unless their policy had a restoration benefit. This would also mean that due to the claims made, the policyholders will not be eligible for no-claims bonuses, which help discount future premiums or increase the sum assured.

Only a few insurance providers are ready to cover the elderly, keeping in mind their higher health risks. But this is not the case with the young.

Krishnaraj and his wife had a much bigger insurance marketplace with several options to choose from, including riders and add-ons. Conversely, the father might have to pick from the few options that exist for those of his age group. The restrictions on coverage for the elderly also mean that you must make the most of your employer-provided group coverage. In many cases, this is the only coverage your aging parents will get.

More on that, and how you can beat the system, in an upcoming chapter.

The Claims Experience

Managing insurance claims is important. It requires attention to detail. I have managed multiple claims: my wife's delivery expenses, a family member's hospitalization costs during a trip to Italy and that of another kin's heart procedure.

I split my wife's maternity claim. I covered 50 per cent of the costs via my company's group policy and the rest from my personal floater plan, which my wife is a part of.

If you possess multiple policies, you are allowed to split your claim among them. It is common to make the first claim via the office coverage. This also preserves your personal coverage, keeping its benefits intact.

For my trip to Italy, the claim was made on a travel insurance policy. As you may be aware, it is advisable to travel to foreign countries only with a travel cover. Hospitalization without coverage in countries such as USA could financially hurt you. Travel insurance, which typically deals with cancellations, delays, lost baggage and theft, can also cover hospitalizations.

So there we were, on a family holiday in Italy, and a family member needed to be rushed to the hospital in a life-threatening situation. The hospital staff in that Italian hospital were professional and friendly even as we navigated the language barrier between us. We had taken the travel cover from a private insurance company. Thankfully, the experience was smooth. Though I was in a foreign country, I was able to get the required coverage. With a travel cover, you must report your case as soon as you are admitted and not when you get the hospital bill. The claim requires documents of admission, diagnosis, test results and anything material to the claim.

I had to manage the claim without a third-party administrator (TPA), which is an intermediary between the insurance provider and the insured. Its job is to facilitate the claim.

One must register with the TPA upon admission, or prior to admission in some cases, such as those involving maternity claims. Big hospitals have TPAs attached. They process a lot of the difficult-to-understand documents, like those of diagnosis, prescriptions and bills between the hospital and insurance company.

Cash claims are tricky. If the total expense exceeds the first policy coverage or sub-limits, then the policyholder must seek coverage from the second policy. In such cases, cashless claims are always easier and seeking reimbursements is tough due to the amount of paperwork involved.

I think filing insurance claims is an important skill for any person. It requires diligence, planning and working with the right insurer, who can give you the required support in your moment of truth—when you make the claim.

I have found that for specific custom requirements, such as health insurance porting, life insurance top-up and claim reimbursement management, working with an insurance broker comes in handy. The only one I really like and trust is First Insurance World. They do amazing work. In one instance, they helped someone I know with their car insurance claim during the 2018 Chennai floods, though it was declined initially.

When You Should or Shouldn't Make Claims

After a claim-free year, the insurer gives you a no-claim bonus (NCB). This could fetch you a discounted premium on renewal or it could increase your sum assured by a fixed per centage till it reaches a cap. NCB benefits vary from one policy to another.

For example, one policy increases your sum assured by 10 per cent for each successive claim-free year till the bonus coverage reaches 50 per cent of the original sum assured. This essentially incentivizes wellness. The better health you have, the better your coverage will be. When you make a claim, the NCB stops, and the benefits attached to it are reset. The clock starts again, after which your NCB accrues from zero.

Therefore, ideally, you should avoid making petty claims. Let your health insurance take care of bigger costs, such as hospitalizations, surgery or complex daycare treatments. While you can make other eligible claims, you should also understand the impact on your coverage and premiums.

Sushma is an Early Jobber and a YouTuber. She has a health policy of ₹10 lakh with an NCB of 10 per cent annual increase in the sum assured. She made no claims for three years. This increased her sum assured by ₹1 lakh per claim-free year to ₹13 lakh. In the fourth year, she made a petty claim of ₹15,000 after a daycare procedure at her local hospital. As a result, instead of her sum assured increasing to ₹14 lakh with another year of NCB, it ended up getting reduced to ₹10 lakh. Then she had another claim-free year, and the NCB started accumulating once again.

The base sum insured remains unaffected. Claims only impact the NCB. Therefore, be calculative and extract the maximum value from your coverage.

Why Buy Insurance If Your Employer Covers You?

Kalpana, a Moneymooner, works as a digital marketer. As she neared her fourth work anniversary, she found herself out of work. Her company wound up after suffering crushing losses during the Covid-19 pandemic. What happened next was worse: Kalpana tested positive for the infection and had to be quarantined in a private hospital. She also had asthma, which, in turn, complicated her health condition.

Though she recovered well, she incurred heavy medical expenses. Having lost her job, she did not have employer-provided health insurance coverage. Being young, she had regrettably not bothered to buy her own policy. She came to understand how it would have cushioned her precious savings after losing her job.

It is extremely important to have your own coverage. You might have to face unfavourable situations like unemployment. You will no longer be covered by your employer company. On top of that, if you have poor health, it would mean no insurance provider would sell you a cover.

If you remain employed, even with a pre-existing health condition, your group coverage can protect you. But the existing health condition may become the reason why you cannot buy a personal policy.

Recently, my mother told me that Rotary Club and Star Health joined hands to provide health insurance to children who had survived five-plus years after cancer.[34] Kudos to them!

Once you have a serious disease like that, no new policy—health, life or even travel insurance—is available, unless it is via your employer.

Therefore, I cannot emphasize this enough. Your employer-provided group coverage may sometimes be good enough. But you may need more. You will not be employed forever, and it gets tougher to buy insurance as you age. With pre-existing conditions, the difficulties increase—it is ironic because this is right when you are in maximum need of a coverage.

It is true that health insurance premiums increase with age while life insurance premiums are fixed when you purchase them. But at least, when you lock in the coverage, you can expect to be treated fairly.

Group coverage is great when available. It is often the reason young people do not consider buying additional health insurance. It should be understood that losing group coverage can leave you financially vulnerable.

The iron beetle is unbreakable with its shell. And that is why you, too, should not go a single day without coverage.

Port Your Coverage When You Leave Your Job

Abdul had a problem with his insurance coverage. He was exiting the job he had been in for six years. He was going to another company. Though the salary being offered in the new company was better, the group health coverage was not.

Abdul could have bought a new health policy from the market for himself. But that would have come with waiting periods—something his group cover at the old job did not. Leaving the old job translated to losing the coverage, and his market-bought policy would have then needed him to start his waiting periods from scratch. That would have been problematic.

He was faced with a bigger problem: the group policy also covered his parents, and it would have been difficult for him to get another policy from the market for them due to their advancing age and health conditions. But he played it smart. He took his previous employer's permission to keep his group policy. He approached the insurance provider, paid the premium and converted the group policy into two personal policies—one for himself and another for his parents.

Despite having taken new policies, he was accredited with the waiting periods already served in the group policy. The waiting periods did not start afresh. His parents' coverage continued unbroken.

If you have the privilege of working for an employer that provides great health coverage, do not waste it. Port the policy when you leave that job, continue with the coverage—it will help you protect your family because getting coverage for your parents only gets tougher with time.

There is another way porting can be done. When your policy is due for renewal, you have the option of shifting it to another insurance provider. This ensures you will not lose the waiting periods already served when the term for your new policy begins.

I, for example, ported my policy recently when I found out my old policy provided a high sum assured but a low maternity sub-limit. Another recent experience helped me learn that only 50 per cent of the costs of robotic surgeries, a comparatively new development, are covered.

I am wrapping my head around the fact that though my total coverage might be greater than the amount billed to me by the hospital, the insurance payout might be much lower than the hospital bill.

I am still to fully understand how this works.

Reminder: Lock in While Young

This needs to be repeated.

1. Buy health insurance when young. Lock in your coverage at low costs and enjoy the savings as you get older.
2. Your employer-provided coverage is not enough. You could lose that coverage any moment. Buy your own coverage from the retail market.

3. It will be much harder for you to get coverage once you are older or if you are diagnosed with a health complication.

4. While you are young, you can easily complete your waiting period without suffering any setbacks. Once old, there are chances you might suffer a health problem in the course of the waiting period.

5. Do not wait to be a Wealth Warrior to buy health insurance. Buy it when you are an Early Jobber. Your older self will thank you for it.

Getting your financial fundamentals right in your youth makes the climb to Serenity easier. If your finances are unharmed in your youth, you are better positioned to fulfil your aspirations in life.

Life Insurance and Who Needs It

The subject of life insurance is a morbid one. It forces you to ponder over your mortality. It pushes you to visualize the day your family will bid you goodbye. With your departure, what will that day—and the rest of their lives—be like for your family? It is an unpleasant thought indeed. However, for practical purposes and for the benefit of our dependents, you must deliberate upon such scenarios without delay.

A life insurance policy is a financial armour for your family. Your family's goals—educating the child, paying off the home loan or taking care of the aging parents—still need to be completed even after the event of your untimely death.

I had let my first life insurance policy lapse. But I have tightened up now. I think of coverage before anything else. Once I got married, I bought a term plan. Then, as I did with my health cover, I doubled the coverage when my daughter was born.

Life insurance ensures that your family is not forced to give up on their goals when you are not around. Your family's grief will be limited to your death and will not accrue from any financial problems.

Who needs life insurance? The simple answer to this complex question is that anyone with financial dependents and financial liabilities should get this coverage. It is assumed that the average policyholder is not able to accumulate enough wealth for the sustenance of their dependents. Therefore, insurance is needed to pad up the wealth the policyholder will leave behind.

Dependents could be a spouse, children, parents, other family members or even unrelated persons. Some dependents are legal heirs. Personal liabilities, just like assets, get passed on to one's legal heirs. Therefore, a pending home loan or obligations such as expenses caused by one's death should not be allowed to weigh down one's dependents. Conversely, those without dependents or liabilities probably do not need life coverage.

However, if you are a young person—an Early Jobber or a Moneymooner—who expects to have dependents, get married or start a family, you, too, can get coverage in anticipation of your future needs.

Just like with health insurance, the benefit of starting young is the lower cost. You could get your dependents covered for a fixed length of time—for example, till your retirement, or you could even take a full-life cover, which ends when you turn 99.

How Much Life Cover Do You Need?

This is one of the most important questions in money management. For the benefit of our dependents, it needs to be thought about seriously.

There are many ways to calculate your life insurance requirement. Truthfully, none of them can accurately tell you how much money your dependents will need after your death. The point, however, is to make a guess that is good enough.

Make a pragmatic assessment of your insurance needs. The assessment must be based on factors such as your age, current income, family's goals, the dependents' income needs, inflation, and your current assets and liabilities.

Let us say you are 30 years old, have a non-earning spouse and a three-year-old daughter, and your annual income is ₹10 lakh. You have planned to retire at the age of 60. Your current savings are ₹15 lakh. You have a car loan of ₹5 lakh. Your existing life coverage is ₹20 lakh.

Let us do a simple calculation here.

To account for your spouse's income needs for the next 30 years, you need at least ₹3 crore—current income multiplied by the number of years left to retirement. This is the income replacement method for calculating life coverage needs.

To this, you can add your family's other needs: the child's education, aging parents' healthcare and something to take care of your spouse after their retirement. Let us assume the values of the above are ₹75 lakh. Add another ₹5 lakh for the car loan balance. This takes the coverage requirement to ₹3.8 crore.

From that number, subtract existing savings and coverage (₹35 lakh in all). This means that you need additional life coverage of ₹3.45 crore. This number also assumes that your family will invest this sum to allow it to grow and spend it in a staggered manner, so that it lasts them a lifetime.

If this all sounds too much, it is because it *is* a complicated subject that requires careful thought. You could buy a coverage at once or you could take a calibrated approach and buy additional policies as you grow older and your responsibilities increase.

So how much thought have you given to your life coverage? Is it enough? If not, how much is enough? These are extremely important questions you need to ask yourself.

My term insurance, for example, has a sum assured of 10 times my annual income. I wanted to protect my wife and child with 10 years' worth of my income if I were to die today. I feel good about this. I am at peace knowing my family will be fine.

First Life Policy? Buy a Term Plan

There are many forms of life insurance. Traditionally, endowment and cashback plans have been favoured. Then came market-linked insurance plans. These combine insurance and investment.

Table 7

What Does a ₹1 Crore Cover Cost?			
Policy Name	Annual Premium at Age 25	Annual Premium at Age 35	Annual Premium at Age 45
LIC Tech Term	₹8,515	₹15,293	₹31,648
SBI Life eShield	₹8,354	₹15,541	₹33,111
HDFC Life Click2ProtectLife	₹9,230	₹16,267	₹36,116
ICICI Prudential Life iProtect Smart Life	₹9,259	₹16,935	₹36,304
Max Life Smart Term Plan	₹7,948	₹13,849	₹31,882

Costs of life-term policy from top-five life insurance providers as per first year total individual and group life insurance premium collected for the period ending 31 March 2021. Data pertains to life-term insurance cover of ₹1 crore for a 30-year tenure for male individual (non-smoker), residing in Bengaluru, and the respective age is correct as of 10 June 2021. Premium paying term = 30 years. Data is indicative. Actual premium may vary from the data mentioned in the table depending on the health condition of the insured and other factors.

But if you are shopping for your first life cover, let it be a term insurance plan.

If you die or are diagnosed with a terminal illness during the policy tenure, it will cover your dependents. It should be noted that it offers no investment benefit, no maturity value, no rate of return and no surrender value. It covers you for a fixed number of years and then it ceases.

This is so because it is a pure insurance product. It is cheap in comparison to other forms of life insurance that also combine investment and saving. With the focus on covering risks, it provides you the kind of meaty coverage you need. Hence, it is considered the best form of life insurance now.

For example, a 30-year-old looking for a life cover of ₹1 crore for 30 years can buy a term insurance plan from the retail market. The annual premium on this policy would range between ₹9,500 and ₹14,000, depending on who is selling it. For most people, it would not even be possible to buy a similar-sized life cover through traditional insurance policies.

For example, a well-known government-owned insurance provider sells an endowment plan of ₹1 crore for 30 years to a 30-year-old for around ₹3.15 lakh per annum. Hence, it makes sense for Early Jobbers and Moneymooners to lock in to their term coverage at a young age and enjoy low premiums and high coverage for any length of time.

Term coverage is available in many avatars: basic coverage, increasing or decreasing coverage, with riders and add-ons, full life coverage, and so on. One thing is clear: regardless of the variant you buy, a term plan is the best way to cover your dependents.

Pro tip: buy insurance from insurance providers that have a high CSR, which refers to the number of claims every 100 claims the insurer has settled in a year. Go for insurers that have a CSR above 95 per cent.

Table 8

A Few Well-Known Term Insurance Add-Ons			
Accidental Death	**Critical Illness**	**Terminal Illness**	**Premium Waiver**
The policy pays a lump sum over and above the basic sum assured if the policy holder's death is caused by an accident.	The policy holder receives a one-time lump sum if diagnosed with a critical illness defined in the policy.	If the policy holder is terminally ill and likely to die soon, the policy pays out the sum assured immediately.	Some policies waive off future premiums when the policy holder has a critical or terminal illness or a disability.
Disability	**Monthly Income**	**Return of Premium**	
The policy holder receives a benefit if partially or fully disabled.	Apart from the sum assured, the nominee is also paid a monthly income for a fixed period.	The premiums paid are returned at the end of the term.	

Based on market research. Riders and add-ons may continue or be discontinued as per the insurance provider's business policies, regulatory requirements or market needs. The above-tabled benefits may or may not be provided by all insurance providers. Each life insurance policy has unique benefits, and you must buy the one with benefits suited to your financial needs.

Don't Mix Life Insurance and Investments

Traditional life insurance policies such as endowment plans have allowed people to combine coverage, investing and tax-saving in a single instrument. Hence, many people still treat life insurance as the solution to all their financial needs.

They achieve their tax-saving objectives. But sometimes, in exchange, they get low returns on investments, low liquidity and—ironically—shockingly low coverage.

After the global financial crisis in 2008, Hemant, the co-author of this book and then a journalist in New Delhi, wanted to buy a life policy. He had had enough of market-linked insurance policies. He decided he wanted something safe. He also wanted to save income tax. Still an Early Jobber and unaware of the ways of the financial world, he bought an endowment plan from his bank relationship manager. The annual premium was ₹40,000 plus taxes. Cut to the end of the policy's 10-year term in 2020: the policy matured and paid out ₹5.31 lakh. Hemant calculated that this worked out to a mere 4.3 per cent returns per annum.

It was a shockingly low return. In the same decade, assured income instruments as well as stock markets had provided double-digit returns. The inflation rate was around 6 per cent. So by earning just 4.3 per cent over a period of 10 years, Hemant earned negative returns of 1.7 per cent per annum. He calculated that had he instead invested roughly the same amount as monthly instalments (₹3,400) in the same brand's tax-saving MF, his investment would have grown at 10.2 per cent per annum, giving him ₹6.82 lakh in the same timeframe.

Had he opened a Public Provident Fund (PPF) or merely contributed to his office PF instead of the endowment plan, he would have earned a comfortable 8.5–9 per cent per annum, fetching around ₹6.5 lakh in 10 years.

Over a 10-year period, if you invest ₹100 with negative returns of 1.7 per cent per annum, you are left with ₹84.3. If you invest and get 8 per cent growth over the same period, you get ₹216.

Hemant also came to understand that investment-based insurance policies have long lock-ins. This means you cannot dip into this investment without suffering losses. Therefore, liquidity is a major issue in this style of investing.

What were the key learnings for Hemant?

1. Never mix investment and life insurance. Separate the two; get the best of both worlds—good coverage, better liquidity and higher returns. If you mix the two, you would get the worst—low coverage, poor liquidity and negative returns.

2. Never go without term coverage when you have financial dependents. Buy a term plan and put your savings in PF or a tax-saving MF. Over the long term, this combination is likely to work better than investing through traditional insurance.

3. Do not make your financial mistakes long term because the losses compound with time. For example, committing to the aforementioned policy for 30 years instead of just 10 would have led to more profound losses. At the same rates of return, the endowment plan would have returned just ₹28 lakh whereas the MF would have returned ₹79 lakh.

4. Playing safe is actually a big risk. In wealth creation, embracing the right degree of risk is necessary.

We will cover investments, risks and rewards in 'Strengthen'.

Get the Longest Possible Coverage

Dharan and Swati were a DINK (double-income-no-kids) couple. Both had well-paying bank jobs. However, a lung infection turned critical for Swati and she was unable to continue working. Dharan decided to obtain a life insurance policy that covered him until the age of 50. He outlived his policy only to pass away from a heart ailment at the age of 52. Swati, who continued to be unemployed, would have undoubtedly benefitted had the term policy extended for another 10–15 years. She had to manage their life savings and medical expenses. While the expenses had grown, the savings had shrunk.

When buying term insurance, cover yourself for the longest period necessary. The term could end with your retirement or 10–15 years after retirement or cover you for your entire life. The longer the term, the higher the premium. Note that you do not necessarily need a full-life cover, just an optimally long one. The term coverage should be based on your unique needs. It needs to exist for as long as your dependents may need it—and remember that their needs will evolve over time.

The Bells and Whistles of Life Coverage

Insurance is indemnity against the hospital bill. But what about things like loss of income while you are in the hospital?

As this thought crossed my mind, I decided to buy a ₹1.5 crore critical illness rider with my term insurance. This is to cover situations where I am critically ill and unable to work. With a critical illness rider, the term policy can pay out while the policyholder is alive. The benefit is received upon diagnosis.

There is much more to term coverage than just a basic sum assured. Just like with health insurance, you can add riders and add-ons to your policy and make it more comprehensive. Of course, these additions cost more money and you should pick them carefully, depending on your unique needs. For example, if you spend a lot of time driving long distances, an accidental death benefit may be useful. If your family has a history of certain critical illnesses, a critical illness rider can be taken.

In hindsight, I should have bought more of this coverage in my 30s. It would have been cheaper for me. Now in my 40s, the costs are twice as much. To be fair, the need did not hit home till I got married, bought a house with a home loan and had a baby.

Cutting Your Losses

Bad insurance decisions need not be permanent. There are ways to cut your losses.

Joseph, a Moneymooner, had just started his second job as a visual designer in Bengaluru. He understood the pay bump came with enhanced financial responsibilities. He wanted to save, invest and insure. The 30-year-old took a friend's financial advice. He made the classic mistake of trying to save taxes, invest and insure with a traditional life insurance policy with a cover of ₹30 lakh for 25 years. Joseph bought the policy believing that the coverage would help him secure his future. A week later, Joseph did the math. The penny dropped.

He realized that the annual premium of nearly ₹1.20 lakh on the policy would take care of most of his tax-saving needs. But accounting for the inflation over 25 years, the policy proceeds may not cover his life expenses for a single year after he turns 55. Furthermore, he understood that the life cover was inadequate and could leave his family in financial turmoil. Had he tried to surrender the policy before its term, he would have suffered heavy losses. For example, in the first year, he would have got zero rupees back.

Investment-linked insurance plans such as these have a heavy commission structure. It has been common for insurance agents to earn as much as 25 per cent of the first year's premium as commission. In the subsequent years of the policy term, the commission gets smaller. However, it may remain as high as 5–7.5 per cent even in the later years. The high commissions erode value of investments. In 2022, IRDA stated its intent to cap commissions at 20 per cent, which is a consumer-friendly move.[35] Imagine investing ₹100 and immediately starting that investment journey with a 25 per cent loss.

Joseph realized his best option was to exit the policy immediately. He used the free-look period in which policyholders can return their insurance policy and claim a refund.[36] This needs to be done within 15 days of the commencement of the policy.

He took back his first premium, bought a term plan of ₹1 crore and invested the rest in a mix of tax-saving MFs and PF.

Insurance Disasters and Knowing Your Rights

Insurance claims need to follow the policy's terms and conditions. Claims—whether for life or health insurance—are rejected broadly due to the following reasons:

1. The claim was ineligible or against the terms of the policy. For example, the claimant was involved in a case of drunk driving, thus violating the policy terms. Therefore, it is extremely important to understand the exclusions in your insurance policy.

2. Disclosures were not made by the policyholder. For example, a policyholder suppressed the information that he had had a heart surgery a few weeks before taking the policy. Making all necessary disclosures about your age, income, health conditions or family's health history are critical to getting coverage.

These bits of information impact your insurance underwriting—the price acceptable to your insurance provider for your coverage. In the second case, limitations apply. For example, Section 45 of the Insurance Act, 1938, states that no life insurance claim can be denied after three continuous years of coverage, whether from the start of the policy or from its revival. The law says the insurance provider must use this three-year period to call the policy into question for any reason, such as concealment of facts and fraud. After the end of this window, it must honour any claim.[37]

When the insurance provider can establish fraud or suppression of material facts, it can contest the policy, deny claims and even return the premiums paid—but only within the three-year period. Similarly, for health insurance, the IRDA says no claim can be rejected where a policy has completed eight continuous years, except in cases of 'certified fraud and permanent exclusions'.[38] The regulatory body has done some fabulous work on this front. It standardizes the rules. It removes discretionary controls through which claims can be denied. That said, the onus lies on both parties—the insured and the insurer—to ensure that material facts are correctly disclosed and accepted into the policy.

Hence, you must pay close attention to your insurance application. Carefully verify that the information has been shared correctly and not left blank or open to misinterpretation. Do not trust strangers to fill out your forms. If a vital piece of information is missed, a claim may be denied. It is possible you will no longer be alive to fix the error, as a result of which your dependents will suffer the consequences of a claim denial.

There is also the matter of creating wills, nominations, keeping your family informed about your financial affairs, and which of your nominees get to benefit from your insurance coverage.

We will cover this in greater depth in, 'Serenity.'

Look beyond Tax Savings

Table 9

Saving Taxes with Insurance				
Section of the Income Tax Act	Tax Deduction Up To	For Premiums Paid On	For	Ages
80C	₹150,000	Term plans, endowment plans, cashback plans, unit linked insurance policies, annuity plans	Self	No bar
80D	₹25,000	Health insurance policies, top-up policies, preventive health check-ups	Self, spouse, dependent children	Up to 60
	₹25,000		Dependent parents	
	₹50,000		Self, spouse, dependent children	Above 60
	₹50,000		Dependent parents	

Life and health insurance policies help you save income tax. The premiums you pay towards these policies provide tax deductions, which are subtracted from your total income. This reduces your income, but also your taxes. For example, if your annual income is ₹7 lakh and if you claimed no deductions, you would pay ₹54,600 as income tax under the norms in 2021. However, if you purchased life insurance with premiums worth ₹1.5 lakh, and health insurance for yourself and your parents worth ₹50,000, your income would reduce to ₹5 lakh. At that income level, you pay no income tax.

One of the great benefits of health insurance is that you can claim deductions for health insurance bought for your parents as well. If you are under 60 and you have dependent parents over 60, your deductions could go as high as ₹75,000 under the current norms. However, do not let tax-saving benefits dictate your insurance purchase. You buy insurance for financial protection. The tax savings are a useful by-product of the exercise.

If you buy life and health insurance keeping only tax benefits in mind, you are likely to under-insure, which can be risky.

Protecting Your Wheels and Property

Lastly, let us not ignore the importance of owning vehicle and property insurance. It is mandatory by law to insure your vehicle. It is useful to protect your house and the goods within.

Law requires you to own, at the very least, a third-party insurance policy for your vehicles. A third party is anyone other than you or the insurer who could suffer damages in an accident involving your vehicle. To cover damages to self and to one's own vehicle, you need comprehensive vehicle insurance. Just like life or health insurance, vehicle insurance, too, has variants, riders and add-ons that provide you higher levels of protection.

For example, if you were on a highway and your car broke down in the middle of nowhere, would you not want your insurance provider to tow your car to the nearest workshop and lodge you overnight while you wait for the repair work to be over? This, and much more, is possible through comprehensive insurance, ensuring peace of mind for you in your moments of difficulty.

Similarly, would you not want protection for your precious possessions and house in case there was a natural calamity like an earthquake or a cyclone? Home insurance is not mandatory, but it is good to have. It can be taken by both property owners and renters. Tenants can take this insurance to protect the contents of their home against natural calamities, theft, fire and various man-made damages.

Nature has not given us a thick armour like that of the diabolical ironclad beetle. But there is insurance—and that makes our lives easier.

III

SAVOUR: ENJOYING YOUR MONEY

THE BOWERBIRD

Evolutionary biologist Jared Mason Diamond has called bowerbirds 'the most intriguingly human of birds'.[1] Ornithologists recognize these birds as an avian species a class apart. Found in the tropical forests of New Guinea and Australia, they are intelligent, creative and have a heightened sense of aesthetic. A 'bower' is a dwelling, a shelter made with tree branches and vines. The bird gets its name from its ability to create attractive shelters for itself.

Male bowerbirds express their creativity by building intricate nests highlighted with different shades of colour to attract potential mates. Australia's satin bowerbird, for example, loves everything blue. It finds blue things, be it pieces of glasses, flowers or plastic items. Using these, they decorate their nest to attract females.

The bowerbird's nest shows its skill and wealth. It represents its optimistic materialism. This wild bird symbolizes grace, individuality, self-acceptance and the ability to give and receive love. It serves a reminder that expression, beauty and fulfilment are also human needs. Therefore, no money management plan can be complete without the allowance to savour life on one's own terms.

And that is what this section—Savour—will cover.

We will look at how we can enjoy the many flavours of life—the fulfilment of aspirations, self-expression and living a life you have dreamt of—without compromising on financial security. We will also delve into how all of this is possible by living within your means, and by smart use of credit cards and loan products, which are tailored to deliver your desired lifestyle.

THE 5S PYRAMID
BankBazaar

Serenity ← Credit score, Debt-free assets, Retirement

Home, Assets, Investments → Strengthen

Credit card, Personal loan, BNPL
Savour ← → You're here

Insurance: Health, Term, Vehicle, Property → Secure

Save ← Savings, Fixed deposits, Liquid mutual funds

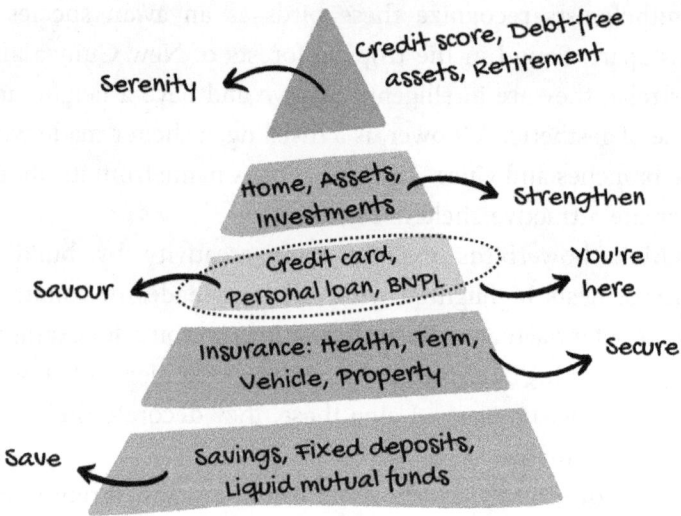

Enjoy Your Money within Limits

The year was 2005. After attending graduate school, I had started working in New York City for Deloitte Consulting. There, I constantly felt that everyone around was driven, ambitious and wanted to get to the next stage in their lives. In that sense, the city had the same energy as big Indian metropolitans like Mumbai.

I started this phase saddled with a student loan. A loan taken in American dollars was hard to pay with an Indian income once I moved back to India to start BankBazaar. The Indian rupee devalued against the dollar over the years. My payments had less and less impact over time in helping me pay the loan.

I focussed on making the minimum payments, i.e. just the monthly instalments. This was a mistake. I should have paid more. If I had pre-paid even 5 per cent of the outstanding loan every year, I could have closed the loan in five years. In the end, it took me 10.

I think of that experience each time the matter of loan payment comes up. For example, during the 2020 pandemic lockdowns, the RBI allowed a six-month moratorium on loan payments. It allowed financially stressed borrowers to pause their loan payments between March and September 2020. In the normal course of events, missing a loan payment invites penal charges and a credit score drop. But this was a special case. The RBI said nobody choosing the moratorium would be penalized.

For borrowers who had lost their incomes in the lockdown, the moratorium was a fair option. But there is no such thing as a free lunch. If you take a home loan at 8 per cent for 20 years and miss the first six EMIs, 27 more EMIs would be added to your loan. This is how compounding interest works. With the moratorium, you can avoid penalties, but your loan would get bigger.

The moratorium math impacted each borrower in their own unique way. But we advised BankBazaar customers to take the moratorium only if they absolutely needed to. And for those who did, we suggested methods to minimize the hefty interest they were about to incur. These methods essentially required them to pay more than their minimum dues—what I should have done with my own student loan.

Coming back to my life in New York, I had other priorities. I continued to have fun in the city. Living in New York City obviously came with high expenses. My friends and I were freshers starting out in one of the biggest cities in the world. We had to be careful. But we also wanted to savour life in the 'Big Apple'. We lived in a shared apartment in West Village. It could be compared to living in Indiranagar in Bengaluru. The place was spacious and well-connected. Just like Indiranagar, it would have been difficult for me to afford the place as an individual. But the three of us got together to split the rent. It allowed us to live in the heart of the city. Neither Indiranagar nor New York City is cheap for anyone starting out. You need to have a sense of proportion.

I eventually learnt that there were always interesting things to do in New York City, no matter what your budget was. You will find restaurants that serve you $4 meals. You will also find ones that charge $400 per meal.

I knew I was going to live in this city only once. So I ate out, partied and even travelled to Brazil, Argentina, Colombia and Mexico. I did not save much in that phase.

This brings me to my point about personal finance thumb rules. They are handy and help develop a sense of proportion and discipline, which you need to live life within your means and to achieve your goals.

In their 2005 book, *All Your Worth: The Ultimate Lifetime Money Plan*, United States politician Elizabeth Warren and her daughter Amelia Warren Tyagi popularized the 50-30-20 thumb rule for monthly budgets.[2] As per this thumb rule, monthly income must be set aside as per a per centage for each important expense head. Just as you would enjoy a balanced diet for a healthy and happy life, you must balance your money allocations for a healthy financial life.

The Warren split requires 50 per cent to be set aside for essential monthly expenses. These can be for rent, groceries, utilities, education costs or insurance payments. Then, 30 per cent can be spent as per your discretion—visiting the mall, upgrading your gadgets or taking a vacation. Lastly, the 20 per cent should be set aside for savings and investments—the minimum amount of money you need to compulsorily lock away.

You could come up with your own ratio based on your circumstances, like Sandhya, a 27-year-old, who works in the robotics department of a multinational company in Bengaluru. She wanted to start a disciplined savings plan using the Warren split. However, she tweaked the per centages to suit her circumstances.

Since Sandhya planned smartly in the early days of her work life, she was able to reward herself with an increase in her discretionary spending.

With a take-home income of ₹70,000, she decided to allocate 50 per cent to her emergency fund. She planned to accumulate it for one year. She wanted to live frugally while she built her emergency fund. So she allocated just 20 per cent of her income to discretionary spending and only 30 per cent to monthly expenses. By the end of the year, she had an emergency fund in place, but now wanted to focus on investments. So she flipped the equation again. She eased up on savings and decided to allocate 50 per cent to monthly expenses. She maintained her discretionary spending at 20 per cent and decided to invest the remaining 30 per cent.

When she feels the need to indulge in a discretionary expense on occasion, she uses her credit card. She understands that she needs to pay the credit card dues in full once her paycheque arrives and make the adjustment in the next month's savings plan.

The bowerbird does not complete its incredible construction in a jiffy. Its work is a meticulous, well-thought-out effort and a construction marvel to behold. Your financial plans also need to be carefully constructed and monitored. The objective of money management is to savour the joys it brings with it, much like the bowerbird in the wild.

The Difference between Wants and Needs

> *Our life is frittered away by detail.*
> *Simplify, simplify, simplify!*

—Henry David Thoreau, *Walden*

Wants are things that you desire, but they are not essential to your existence. Needs, on the other hand, are critical and necessary in your life. To paraphrase an economics lesson, wants are needs backed by purchasing power. For instance, water is a physiological need, as Abraham Maslow would tell you. But drinking only bottled water is a want. A car may be a need, but seeking a particular brand might be a want.

The two seem similar, but you need to learn to differentiate between them. This is critical to your financial health.

Table 10

Eisenhower Matrix	
• Do First: First focus on important tasks to be done the same day.	• Schedule: Important, but not-so-urgent stuff should be scheduled.
• Delegate: What's urgent, but less important, delegate to others.	• Don't Do: What's neither urgent nor important, don't do at all.
MoSCoW Method	
• Must Have: The most important things you can't function without.	• Should Have: Things that are important yet not absolutely vital.
• Could Have: It would be nice to have these.	• Won't Have: You can do without these.

There are many ways to arrive at financial decisions.

Let us look at the MoSCoW Method.[3] It stands for Must Have, Should Have, Could Have and Won't Have. It is a prioritization model devised by Dai Clegg to help make business decisions. It helps you list your wants and needs under these four categories before you can discard what is not a priority in your current timeline.

Another model to separate wants and needs is the Eisenhower Matrix.[4] It was initially developed for productivity, but can be easily customized for wants and needs.

What are its takeaways? If something is important, do it now. If it is urgent, but not important, delegate it. If something is not urgent but important, schedule it for later. If it is neither important nor urgent, avoid doing it.

What is the point of this prioritization exercise? It will help you understand you need not deny yourself what is truly important to you, and also ruthlessly cut out what is not.

The bowerbird spares no effort in creating its attractive dwelling. It remains steadfastly focussed on what matters. It cannot be distracted by something that does not.

Overlaps between Wants and Needs

Neha, a Moneymooner, wants to fulfil some of her aspirations with every salary hike she receives. Being a cycling enthusiast, her goal is winning a championship someday. She wants to upgrade her bicycle to a swift carbon-based model. She listed it as a want. However, when she grouped it under a need like regular exercise, she justified the high cost.

She followed the MoSCoW method to arrive at her decision. The bicycle did not categorize as a 'won't have'. She could not do without it. It loosely categorized as a 'could have'. She had the purchasing power to turn her want into a need. It was certainly a 'should have' because it was to help her train for competitive cycling. And it most definitely was a 'must have' considering her need for physical fitness.

Her wants and needs strongly aligned in this case. With a desk-based job, cycling was her go-to enjoyable and strenuous activity. It ticked many boxes, including being part of a cycling community, which helped her maintain her social life and disconnect from work-related stress. It helped her go ahead and purchase a bicycle of her choice, even though it was costlier than a regular one.

Needs and wants can be different for different people. You need to devise your strategy to make the most of life when it comes to enjoying your money within limits.

Lifestyle, Consumption and Borrowed Money

Life must be savoured but while living within one's means. In the grand scheme of your financial life, more of your money must go towards pursuits that make you financially stronger. Likewise, you must reduce the flow of money towards pursuits that financially weaken you.

Most of your money will go towards 'must have' pursuits. Lesser money should flow into 'should haves' and 'could haves'. The 'won't haves' should be aggressively minimized. This also applies to your borrowing decisions.

BankBazaar, the credit marketplace I co-founded, helps you buy loans and credit cards from a variety of banks. But even as I market these loans, it is my responsibility to remind borrowers what loans should and should not do. Borrowing can be either constructive or destructive to your finances. You can borrow to create assets, whose value appreciates with time, or you can borrow for sunk costs.

For example, a home loan helps you buy property whose value will increase as the years roll by. An education loan finances the ladder to a career that will help you become prosperous. A business loan will help you take your enterprise to new heights. This kind of borrowing helps you become financially stronger.

On the flip side, you can also borrow to finance lifestyle choices and consumption. For example, a car loan helps you buy the ride you always wanted. But a car is a depreciating asset—its value reduces with age. You will sell it at a value far lower than the price you paid for it. Discounting the utility you will derive from the car, the more you borrow for it as a depreciating asset, the more money you lose over time through the interest paid on the loan.

Similarly, credit cards help you finance your shopping, entertainment and travel requirements. You get deals, discounts, rewards and cashback. You get no-cost EMIs for 6–12 months. But if you were buying groceries on your credit card and then delaying your card payment, the interest on your dues will make your groceries costlier. This is bad for your finances.

This also takes us back to the earlier lesson about the 50-30-20 rule. You must finance your lifestyle with your own income—both your basic needs as well as discretionary wants. If you lived on borrowed money and paid heavy interest, your finances will be in trouble. We are living in a time when credit is easily available. We are inundated with prompts to take a credit card or a loan. While these instruments help finance our aspirations, they can also create financial traps that we should all try to avoid.

And so this chapter is going to be about making the best use of small loans, and laying a strong foundation for your credit history.

Borrowing for Lifestyle

Vikram is an avid photographer, who loves to travel to scenic locales for his shoots. The Wealth Warrior created a travel fund for this pursuit. Occasionally, he took a personal loan to finance his foreign travels.[5]

Personal loans can be taken for any use. You might take it for funding a holiday, buying a gadget or financing a hospitalization. Nearly every bank provides one. All they ask you to do is to not use the loan for speculative activities such as betting on stock markets.

A personal loan does not require a collateral—the asset you pledge to the lender as security. A collateral could be gold, a fixed deposit, property papers or anything of value. The collateral is returned to you once you have repaid the loan. Conversely, if you fail to repay the loan, the lender reserves the right to sell the collateral to recover the unpaid dues. Loans that require collaterals are secured.

The unsecured nature of a personal loan makes it costlier than secured loans such as home loans. In early 2022, home loans could be availed at interest rates starting around 6.5 per cent. Personal loan started at around 9 per cent.

Photography is an expensive hobby and so is travelling. However, Vikram being brilliant at his work, shot enough photographs for a gallery exhibit. There, he sold his work. While the personal loan financed his travel costs, it was the exhibition that helped him make profit.

Vikram borrowed to finance his lifestyle. But he also balanced the costs of borrowing smartly by making the pursuit pay for itself. It was money well managed.

Meanwhile, Vikram's friend Sanjay, also a Wealth Warrior, has yet to catch up on the concept of good and bad borrowing. Sanjay loves gadgets. Every time an upgrade is available, he goes for it. Be it a phone, a music system or a video game console, he wants all the latest technology.

He enjoys being the tech expert in his social circle. The problem rests in the fact that he often bought these items on credit. He has an ongoing personal loan for a laptop purchase. He also has dues on two different credit cards from a mobile and music system purchase. The interest on these loans is not easy to pay. Sanjay offset these costs through buyback offers or by selling old gadgets online. But this is not enough.

Sanjay has come to realize that being in debt to finance his lifestyle is not a good idea. He is now toying with the idea of starting a tech review podcast and video channel. He hopes to make an income from his reviews and receive gadgets directly from manufacturers.

Let us understand Sanjay's situation through the Eisenhower Matrix. He was prioritizing ways on how to get out debt. That was his 'Do First.' Starting the podcast was his 'Schedule.' Getting gadgets directly from the manufactures became his 'Delegate.' Not taking more loans was his 'Don't Do.' He realized he could not afford worsening his debt.

Unsecured Credit and How It Helps You

There is a glut of unsecured loans in the markets. Alongside banks and non-banking companies, there are lending start-ups and fintech companies offering easy access to liquidity to anyone who needs it. I am sure you have received many calls and text messages about loan offers. The pandemic has caused liquidity problems for many. People have suffered income uncertainty and need help with their finances.

Some years back, we just had personal loans and credit cards as unsecured credit products. Now we also have Buy Now Pay Later (BNPL) loans. All these options are available to the right borrowers with just a few taps on their phone screens. Fill out your personal details, complete your KYC process and get your loans sanctioned—sometimes in minutes.

Thanks to changes in lending regulations, the KYC process can now be done from your home via a video call. Gone are the days when you had to queue up in a bank, submit your photocopied documents and then wait for days to get your loan. The RBI is to be congratulated for these progressive regulations, which have not only empowered consumers but also encouraged tremendous innovation in fintech—a domain in which India is a world leader today.

The young are rapidly turning to these digital loan options. As per a Bernstein report from April 2021, the gross merchandise value of India's BNPL market was valued at $15 billion. This is expected to grow over sixfold to $100 billion by 2025.[6]

With BNPL being a new lending category, its regulations are still being shaped to protect customers. There were concerns around this category that needed to be addressed. The RBI wanted greater transparency over loan charges. It also wanted all BNPL lending to be reported to credit bureaus for the computation of credit scores.

In August 2022, the RBI stepped in to announce new digital lending guidelines. Now, digital lenders will need to provide a one-page fact sheet mentioning all loan costs. They will also have to report consumer data to the bureaus.

Unsecured loans, as I said earlier, attract a higher rate of interest than secured loans, such as home loans. Given how easily they are available, how are they good for your finances? Credit cards, electronic store credit and now BNPLs will increasingly become the first form of credit young people take. Your first loan of any kind initiates your credit history. I would also throw education loans into this mix, though they are less comparable to the other options.

These forms of credit help you fulfil an immediate need, such as paying for a cab ride or buying an electronic item. For an eligible borrower, they are easy to get and easy to repay, and easy to avail again. Your credit card transactions may also provide you incentives, such as reward points, discounts and deals. This is better than spending via cash, which has no incentive.

India has seen an interesting development with no-cost EMIs as a built-in feature on credit cards. With these, you can buy electronics with a no-interest loan that can be paid off in 6–12 months. For example, with BankBazaar's co-brand credit cards, you have no-cost EMIs on Amazon with access to offers delivered to customers on the first of every month for laptops, TVs and household appliances.

Most importantly, these forms of unsecured credit also help you develop a credit history, which becomes pivotal to your financial life and forms an important component in your 5S Pyramid.

Your credit history is a snapshot of your financial health. No matter what you earn, how much money you have in your bank and where you live, your credit history sticks to you. If you pay your loans on time, it will reflect positively on your credit history. If you are late, have loan defaults and have not been able to fully repay your dues, your credit history becomes toxic.

As a nation, we are still coming around to the concept of credit score. We have much to learn about the long-term repercussions of our credit behaviour. As per BankBazaar's 2021 Aspiration Index survey, 27 per cent of the respondents did not know that their credit scores impact their loan interest rates.

We will come to what a credit score is shortly. But as of now, you should know that it dictates whether you will be able to borrow, how much and at what cost. Therefore, while unsecured credit is easily available, it is critical to use it in a disciplined manner, else it could hurt your credit score and jolt the 5S Pyramid.

We will talk in depth about what credit history is, how it is scored and how it impacts you. We will also look at why you need to reach Serenity, the summit of our 5S Pyramid, with a credit score over 800.

How to Get Your First Credit Line

A BNPL

BNPL loans are a fast-growing loan segment. They are being sold by fintech lenders, large non-banking lenders, e-commerce players and even some banks. BNPLs have been around for some years now. Ride-sharing and food delivery apps as well as several e-commerce platforms have had them as payment options. These loans typically range from a few thousand rupees to a lakh. With the pandemic, the demand for BNPLs shot up. The period saw a change in the way people make transactions. It happened because of two fundamental reasons.

1. Job losses and pay-cuts due to the ensuing lockdowns made it difficult for many people to spend money freely.
2. An increasing number of people turned online even for their essential expenses, like groceries and utility bills, in addition to their discretionary purchases. Thanks to these factors, BNPLs proliferated.

The loan does what its name suggests. It allows you to buy something and pay for it later. The merchant, typically someone on an e-commerce platform, allows you to pay from options such as cash on delivery, debit or credit card, or a BNPL. If you choose to pay via a BNPL, the payment is done on your behalf by the BNPL loan provider, with whom you need to register your loan account.

If you use the BNPL option and later repay the loan provider in the interest-free window, you can avoid paying interest and penalties. You typically incur no charges for using this loan, not even processing fees. The loan allows you to delay your payments at no cost, provided you repay the dues on time.

The loan provider makes his money by taking a cut from the merchant.

Consumers, especially Early Jobbers and Moneymooners, are looking for simplified microloans to manage their recurring and occasional purchases in a better manner. Lenders often prefer borrowers with a credit history when disbursing a home loan, car loan or a personal loan. But often for BNPLs, lenders are open to borrowers who are new to credit.

But remember, what has been borrowed also needs to be repaid. If you do not repay in a timely manner, your credit history will get wrecked.

A Credit Card

It is easy to avail a credit card. Let us see how it can be done:

1. If you are a salaried person, check with the bank where you have your salary account. They would normally create a pre-approved credit card offer for you. You can avail it with minimal paperwork.

2. If you do not want to apply for a card from your bank and are interested in seeing what other offers you can get from other banks, go online. For example, on a lending platform such as BankBazaar, your pre-approved loan and card offers from various banks will be listed in one place. You can choose the offer you like.

3. Things are trickier for the non-salaried. What if your income is unstable? What if you have no income? The bank will see you as a high-risk borrower. But worry not. You can still get your credit card. For that, you will need to pledge an FD with the bank as collateral. The bank will give you the card with a spending limit of up to 90 per cent of your deposit. There is another

way for those with unstable income to get a credit card. They can get an add-on card through a family member's credit card. The add-on card is a sub-account of the main card. Though the cards share a spending limit, the add-on has its unique card number. For practical purposes, it is one account with one spending limit, and the main account holder is responsible for repayment.

Before you apply for any credit product, remember to check your eligibility and have your documents in order. Banks do like salaried borrowers because of their income stability. They may still impose other eligibility criteria, such as a minimum salary (typically, ₹30,000 and above) and a minimum number of months spent in your current job. Thanks to digital KYC, it is easy to sign up for a credit card if you have proofs of identity, address and income as required by the bank.

So stay safe at home, grab your documents and go online.

Keep Track of Your Credit Score

Procrastination is like a credit card:
it's a lot of fun until you get the bill.

—Christopher Parker, actor

Here is a rule of thumb I would like to suggest.

Any person with a running loan or active credit card should check their credit score once every month. A credit score is a three-digit rating given to borrowers for their credit behaviour. The rating ranges between 300 and 900. The higher you score, the better, 900 being the elusive, perfect score.

The credit score is a measure of your credit health. By extension, it is a measure of your financial health. It shows how you have managed your dues in the past. This can also indicate how strong or weak your finances have been. All the loans and credit cards you have taken, each month you have been late with your EMIs and each loan you have closed shows up in your credit report. It lays bare your credit history and assigns you a score on the basis of your credit behaviour.

Good credit behaviour is paying your EMIs and credit card dues on time for several years in a row. This alone has the highest positive impact on your score, pushing it higher. Delaying your dues, having an unpaid credit card balance and applying for too many credit cards or loans in a short span will lower your score. Closing a loan or card account without full repayment of your principal and interest can destroy your score.

Your credit behaviour stays on your record. When you apply for a loan or credit card again, the lender looks at your credit report and sees what you had been up to in the past. The widely acceptable benchmark of a good credit score is 750. If you score beyond that, lenders will like you. They will reserve the best loan offers, ones with the lowest interest rates, for you. If your score is low, you will pay a higher rate of interest. If your score is very low, your credit application may be rejected and you may not be able to take a new loan or credit card.

There is no getting away from your credit history. Bear in mind, the credit score will only specify whether you repaid or failed to repay your loans on time. It does not take into account why you were late. You might have missed payments due to loss of income, a hospitalization or a lockdown. You might have been wilfully negligent and refused to pay despite having the means to. For the credit score, a late payment is a late payment regardless of your reasons.

When you borrow from a regulated lending institution, such as a bank or a non-banking company, your credit activity will be reported by the lender to credit bureaus such as Experian and TransUnion CIBIL. The bureaus receive this data, put it through their own unique credit scoring mechanism and give you a score.

It is very easy to check your credit score online. The credit bureaus must offer you one free credit report every year. Nevertheless, you can get unlimited free reports and score checks via websites such as BankBazaar.

My credit score is 862. What is yours?

My First Credit Card and the Add-On Experience

I got my first credit card in USA. It was an American Express student credit card with a small credit line. It was given to me as soon as I started my studies for graduation. I used to buy groceries with it. This was my first experience with shopping at big American supermarkets in 2003. I was good at paying the credit card bill in full every month. This boosted my credit score in USA. At that time, I also had a large student loan from an American bank, which funded all Columbia students without collateral.

I was not repaying the loan as a student. So the credit card was key to improving my credit score. American Express had issued the card to me with a small credit limit considering my admission to a reputed school. The small limit helped mitigate initial risks to the lender. They kept increasing my spending limit as I kept paying my bills.

I had learnt about credit score in USA, as it was required for everything including a phone connection and renting a house. India, on the other hand, was slowing moving to this paradigm—at least as far as lending was concerned. When I returned to India in 2007, the first credit card I took was a Deutsche Bank add-on card connected to my parent's account. Later, IndusInd Bank acquired the Deutsche Bank credit card portfolio. I received an IndusInd card then.

In these days of bank mergers and acquisitions, you will find many consumers making a similar switch. They will need to consent to receive the acquiring bank's credit card in lieu of their current credit card, which is being discontinued.

Interestingly, getting an add-on card did not help me create or improve my credit score. In fact, the reason I had an add-on card was because without a credit score in India, I was ineligible for a credit card. The American credit scores with TransUnion and Experian are completely different from Indian credit scores with the same credit bureaus. So my good credit history in did not translate to any benefit in India.

The add-on card gave me a credit line. But it kept me out of the benefit of developing a credit score. There is also a mistake I made with my first Indian credit card. For over a year, I paid only the minimum amount or partial amount and started carrying a monthly balance.

Those days, I was short on cash as the company was in its nascent stages. We also did not have the option to convert credit card purchases to EMIs as we commonly do now.

In hindsight, I realize I should have ideally cut my costs to live within my means or alternatively relied on lower cost credit, like a personal loan. That would have been cheaper due to lower interest rates.

But soon, by a combination of reducing my discretionary expenses and increase in my salary, I was able to pay off my credit card dues. Since then, I have been more careful in paying off my bill in full and using my credit card for its many benefits.

Being Late Is Costly, Very Costly

Syed, a Wealth Warrior and a digital marketer, found himself abroad for work. Before leaving India, he had purchased a book from an airport shop. It cost just ₹250 and Syed used his credit card to pay for it.

Syed's card spending limit was ₹1.5 lakh. Financially, he was well-organized. He had already paid off a car loan and a home loan. He had no late loan payments on his record. As a result, his credit score was an impressive 844. The book purchase had happened at the end of the credit card billing cycle. Syed was going to stay abroad for several weeks. While there, Syed missed his credit card due date and could not access payment options to repay his card dues. A late payment penalty of ₹300 and interest was applied to his dues.

Credit card users must make a minimum payment each month to avoid late payment penalty. This minimum amount is normally 5 per cent of the dues, subject to a lower cap set by the bank. Syed's minimum due amount was ₹200.

The penalty and the interest did not hurt. As soon as Syed returned to India, he paid the dues in full. What hurt was the precipitous decline in his credit score. In the first month, Syed's score fell to 776. Though he had paid his dues, his score fell some more to 727 the next month.

He was planning to take a new home loan of around ₹50 lakh. At the credit score of 844, his home loan interest rate would have been a rock-bottom 8.60 per cent. But because of the decline in his credit score, he would now get the same loan at 9.30 per cent. The interest on the first loan was ₹54.89 lakh over 20 years. The interest on the second would be ₹60.29 lakh. The missed card payment of just ₹250 was now going to cost Syed an additional ₹5.40 lakh in home loan interest.

He decided to delay his home purchase and fix his credit score first. It took him six months of disciplined credit card use to take up his score to 840.

This, unfortunately, is the story of many. We take our credit card payments lightly. We think a delay of a few days will not harm our finances. What is in a small penalty? But that is far from the truth. Credit is available easily, but it still needs to be repaid—in full and on time. Not doing so will prove costly in ways you may have not even thought of.

The Secret Sauce to 800

It does not take much to get a credit score of 800. It is not rocket science. Timely repayment is enough. However, there are other things that help, too.

Prince, a Wealth Warrior from Bengaluru, has a strategy to keep his credit score high by using his credit card. We can learn from his example:

1. Always pay dues and EMIs on time. If you cannot pay the entire dues, at least pay the minimum. Avoid missing even a single payment and that will positively impact your credit score. A few years ago, Prince used to be wayward with the repayments of his dues. He took care of it later and automated his credit card payments. He instructed his bank to clear his dues before the deadline. He has never been late since then.

2. Avoid spending more than 30 per cent of your spending limit. A high credit utilization ratio (CUR) moderately hurts credit score. What is CUR? It is the per centage of your available spending limit in a month.

   Let us say you had two credit cards, each with

a spending limit of ₹1 lakh. You spent ₹55,000 on one card and ₹75,000 on another. Your total spend is ₹1.3 lakh out of a total limit of ₹2 lakh, so your CUR is 65 per cent. This is very high. It will pull your score down. Keep it to 30 per cent or less, and do not forget the first rule: always pay the dues on time.

3. Try paying in full. If you keep paying minimum amount due, your dues will keep increasing because interest adds up. If the dues increase, your CUR increases, which we know is bad for your score.

4. Hold on to your credit card. Do not cancel it unless necessary. The older your credit card is, the better it is for your credit score. It shows you have held on to this credit line for many years without getting into trouble with it. That shows creditworthiness. It might be possible you do not like your card and want a better one. You could just ask your bank for an upgraded card with better benefits. That is what Prince did. He cited his credit discipline, increased income and relationship with the bank to get an upgraded card. Had the bank not agreed to his request, he would have simply got himself an additional card from another bank.

5. Do not apply for too many credit cards or loans in a short span of time. Select one option thoughtfully as per your eligibility and apply for it. Each time you apply for a credit line, the lender checks your credit history. This is called a 'hard' check of your credit score. Each hard check mildly lowers your score. Several hard checks can substantially lower your score.

6. Use your credit card. Do not just keep it in your wallet. An active credit life with timely and full repayment will improve your score bit by bit, and provide you

rewards, deals and discounts, which other modes of payment may not.

7. Do a monthly 'soft' check to track your credit score progress. Soft checks are your own credit score checks and can be done as many times as you want. Soft checks do not harm your score. Monthly checks are also important because they can help you identify errors in your credit report, which can then be flagged to your lender and credit bureau. Errors can also damage your score.

Your credit score as well as all loan accounts are linked to your PAN. If someone were to fraudulently or erroneously use your PAN to take a loan, the loan would get tagged to you. If there would be a default on this loan, your credit score would suffer. Errors flagged to the credit bureau and lender must be rectified.

8. Do not take the option to 'settle' your loan or credit card dues. This option is given by banks to defaulting borrowers unable to pay their dues for any reason. Through it, the bank asks you to pay a fraction of your dues towards interest and principal, and consider the loan account settled. For example, suppose you defaulted on dues of ₹4 lakh and the bank asked you to pay ₹1 lakh to end the matter. It sounds like an easy way out. But taking this option will destroy your credit score. The settlement will become the basis for rejection of your future loan applications. The settlement will underscore your inability to service past loans. Lenders will see you as a high-risk borrower.

Therefore, aim to pay your dues in full, even if you are not on time. The only acceptable account status from the point of view of your credit score is 'closed'. It means the loan principal and interest were paid in full.

Credit cards are a double-edged sword. Use them badly and they will wreck your finances and your credit score. Use them well following the above eight points and they will help you develop financial clout.

Before BNPLs, using credit cards was the only way you could build your credit score without paying interest, which means repaying your dues on time. The clout of a great credit score will help you to keep borrowing at favourable terms, be it for buying a house or a car or anything else, propelling you towards Serenity.

Tracking Your Credit Report Errors

When it comes to your credit history, a lot could go wrong despite your best efforts. I could cite my own example.

I made my first credit score check in India in 2017. We had launched the credit tracker dashboard on BankBazaar at the time. Customers use the tool for free credit score checks. My check showed my credit score was above 800. That made me a prime borrower. The rude shock was finding out that five out of my 200 EMI payments had been marked late.

Digging deeper, I found that the late payments were on a car loan. The bank from which I had taken the loan had marked them late despite all my payments being timely. This would have damaged my credit score. I later realized that the bank had not cashed the cheque for my first EMI. Often, the first EMI on a car loan is collected in advance, right when the loan is disbursed. So while my payment had been made, the bank had erred by not depositing the cheque and had gone on to report me as late.

At the time, I did not have the bandwidth to write to the bank and the credit bureau with proof of payment. These are some of the pain points around credit scoring that inspired BankBazaar to launch the CreditStrong dashboard, which has a chatbot through which you can complain about your credit report issues and get them fixed. CreditStrong also has a credit fitness advisor. It tells you how to improve your credit score—necessary to keep you steady on your climb to Serenity.

Don't Be MAD

> *With great power, comes great responsibility.*
>
> —Uncle Ben, *Spiderman* (2002)

Have you considered what may happen if you pay only the minimum amount due (MAD) on your credit card bill? Let us look at a theoretical example.

Kanishka, a happy-go-lucky Early Jobber, loved to splurge using her credit card. Let us say that Kanishka's MAD is 5 per cent of her dues, subject to a minimum of ₹500. Assume she spent ₹1 lakh on her credit card and decided to pay only MAD from here on.

The typical credit card interest rate is 4 per cent per month. How long do you think will it take Kanishka to repay her dues? Six months? One year? Two years? Three years?

Think about it. If she pays 5 per cent every month and her monthly interest is 4 per cent, she is effectively repaying only 1 per cent every month. Theoretically speaking, at a rate of 1 per cent per month, it will take Kanishka 36 years and nine months to repay her dues of ₹1 lakh.

Sounds insane, right?

In those nearly 37 years, she would have completed most of her adult life, retired from work and would be looking forward to living her life at an easier pace. But she would still be in debt from that one-time credit card binge in her youth. Apart from the debt of ₹1 lakh, she would have paid ₹3.15 lakh as interest. This is assuming she did not use the card again. If she did, her dues would be higher.

What is the lesson we need to look out for? MAD leads to mad debt. Pay your credit card dues in full because the interest charges are high and would take forever to pay off with MAD.

Make Your Credit Card Work for You

That is correct. Let your card do some of the heavy lifting for your financial progress. If you want to savour life, like the hard-working bowerbird, you might as well make use of all the help coming your way. A credit card, when used smartly, can give you several benefits and help you savour life better. These benefits include cashback, redeemable reward points, discounts and deals, curated lifestyle experiences, travel benefits and much more.

Each time you pay a bill with your credit card, payment networks such as Visa and Mastercard make a little money. That money comes from the vendor. For example, if you paid ₹1,000 for your dinner using your credit card, 2 per cent or ₹20 will go to your card's payment network. The restaurant will get ₹980.

The networks pay back some of these charges to you in the form of benefits.

During the pandemic, BankBazaar tracked an explosion in online spends. This was caused by customers wanting to transact from the safety of their homes. They no longer benefitted from free movie tickets, free petrol, airport lounge access or discounted fine dining, which their cards offer. These were of little use while they were stuck at home. They wanted their online spends to be incentivized. So BankBazaar used the opportunity to launch FinBooster, a co-branded credit card in partnership with Yes Bank. The card gives its users higher rewards for online spends for apparels, groceries and food—things they cannot do without.

Your credit card should either help you in your current lifestyle or help you access the lifestyle you want. When this happens, you are rewarded for doing the things you need to or want to do. As you savour life, the savings add up.

Personally, I use credit cards extensively for all payments. I enjoy using the reward points and cashback to pay for my card bills and fuel costs. I also enjoy the no-cost EMI offers with which I can plan my electronic purchases with no interest or processing fees.

I also like the fact that it is easier to reverse disputed charges on my credit card. For example, if you erroneously swipe your debit card twice, the money will go out of your bank account twice. But with a credit card, you could call up the card company and get the disputed charges fixed in no time.

How Chris Hutchins Hacked the Credit Card Game

If you love shopping and dining, you need a card that adds to your experience. If you are a frequent flier, you need a card that provides free air miles, lounge access, priority boarding, travel insurance and hotel deals.

Few people in the world have been able to understand this and make their credit cards work for them better than Chris

Hutchins. The Wealth Warrior and former Google employee went to extreme lengths to maximize reward points from his credit card spends. By brilliantly optimizing his expenses and gaming the system, Chris accumulated close to 12 million points from his credit cards.[7] The points allowed him to accomplish his passion: travelling the world for free.

At last count, he could convert his points into 250 flights or 1,000 nights in nice hotels. He can travel to any destination without worrying about the costs. Doing so, he has been able to visit 60 countries.[8] Chris realized that every time he spent a dollar, he could get an air mile. These are airline reward units that can be exchanged for free plane tickets. Chris decided he was going to rack up air miles as fast as he could. His love for travelling drove him down the rabbit hole of reward points, terms and conditions, and the financial hack of a lifetime. He maximized his points so efficiently that he no longer had to pay for his trips.[9]

In 2021, Chris had 10 credit cards, 20 bank accounts and 20 reward point accounts. His wife, Amy, has her own credit cards. At one point, he had 65 bank accounts. His friends and wife first thought he was being cheap. But they came around. They even helped fuel his thirst for rewards.

During his team outings and office off-site meetings, Chris would volunteer to pay for his groups' bills. He would later be reimbursed by the company. Settling these large bills for the whole group allowed Chris a way to accumulate a lot of points quickly on his credit cards. He also started organizing parties for his friends. He became their go-to person for planning their bachelor parties and weddings. The process was the same. Chris would pay the bills from his credit cards and earn his points. His dues would be reimbursed by friends.

When he was about to get married to Amy, the two wanted

to shoot a video of the event. But the budget would not permit it. He eventually found a videographer whose dream was to visit Seychelles. Chris offered to fly her and her husband to an all-expense paid trip to Seychelles for the wedding, provided the videographer shot the film for free.

Chris used his rewards to make all of this happen. But he also made it a point to educate anyone following his example. He said, 'I would actively try to pay down those credit cards to a zero balance before you enter the points game because any amount of points is not worth the interest.'[10]

That is correct. Interest on these large-sized dues could hurt your finances. Chris has benefitted from the rewards in the system. But the system would stop working for him if he started racking up interest on his lifestyle choices. This leads us to an important question: how many credit cards is too many for you? We will find the answer to this question later in the chapter.

The Rush for Premium Cards

At BankBazaar, we have seen a continuous rise in demand for premium credit cards—they typically attract annual fees. Depending on the type of card, the fee can range from a few hundred rupees to a few lakh.

Free credit cards do not attract any annual fees. Some premium cards also waive off their annual fees if you achieve a spending milestone, such as ₹1 lakh in a year. Though they attract a cost, premium cards often pay for themselves. They are increasingly what credit card hunters want because such cards unlock high spending limits, lower interest rates and premium lifestyle benefits.

In 2020, we at BankBazaar saw a 115 per cent increase

year-on-year in the demand for premium cards. Non-metro cities were not to be left behind. Their demand for such cards rose by 240 per cent in the same period. Among women, there was a 173 per cent increase. Among the age group of 25–45, there was a 128 per cent increase.

The fees on these cards are not a deterrent because such cards can pay for themselves. More Indians are looking to own a second or third credit card tailored in the premium category. Indians want to savour life, much like the bowerbird, who works very hard to find colourful things to decorate its nest with. Sometimes, you must take a step back to go two steps forward.

Inside the World of Super Premium Cards

Then there are the luxury credit cards. Credit card companies give them only to the ultra-rich. These are the highest of the high-end credit cards, sometimes made of precious metals and stones. They can attract lakhs in annual fees and often have no spending limits. You can buy literally anything off them.

Through these cards, you get unlimited lounge access, concierge services, and curated experiences, such as fine dining served by the world's best chefs, priority bookings, discounted chartered flights, gift vouchers of luxury brands, golf and sailing lessons, and much more. There are even things money cannot buy, but the card company may go out of its way to get them for you.

Take the example of the legendary American Express Black Card, one of the most exclusive cards in the world. It is made of titanium and has no spending limit. The Internet is full of stories about the card. One story reported in many media outlets goes like this. A customer wanted some sand from the

Dead Sea for their child's school project on the Holy Land. The card company reportedly sent a concierge by bike to the Dead Sea, collected the sand and had it couriered to the customer in London.

Snopes.com, the well-known fact-checking website, decided to investigate stories about this card, in particular the rumour that it could help you buy anything. Its conclusion: the rumour was true.[11]

Super premium credit cards are typically offered on invitation to a very small number of customers on the basis of their net worth, relationship with the bank, income or credit history. In most cases, you cannot apply for one.

That is the kind of financial clout and creditworthiness one can aspire to have as they make their ascent to the top of the 5S Pyramid.

Debt Spirals and Catching Them Early

You can land in a debt spiral when you take more loans to pay off existing loans and end up getting pulled deeper in debt. This can happen for many reasons. It could be due to undisciplined use of loans and excessive borrowing. It could be because you borrowed from loan sharks—unregulated lenders who charge sky-high, hard-to-pay interest and harass you for payments. It could also be for reasons beyond your control, such as an economic or health crisis, which hurt your ability to service your loans. Sometimes, your income is insufficient to pay your loans. And you may not have an asset, such as gold, to liquidate to pay the loan. The only way forward might be to borrow some more.

This is the point at which you risk getting into a debt spiral. Consider it the event horizon of a black hole from where there may be no return. Do not allow yourself to reach this point. When you have borrowed money, it is your moral, legal and financial obligation to pay it back—preferably with your own funds. If you require new loans to repay old ones, your debts may start to hurt.

It is easy to get a credit card or a personal loan these days. With easy money abound, it is also easy to fall into bad financial habits, such as not repaying your dues in a timely manner. The consequences of a debt spiral are profound. It can hurt you financially, strain your income and ruin your credit score. It may lead to social isolation due to your lack of creditworthiness. All this combined can hurt your mental health too.

Beware of the urge to live off borrowed money. Also be cautious of your income, health and life risks. Lower them by provisioning for an emergency fund and buying health and life insurance. That way, you will not have to borrow your way out of an emergency.

Getting Out of a Credit Card Debt Spiral

What if you are already in this spiral?

Let us examine the case of Vicky, a Moneymooner who ran a local chain of grocery shops. Vicky had piled on dues of ₹3 lakh on his credit cards. He was anxious to repay his dues. He had an MAD of 5 per cent, but the interest was 4 per cent. This meant that he had to repay at least ₹15,000 a month as MAD, assuming he made no further use of the cards.

The pandemic stifled his business. Interest was piling rapidly on the credit cards. But Vicky decided to have positive intent—he was going to pay his dues one way or the other. So here is how he did it.

1. He stopped using his credit cards. Fresh use would immediately attract interest. This would not help him.
2. He took stock of his dues. He ranked them by size, interest rate and charges involved. He decided to target the dues with the highest interest rate. This would be his credit cards.
3. He liquidated some gold and sold some of his high-end electronic items. This helped him raise some cash. It acted as a lump sum payment towards the dues. This lowered the pressure of piling interest.
4. He worked towards stabilizing his income, which made repayment easier. He also cut down on discretionary expenses and diverted more of his income towards debt payment.
5. As he made progress on his payments, he asked the bank for a loan consolidation option. This allowed him to combine his dues and pay them off in one shot. It left him with a single, consolidated loan that attracted an interest rate of 12.99 per cent. This loan would be easier to repay than the credit card dues that attracted interest at 4 per cent a month, on which the interest would effectively be 60 per cent a year.

As said, borrowing to pay existing loans is a bad idea because it pulls you into a debt spiral. So why is Vicky's loan consolidation a good idea? This is because if you have the financial discipline to pull it off, it makes sense to refinance several high-interest loans into a low-interest one. This is, however, not an option every borrower can take. If you are already struggling to pay your dues, have an instable income and do not have any collateral to pledge, you are going to struggle to get a fresh loan.

Vicky was able to get the consolidated loan only after he

got reasonable income stability. The lower interest rate pinched him less. This arrangement allowed him to immediately pay off his expensive credit card debt. A personal loan comes in handy if the credit card debt is steep. This option seems to offer an instant solution to get out of a debt spiral. But remember: it is just another opportunity to develop and improve your money management habits. Money should be savoured responsibly. It should not create stress. The bowerbird's beautiful abode helps it find fulfilment. It cannot be a source of pain for it.

How Many Credit Cards Should You Own?

This is a tricky question. There is no single answer. You can have one or many, or none whatsoever.

Since 2015, I have had a Citibank travel miles card which is for airlines miles. But recently, I have been converting my points to Amazon gift cards to buy books for my daughter. A FinBooster co-brand card by BankBazaar and Yes Bank is the one to which I have been moving all my expenses. The accelerated digital rewards on online dining, which we use at least twice per week, and the CreditStrong credit fitness advisor are helpful.

I also use the SaveMax co-brand card by BankBazaar and RBL Bank for my fuel and groceries to get accelerated rewards, and to access the no-cost EMI offers on hospitality and travel. I have an Amazon credit card that I use on the website for the 5 per cent cashback for Prime customers. Lastly, I have an American Express corporate card for corporate expenses only. It is a charge card and must be repaid in full the same month by the company.

What are the key differences between a charge card and a

credit card? With the latter, you can get away with minimum payment and have a defined spending limit. In the former, the spending limit may not be defined, but the dues cannot be carried over to the next month. In the end, what matters is credit discipline. If you have it, get as many cards as you can maintain without getting into financial trouble. Chris Hutchins is a good example to illustrate the point.

Should you have no credit card whatsoever? Is that a good option?

There runs a thread among the credit-averse that they should not borrow for anything. They may think it is trouble or they probably lack the discipline required to use one. In being credit-averse, they miss out one of the easiest ways to develop a credit history, which unlocks many benefits we went over earlier—discounts, rewards or getting a loan in the future.

We have seen the methods through which you can use a credit card in a disciplined way and avoid trouble. However, the choice to not own a credit card is entirely yours and so are the costs.

Those who are credit-averse might need a loan at some point in their lives. If they are new to credit and have no history, the lender may charge them a higher interest rate. That is one of the costs of never availing credit. But if they use their credit card in a disciplined manner and develop a good credit history, they will get a cheap loan at a low interest rate.

Next, should you have one card or many?

If you have one card that incentivizes most of your usual spends, gives you the rewards you need and helps you access the lifestyle you need, you may not need another card.

It may so happen that you feel the spending limit on such a card is low. If so, you may simply ask your bank to increase your spending limit on the basis of your recent credit history.

Most banks would do this for long-term customers, who have strong financials and a clear credit history. But what if your card is not adequately incentivizing your spends? For example, you recently started extensive travelling by road and you need a credit card that incentivizes your fuel spends. If so, you may simply get a card that accommodates your new requirement.

What you should not do is get multiple cards offering the same kind of benefits. Your aim should be to own multiple cards that maximize incentives for you. This helps cast a net wide enough to catch the maximum number of deals, discounts and rewards.

Lastly, it would be good if we regularly reconsider what can be an appropriate number of cards for us. If you had cards you did not use, that you had a hard time keeping track of, or had high charges that did not pay for themselves, you may be better off cancelling them.

If you do not use your card, you need to know the new rules. The RBI has said that credit card companies must intimate customers about a card that has not been used for one year.[12] If the customer does not respond to this reminder within 30 days, the card may be closed, subject to the payment of any dues. The problem with cancelling cards, as I mentioned earlier, is that you lose the positive credit history associated with them, and this could marginally lower your credit score.

You would also lose part of your overall spending limit. Since you would then spend a higher per centage of a smaller spending limit, your CUR would increase, which would hurt your credit score.

So for example, if you have two cards with spending limits of ₹50,000 each and you spend ₹30,000 a month using both, you have an overall CUR of 30 per cent. But if you close one card and continue spending the same amount via one card, your

CUR will rise to 60 per cent. The higher CUR can negatively impact your score.

If you must cancel any credit card, redeem the associated reward points, pay off the dues and get a no-dues letter from the bank. The bank needs to close your card within seven days of receiving your cancellation request, assuming you have cleared all dues.

Do not forget to track the credit score impact of the cancellation in the months to follow.

How Many Loans Are Too Many?

This also brings us to a related question. How many concurrent loans should you have running?

The answer is simple: as many as you can afford. But there are varied things to consider here.

It is common for people to have a combination of debts running concurrently at any point. Typically, these would be a mix of the following: personal loan, car loan, home loan or credit card dues. Each loan adds an EMI that you need to pay. Each EMI reduces your disposable income. The lower your disposable income, the greater your financial stress.

Each additional loan also pulls down your credit score. Lower scores mean higher loan interest rates. This could potentially make each additional loan more expensive, thus squeezing your income even more.

Even then, as long as you are able to comfortably pay them off, nobody can stop you from taking additional loans. Many experts say your monthly dues—all loan payments and credit card dues—should not exceed 40 per cent of your income. The comfort zone lies in different places for different people. If your monthly income is ₹50,000 and your EMI takes away

40 per cent of it, you would be left with ₹30,000. This may make subsistence tougher in a large city. If your monthly income is ₹2 lakh and you had to pay 60 per cent as EMIs, you would be left with ₹80,000, which may be enough for your subsistence.

The more money you owe, the greater the strain on your income. If you were to lose your income for any reason, the financial stress upon you would be enormous. Therefore, in the ideal scenario, you should pay off existing debts before you acquire new ones.

How to Deal with Pre-Approved Offers

While using your preferred digital platform for banking, e-commerce, personal finance or dining, you might have come across an invitation to apply for a pre-approved loan or credit card. On the basis of your relationship with them as well as your banking activity, your bank assesses your financial health and creates the offer for you.

Pre-approved offers are useful. With them, you do not have to go through the rigmarole of seeking out the bank, filling up application forms, handing over your photocopied documents and then waiting for several weeks for your loan to be disbursed. Banks with whom you have had no prior relationship need that time to evaluate your creditworthiness and financials. However, your own bank knows you and creates offers that are tailored to suit your finances. Such an offer can be availed quickly and with minimal paperwork.

However, just because you are eligible for a loan does not mean you need to take it. Alternatively, you might need to take only a part of it and not all of it. For example, your bank has tailored a personal loan offer of ₹5 lakh. However, your current need is only of ₹1 lakh. Therefore, you should only borrow what you need.

Wealth Warrior Sheena's relationship manager called her about a personal loan being offered at an interest rate of 12 per cent. She had closed out a personal loan that she had taken the previous year when she had to help her parents finalize a land deal. Her excellent repayment track record was the reason for the pre-approved offer. Though tempted to take it up for a vacation, she decided to give it some thought. On the Eisenhower Matrix, this would be seen within 'Schedule'. After analysing her need for the loan through the matrix, she realized taking this loan was not a high priority. It classified as a 'Don't Do' for her—neither important, nor urgent.

It was for the best that she did not take the loan. A month later, the pandemic swept through the world, destroying any possibility of a vacation.

Understanding Your Interest Rates

One of the best things you can teach yourself as you try to manage your money is the matter of interest rates and how they impact you. There is much to learn about interest rates, both at a micro and macro level.

For now, let us look at how loans are priced. Interest rates and how they are charged varies from one loan to another. Understanding the differences could help you save a lot of money.

Nethra and Vijay, an Early Jobber couple, had each applied to two different lenders for a ₹2 lakh personal loan for a tenure of two years. They were offered the same rate by the two lenders. While Vijay got an offer for 12 per cent at a flat rate from a local lender, Nethra got an offer from a bank for 12 per cent at a reducing balance interest rate. What is the difference?

In the flat rate method, you get a simple interest rate calculation. The rate is applied to the whole amount for the whole tenure.

In Vijay's case, a 12 per cent rate for ₹2 lakh for two years works out to ₹48,000. He would have to repay ₹248,000 over 24 months. So his EMI was ₹10,334.

On the other hand, Nethra's interest is calculated each month on the remaining loan balance. The more she pays back her loan, the smaller the loan gets, and the interest she owes reduces each month. Her interest works out to just ₹25,953. Her EMIs would also be much lower at ₹9,415.[13]

Vijay will pay nearly twice the interest Nethra pays. Therefore, it is in their interest (no pun intended) to take a loan with reducing balance interest. And this is the method regulated lenders follow anyway.

Consider credit card interest rates too. The term that cards quote while mentioning their interest rates is annual per centage rate (APR). This, too, is a simple interest calculation on a month-on-month basis multiplied by 12. For example, a card says its monthly interest rate is 3.49 per cent, and therefore its APR is 41.88 per cent, which is merely 3.49 multiplied by 12. This does not, however, mean that your credit card interest is going to be 41.88 per cent. That rate, which we call annual per centage yield (APY), is much higher.

Assume you have dues of ₹100,000 on your credit card and you stop making payments. Your monthly interest rate is 3.49 per cent. After 12 months, your dues would have ballooned to ₹150,931. This gives us an APY of 50.93 per cent! It excludes penalties for missed payments, which would make your dues even higher. While APR does not factor in compounded interest, APY does. Just another reminder: you need to be on top of your credit card dues.

Loan Guarantors and Your Need for Awareness

Risk comes from not knowing what you're doing.

—Warren Buffett,
American businessman and philanthropist

For the right borrowers, loans are easily available. If you have stable income and a good credit score, lenders will queue up to give you loans and credit cards. But if your creditworthiness is low, the going gets tough. So what about those with unstable incomes, low credit scores or the ones who need to borrow beyond their loan eligibility? They might have to pay a higher interest rate, provide collateral or produce a loan guarantor.

A guarantor's presence reassures the lending bank. It makes getting the loan easy. If the borrower defaults on the loan, the guarantor will have to step in to pay the dues. The guarantor is often a person known to the borrower and one who wants to help them get the loan. It is typically a family member, a friend, a co-worker or any loan-eligible person wishing to help the borrower.

Loan guaranteeing is fraught with risk. So let us get two perspectives on it.

1. See it from the perspective of the borrower. Someone is willing to guarantee your loan considering your relationship with them. Therefore, you must ensure full and timely repayment. If not, the guarantor will be at financial risk. Failure to repay the dues would automatically make the loan the guarantor's liability. They would have to pay your EMIs, along with penalties and charges. This could be acceptable in certain situations.

For example, your parents or family members may be willing to help you. However, this is not a position you would want to put a friend or co-worker in. Their finances could get harmed by your actions.

2. See it from the perspective of the guarantor. If you have decided to guarantee someone's loan, be sure you will be able to pay the dues when the day comes and the bank calls on you. For all practical purposes, you have taken this loan yourself. Now, you need to pay what is left of it. Guaranteeing the loan should not impede your ability to meet your own expenses. You should be able to repay the EMIs. If you believe this is not possible, you should not volunteer to become a guarantor. While it would be great to be of help to someone in need, it should not come at the expense of your own financial stability.

Your Credit Score as a Guarantor

Every borrower has a loan eligibility that relies on their income and ongoing loans. The bigger their ongoing loans, the smaller their eligibility for a new loan will be.

When you become a financial guarantor, the loan is essentially yours. Therefore, if you required a loan for yourself, your own eligibility will be limited by the loan you have guaranteed. To give you a simple example, you are eligible for a home loan of ₹50 lakh, but you had guaranteed another home loan of ₹30 lakh. This will bring down your own eligibility to ₹20 lakh.

Even if the borrower is repaying the loan on schedule, the loan would continue to be counted against your eligibility till the month it is completely paid off. As guarantor, if you failed to pay the dues for the borrower, your credit score would be crushed. You will have no option but to pay up. You would not want that, would you?

Be prepared for the risks. Track the loan repayment to ensure the loan is closed out. If the borrower has a poor credit report, think twice before becoming their guarantor. However, if you are committed to being the guarantor despite the risks, ensure you help them rebuild their credit score and get them the necessary counsel to improve their money management skills.

If you would not want this responsibility, avoid being the guarantor.

Finding Your First Wheels

I've always been asked, 'What is my favourite car?'
and I've always said, 'The next one.'

—Carroll Shelby, automotive designer

We now move from savings, insurance and small loans to the stage of life where you are ready to buy your first vehicle. Part of savouring life is also sometimes about having the right wheels. Who does not dream of owning their dream bike or car someday?

The first car I purchased was for my parents in Chennai. I bought it with a ₹5-lakh loan—the same one that had marked my timely payments as late. My second car was bought under a corporate lease programme. It offered me corporate tax benefits.

When it comes to borrowing to make such a dream come true, keep the following points in mind:

1. It does not matter if your vehicle is brand new or slightly used. You could borrow for both. Loans for used cars will attract a slightly higher interest rate though.

2. Remember my point about vehicles being depreciating assets? If you care about accelerating your financial progress, spend as little as possible on your wheels. Applying the MoSCoW Method, a vehicle may be a 'Must Have', since it may make a material difference to your life. Accessories may be 'Should Have', since they are useful but often not essential. Premium accessories may be a 'Could Have', since they are not essential, though good to have. But breaking bank to buy a luxury brand may be a 'Won't Have', since it may impede your other financial goals.

3. The lender owns your car till the loan is paid off. If you miss your payments, the lender reserves the right to follow due process, repossess your car and auction it to recover the dues.

4. The total price of your vehicle comprises the showroom price, road taxes, insurance premium and any other charges as applicable. All these costs combined give us the on-road price. Some lenders will finance all on-road price up to 100 per cent on select vehicle models. Other vehicles will attract 90 per cent or less. Make sure you have the down payment ready.

5. A clean slate of debt helps. If you are not saddled with previous loans and credit card debt, it will be a lot easier to get your loan.

6. Ready your documents for your loan and vehicle purchase. You will be required to furnish proofs of identity, income and address. Make sure you have filed your tax returns as well.

7. Compare your options after checking your credit score. If you have a score of 750 or more, some great offers might be there in store for you. Go online to find out

what the offers are. You do not have to go with the first lender who comes your way.

8. While on the topic of spending frugally, borrow as little as you can, and take the smallest possible loan tenure. If you can pay off your vehicle loan in two years, do not wait to pay it off in seven. This way, you will save a lot of interest.

The word 'frugal' derives from 'bhrūg', which is a Proto-Indo-European word meaning 'to enjoy', possibly a reference to enjoying agricultural produce.

A frugivorous is someone who feeds on fruits. Bowerbirds, incidentally, are frugivores, too. These extraordinarily gifted engineers give colourful expressions to their life's purpose. And what a frugal method they have for this. They collect colourful litter, twigs, flowers and even iridescent insects to build their love nests, defending them from predators and competitors, and sometimes going to occupy them for 20 to 30 years.

This is a good template to apply to our finances.

IV

STRENGTHEN: GROWING
YOUR MONEY

THE BEAVER

A beaver is a lumberjack, engineer and builder packed into one feisty, semi-aquatic mammal. It lives partially on land and spends so much time in water that the Catholic Church once decreed that it was fish, fit to be eaten during Lent.

The second largest rodent in the world, they live in and around the freshwaters of Europe and North America. Beavers are powerful swimmers and can stay underwater for up to 15 minutes. Their thick fur coat over a layer of fat protects them from the cold. Their webbed feet help them swim and so does their flattened and scaley tail. The latter doubles up as a tool to slap the water with to startle predators or to alert the colony about intruders.

The beaver's big talent is its ability—rather its obsessive need—to build dams. With this, it shapes ecosystems not just for the benefit of its own kind but many other species, too. An adult beaver can cut down up to 200 trees in a year. Its incisors work like little chainsaws that can chomp through six-inch tree trunks within an hour. It is quite a sight to see these waddly, cute creatures obsessively gnaw at trees. It may remind you of a puppy working away on a chew toy.

The beaver is nocturnal. It builds dams working tirelessly through the cold and dark. It moves tonnes of wood and rocks over weeks. It carries as much as its body weight with its tiny, digitated hands with somewhat opposable thumbs. The chewed down wood, along with rocks, are dragged into the riverbed to create the dam foundations. Then this structure is cemented with river mud. The dam controls the flow of the river. This creates a pond that provides the calm waters beavers need to create lodges—dry accommodations where they live. Beaver lodges are clever constructions. They are above the waterline, but their entries are underwater to ward off predators.

In the lodge, monogamous pairs start families. Beaver kits often help their parents raise newborns. They also accompany their parents in logging and building missions. After they come of age, the kids are pushed out of their parents' lodges. They must go into the wilderness, use their training and build their own colonies. They must mate before winter. Their survival depends on it. The odds are against them. They must contend not just with predators but also the changing course of rivers and varying forces of the current.

Should a dam get washed by the altering course of a river, a storm or melting snow, beavers have no recourse but to dig deep and rebuild. They have no option but to do so before the cold sets in and threatens their survival.

Beavers are a keystone species. As per *National Geographic*, 'A keystone species is an organism that helps define an entire ecosystem. Without its keystone species, the ecosystem would be dramatically different or cease to exist altogether.'[1]

What can we learn from the beaver when it comes to our finances?

We can learn about growing up, taking responsibilities and building our lives the way we want to. We can learn about assessing and taking risks that are necessary for survival and growth. We can learn about securing our loved ones' future and supporting them for life. We can learn about adapting to the changing tides of life. We can learn that as we strengthen our financial lives, we strengthen the lives of others, too.

So in this chapter, we will cover the all-important matter of growing our money through smart investing, so that it serves not just us but our loved ones as well.

Taking Stock: What's Done and What's Left

Good job making it this far! Now let us take stock of your progress.

THE 5S PYRAMID
BankBazaar

Serenity ← Credit score, Debt-free assets, Retirement

You're here ← Home, Assets, Investments → Strengthen

Savour ← Credit card, Personal loan, BNPL

Insurance: Health, Term, Vehicle, Property → Secure

Save ← Savings, Fixed deposits, Liquid mutual funds

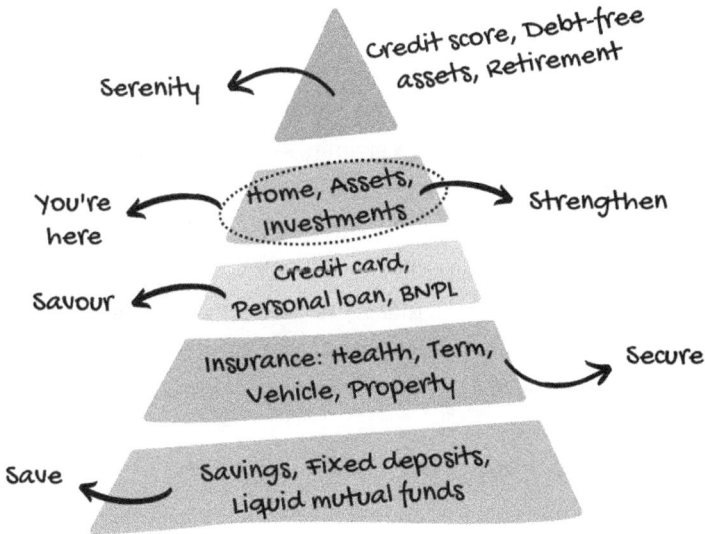

With savings, we have prepared a solid foundation for your financial life. Budgeting, smart saving and an emergency fund have given you a great start to this journey. Then we talked about your coats of armour. With insurance, your health, life and property are secured against life's vagaries. We talked about small credit and opportunities to savour life without getting into trouble. We saw why prioritizing wants and needs, paying your dues on time and tracking your credit score are keys to financial stability.

You can give yourself a pat on the back for coming this far on our climb to Serenity. Now, you have got to fuel up. This climb is about to get tougher. So much more remains: investment decisions, buying a house, preparing your children to face life and planning for retirement. These are some of the toughest things you will do in money management.

Investing is tough. It is a game in which the goalpost keeps shifting. The rules of the game keep changing, too. Strategies need to be formed. Decisions need to be taken. Life-changing opportunities need to be grabbed. When investing, you never stop learning. On the basis of new learnings, you get to constantly optimize your plans for better results.

There are many ways to strengthen your finances. But in a nutshell, the best way is to identify your aspirations and fulfil them by allocating money in the most efficient way possible.

We will now deep dive into how you can fulfil those aspirations, create assets, make your money grow and set up the unshakable foundation for the apex of our pyramid, Serenity. So let us start by taking stock of your aspirations.

What Are Your Aspirations?

If you have built castles in the air, your work need not be lost; that is where they should be. Now put the foundations under them.

—Henry David Thoreau, naturalist and essayist

BankBazaar Aspiration Index is an annual survey of India's aspirations seen through the lens of personal finance. Each year, we ask questions to thousands of Indians about five areas of their lives: wealth, health, relationships, fame and personal growth. Each area has defined aspirations. For example, saving for children's education is a relationship aspiration. To buy a house is a wealth aspiration. To be mentally happy is a health aspiration.

The demographic that answered these questions in 2021 were salaried men and women between 22 and 45 years of age who were digitally aware (having done at least one digital transaction recently) and earned at least ₹30,000 a month. They lived in metros and non-metros all over India.[2]

We asked them three questions about each aspiration. One, 'How important is the aspiration to you?' two, 'How confident are you about fulfilling the aspiration?' and three, 'What is your current preparedness for the aspiration?'

The 2021 responses are tabulated on the next page. The higher the index, the greater the aspiration for India as a whole.

Over the years, we have consistently seen two aspirations dominate the rankings: saving and investing for children's education, and buying a house. But in 2021, we were stunned to see some non-material goals leap ahead in the rankings. Compared to previous years, more Indians prioritized having long-lasting friendships and living near their immediate families.

We interpreted this to be an aftermath of separation from our loved ones through distance and death in the pandemic. India told us in clear terms that its No. 1 aspiration in 2021 was relationships. We craved for community—something we had taken for granted. Seen together, these responses reflected not just India's aspirations, but also their ongoing anxieties.

Table 11

2021 BankBazaar Aspiration Index: Aspirations Important to Indians						
Aspiration	Life Goal	Importance Index	Likelihood Index	Preparedness Index	Aspiration Index	Need Gap
To save and invest money to provide my children the best of education in life	Relationship	93.3	92.7	89.4	91.8	3.9
To have long-lasting friendships	Relationship	92.0	90.3	86.9	89.7	5.1
To buy a house of my own	Wealth	90.7	89.7	84.4	88.2	6.3
To be mentally healthy by being happy in whatever situation I am in	Health	90.6	88.6	84.4	87.8	6.2
To live near my immediate family	Relationship	88.5	87.9	84.5	87.0	4.0
To be able to maintain a nutritious diet	Health	88.6	88.2	83.7	86.8	4.9
To be known as an expert in my field	Fame	89.8	87.9	82.2	86.7	7.6
To be part of a close-knit extended family	Relationship	88.2	87.4	84.2	86.6	4.0
To follow a fixed regime to improve my physical heath	Health	88.8	88.0	82.7	86.5	6.2
To not just be physically fit but also look fit	Health	86.1	86.8	81.8	84.9	4.3

Statement	Category					
To constantly reinvent myself	Personal Growth	85.3	84.8	82.3	84.1	3.0
To be able to stand out distinctly amongst friends	Fame	83.5	84.4	82.9	83.6	0.6
To have enough money to be able to retire early	Wealth	87.0	82.5	79.2	82.9	7.9
To be seen as a go-to person at my workplace/society	Fame	82.5	82.5	82.5	82.5	0.0
To travel around the globe and create memories and experiences	Wealth	84.0	80.7	75.9	80.2	8.0
To start my own business/be my own boss/be an entrepreneur	Personal Growth	82.6	80.6	77.3	80.2	5.3
To pursue avenues that others in my circle have not	Personal Growth	79.0	79.7	78.3	79.0	0.7
To get back to hobbies or passions I haven't had time to pursue	Personal Growth	80.0	79.7	76.9	78.8	3.1
To be an influencer on social media	Fame	79.7	80.0	76.5	78.7	3.2
To have enough money to buy premium products	Wealth	79.0	79.4	74.7	77.7	4.4
(If a bachelor) To spend my own money on a lavish wedding	Relationship	73.7	74.4	71.0	73.0	2.7

The last column in the table represents a need gap. It is the gap between how important the respondents think a goal is and how prepared they are for it. Not surprisingly, the highest need gap in 2021 was regarding a wealth goal for travelling around the globe—a near impossibility for most in the pandemic. Income uncertainty and loss of savings in the pandemic also created a large need gap for another wealth goal: saving enough money to retire early. As we had seen in earlier years as well as in 2021, the least important goal for the respondents was having a lavish wedding—also impossible as a result of strict social restrictions following the outbreak of the pandemic.

Some common themes connect our collective aspirations. We want the security of a roof over our heads. We want our children to get the best education. We want to be mentally and physically healthy. We want money in the bank to retire early, travel the world and buy premium products. The pandemic may have slowed down our aspirations, but it has not cancelled them. We still want to fulfil them.

So let us now see how we can fulfil our aspirations.

Aspirations, Investing and Fulfilment

After my stint in USA, I decided to return to India. With Arjun and Rati, I started to work on getting BankBazaar off the ground. When we started, Arjun had saved up some money. I, too, had a little. We split the investment in a ratio of 50:50. I borrowed from him to complete my 50 per cent share.

I repaid him over three years. It was great that he was able to step up and support me with seed capital. Investors soon showed up. They accelerated our mission of simplifying the loan-buying process for every Indian. I started earning a steady income as the business grew with funding. I finally got into the habit of investing every month in MFs. Too bad I did not start doing this with my first job. I started till I turned 30. My first monthly investment was 10 per cent of my net income. I now invest 20 per cent of my disposable income. One of my goals is to create an education fund for my daughter.

I advise people to start early and save more. People who plan well put away 50 per cent of their net income. That requires discipline and focus. I have friends who do it. But it means being careful about where one spends.

Starting early would have given me some precious years of compounded growth. Lesson learnt. We will understand in this chapter what compounded growth is and what its incredible impact is on wealth creation.

To create wealth, you must invest. Investing regularly strengthens your finances. It helps you achieve any goal you set your mind on. How does this happen?

It is important to have money in the bank. However, we also saw that the returns on savings are abysmal. Savings help you meet immediate needs. But to fulfil your aspirations, you need more than savings.

You need to put your money to work in the investment markets. In the markets, you can buy stocks, bonds, gold, real estate, commodities—even cryptocurrencies if high risk is something you are able to deal with. That way, your money can grow at a much higher rate of return, allowing you to lead the life of your dreams.

Aspirations can sometimes seem impossible to fulfil. But no matter how improbable the goal, if you work at it systematically over the long term, you can achieve it. You must visualize your big dream—your home, a retirement kitty, best education for your kids or anything you want—and work backwards.

You must break down the goal into small, achievable,

monthly steps. What starts off with a small step can become a big leap, thanks to the power of compounded returns. This would, however, not be an easy journey. Investment decisions are rarely perfect. You will make some very difficult choices with regards to the investment vehicles you must pick, drop or stick to.

That being said, you have got off to a great start in your journey towards Serenity. You have saved up to an optimal level. You have secured your finances with insurance. Well begun is half the job done.

Like the beaver, you have toiled through the woods in the dark to prepare the foundation of your dam. You may have been an Early Jobber when you started and progressed to become a Moneymooner. Now, it is time to become a Wealth Warrior, build your lodge and flourish.

The Extreme Importance of Goal-setting

Our goals can only be reached through a vehicle of a plan in which we must fervently believe, and upon which we must vigorously act. There is no other route to success.

—Pablo Picasso, Spanish painter

Goal-setting is one of the most important tasks in money management. Think of it as an exercise in planning a journey. Let us take a long-term goal, such as investing for retirement. We will understand it with the example of travelling from Mumbai to meet a friend in London.

The distance between the two cities is around 7,500 km as the crow flies. There are many ways to complete this journey. But only a few are optimal. You could get there by walking, but this could take you more than a year. You could drive, but that would take you days.

Driving or walking would also need you to make a budget for various expenses: the countless meals, petrol refills, hotel stay, and the costs of visas and taxes to be paid to the countries along the way. This could cost you lakhs of rupees. You could go by sea. This would be comparatively convenient and cheaper. But it would still take weeks. It is, therefore, a suboptimal mode of transport for the journey.

The optimal way to reach your friend would be taking local transport to the Mumbai airport, catching a flight to London, then taking a taxi or train to reach your friend's locality and completing the final few metres of that journey on foot. This journey would take you less than 24 hours. It would have cost you less than ₹50,000 in the pre-pandemic age.

Similarly, it is important to make calculations regarding your journey to retirement. Assume you are 30 years old. You plan to retire at 60. You calculated that you would need ₹10 crore by the time you retire, so that you never have to work again for a living.

Goal-setting is not just picking your target. It is also calculating the optimal time frame and costs needed to hit the target. This is true whether you are flying to London or planning for retirement. For example, trying to save ₹10 crore by parking the money in a savings account would be akin to walking from Mumbai to London.

Assuming you could earn post-tax returns of 3 per cent from your savings account, you would have to save ₹1.7 lakh every month for 30 years to get to ₹10 crore. Here, the costs of investment (₹6.1 crore, i.e. ₹170,000 per month × 30 years × 12 months) are extremely high. There are better ways to reach your goal.

If ₹1.7 lakh a month is too much, and you could save only a reasonable amount of ₹17,000 a month, it would take you 92 years to save ₹10 crore at the same rate of return. Here, the costs (₹1.9 crore) are optimal, but the time frame is not. This plan will not allow you to achieve the goal in your lifespan.

If you saved ₹67,000 a month via a provident fund (PF) scheme returning 8 per cent per annum, you could theoretically hit your goal in 30 years. But again, the costs (₹2.4 crore) are moderately high. This would be akin to taking a luxury steamer from Mumbai to London. It will get you to your destination. There are better ways to get there.

If you invested in the equity market expecting average returns of 12 per cent per annum over 30 years, you would need to invest only ₹30,000 a month. This approximates the ideal cost (₹1.1 crore) in your chosen timeframe. But if we were to nitpick, we can say the costs are front-loaded. It is much harder to pay ₹30,000 today than it will be in 30 years, when that amount will be seen as peanuts due to inflation. You can optimize this plan to make it easier for you today. You can start investing with ₹11,500 per month now. But as your income grows every year, increase your monthly contribution by 10 per cent each year.

So you will be investing ₹12,650 from the second year, ₹13,915 from the third and so on till you reach the thirtieth year, when you will be investing over ₹2 lakh per month. That sounds like a lot today. But inflation and rising income may make it possible for you to invest that much in the future.

This is the step-up investing method.[3] It allows you to start with a small investment and keep growing it as your income increases. This is the best way to break down a big, impossible-sounding goal into small and easy steps. With this graded, step-up plan returning 12 per cent a year, you will hit your ₹10 crore goal in 30 years, though at double the cost (at ₹2.2 crore).

The difference, however, is that the cost is back-loaded. It means you will pay less now, but pay more later. This would strain your income less today, but compel you to make smarter use of your rising income in the future.

You could optimize the above step-up plan to include higher risks for higher returns and raise your returns expectation to 15 per cent. This expectation is not unrealistic. Many high-performing MFs have been able to deliver these returns over the long term. The disclaimer I want to add is that past returns do not guarantee future returns.

With a higher expectation of 15 per cent, your step-up plan could create ₹17.27 crore, or you could start this plan with ₹6,700 a month with an annual step-up of 10 per cent and get to your intended goal of ₹10 crore. The back-loaded cost to you in this plan would be just ₹1.32 crore. This may be the optimal investment cost in the 30-year time frame.

This plan is akin to your direct flight from Mumbai to London purchased at a heavy discount. Thanks to the process of goal setting, we were able to not just define a goal but also find the best way to achieve it.

Headwinds and Tailwinds

The destination we have chosen is Serenity—the apex of our 5S Pyramid. The journey to it has a million little steps. Goal setting helps make completing those steps easier.

However, the path to Serenity is rarely straight. That flight to London is not always going to take you where you want to go. The flight may have to make an emergency landing if there is a problem with the engine. What if you get stuck on that plane for several hours in an unfamiliar country? What if you need to board another flight to resume your journey?

Your flight will not be flying at a uniform pace. It will face headwinds that slow it down. But it will also face tailwinds that will push it towards its destination, helping it recover lost time.

Prakash, a Wealth Warrior planning to retire by 55, has faced these headwinds and tailwinds in his investment journey. He started off investing via an endowment policy, just as many from his generation did. The policy gave him a nominal cover of about ₹6 lakh. After 15 years, the policy will mature. It will pay him ₹6 lakh, along with the bonuses that these policies typically provide. Note that the life cover was not enough to cover his family's long-term financial needs in case of his death.

He was paying a considerable annual premium of nearly ₹50,000 towards this policy. Five years into the investment, he realized the maturity pay-out would mean an annual rate of return of around 6 per cent on his investment. He realized this was too low for him. His flight, instead of flying him to London, had taken a turn for Colombo. Prakash panicked that his corpus was not growing fast enough and decided to surrender his 15-year policy.

He had paid around ₹2.5 lakh in those five years. At the very least, he expected that money to be returned, but he was in for a shock. He only got back 50 per cent as the policy's surrender value, which is the sum you receive when prematurely closing a policy. The value did not even consider his first premium in the equation. He struggled to understand the complex calculations involved in arriving at the figure.

He would have received full value only after the policy's full term of 15 years. He got back around ₹1.25 lakh. He lost the rest. A valuable lesson was learnt. Prakash changed the vehicle he had chosen for his journey. His vehicle would now be MFs. His life cover needs would be met with a term insurance policy.

Not that this was an easy switch. Even with MFs, he has had to calibrate his choices periodically to improve performance, lower risks, optimize costs and increase rewards. He picked an equity MF to start with. But it was not delivering the returns he needed to get to his goal. The fund had been returning 11 per cent on average a year, lower than its peers that were returning 14 per cent. His fund had sunk to the bottom of the MF rankings over a five-year period.

So Prakash switched funds. He also took small, controlled exposure in other high-risk and high-reward funds, which could give him 15 per cent returns over the long term. With this, he started earning the returns he needed to retire early. However, he continued to keep a watch on his MF portfolio to weed out the laggards and bring in high performers.

Then, there comes the last mile connectivity and safely reaching your destination. The flight cannot land in the residential area your friend lives in. When bringing your journey to a halt, you must swap speed for safety. What applies to that jumbo jet applies to your investment vehicle, too.

Therefore, Prakash plans to switch systematically and slowly to low-risk MF schemes as he nears retirement. In my experience, this is what the retired prefer. They want their capital to be safe. Though this would mean lower returns towards the end of the investment journey, it would save their money from evaporating in a market crash.

Start with the Taxes

Tax-planning and investment-planning go together. A good investment plan takes on board the impact of taxes. Taxes eat into your investment returns. You must pay attention to them. This book aims to simplify taxation. But taxation is complicated and connected to one's personal circumstances and the prevalent tax laws. To understand the subject in depth, one can avail professional advice.

It should be remembered that not all investment returns are taxed the same way. Some investments attract higher taxes than others and some do not attract taxes at all. Your investment plan must factor in the layered nature of taxation to get you higher returns.

Many Indians invest because it helps them save income tax. Some investments help you lower your income taxes under various sections of the Income Tax Act of 1961. Not all investments can get you tax breaks, but just a handful chosen by the government.[4]

The higher your income, the higher your taxes. A tax deduction is an amount you can subtract from your total income. This reduces your taxable income. Thus, your taxes get reduced too. Tax-saving investments solve the twin problems of investing as well as saving taxes.

Section 80C is the most popular section for seekers of tax deductions[5]. You can claim a deduction of up to ₹1.5 lakh each year. Under it, you can use a combination of various tax-saving options. Section 80C is popular because it is crammed with many options: life insurance premium, pension plan premiums, National Savings Certificate, PPF, Employees Provident Fund (EPF), Sukanya Samriddhi Scheme, home loan payments, Senior Citizens Savings Scheme, equity-linked savings schemes, National Pension Scheme, five-year FD and education fees paid for children.

If this sounds like a lot, it is so because it is.

If you are an Early Jobber trying to make sense of these

options, worry not. Help is at hand. We are going to streamline these tax-saving investment options.

But first…

Take Stock of Tax-Deductible Expenses

You need to pay taxes only if your income is taxable. So if your income is below a certain level, it is not taxable. Income above that level is taxed at various slabs.

As of 2022, the zero-tax level of income is ₹5 lakh.[6] If your taxable income (income minus deductions) is at ₹5 lakh or less, you pay no income tax. This level is subject to periodic upward revisions as per the Indian government's fiscal and political needs.

Tax deductions can happen not just via investments but also eligible expenses. Chances are you already have undertaken expenses such as house rent[7], education loan interest, your child's tuition fee, contribution to qualified charities[8] or qualified medical treatments[9].

This is not the entire list. There are many of these eligible expenses that give you tax deductions under various sections of the Income Tax Act. Take stock of all the deductions you may be eligible for. With them, does your taxable income come down to ₹5 lakh or less? If yes, you do not need further tax-saving measures. You can move straight to wealth-creation activities.

If not, you need them only to the extent that you come within the ₹5-lakh limit. For example, with those deductions, if your taxable income comes down to ₹5.35 lakh, you only need additional tax-saving measures of ₹35,000 to bring your income to the zero-tax level.

It is important to not go overboard with tax-saving investments. They have limitations such as lock-in periods, in which you cannot liquidate an investment for a defined number of years. If you liquidate a tax-saver within a lock-in, you must pay any taxes it helped you save.

So you must maximize your tax deductions via eligible expenses, insurance payments and investments. When you hit the maximum limit to what you can save through them, you must look beyond them to find ways to create wealth.

Wealth creation is ultimately the greatest purpose of money management—not tax savings.

Investing and Insuring for Tax Savings

Most of you only need three options for tax savings.

First is health insurance for yourself and your family members. Second is term insurance for yourself, if you have dependent family members or financial responsibilities. In 'Secure', we saw how these help achieve the twin goals of tax-saving and essential protection against life's vagaries.

So now let us look at the third option: equity-linked savings schemes (ELSS), also called tax-saving MFs.[10] ELSS is one of the best ways to save money, create wealth, save taxes, have liquidity and pay a very low rate of tax on the returns. It is a silver bullet solution to several problems.

This is it. These three options are all that most people—especially Early Jobbers and Moneymooners—need for tax-saving.

It really is that simple. Agreed?

Exceptions to the Three

Assume you were averse to market risks. You do not like the ups and downs of the stock market and, therefore, do not want to touch ELSS. For you, there is a fourth option: PF. That is it. You need no other tax-saving investment apart from ELSS or PF.

You can invest via your office-provided EPF account.[11] If you do not have this option, go for PPF.[12] PF has been picked for being the highest returns generator among tax-saving debt investments. In 2021, EPF returned 8.5 per cent per annum and PPF, 7.1 per cent. These returns are guaranteed, government-backed, tax-free and your contributions also provide tax deductions under 80C.

EPF has a voluntary contribution facility called Voluntary Provident Fund (VPF). You can now pay ₹2.5 lakh per annum and the interest you earn on this amount will not be taxed.[13] For government employees, this limit is ₹5 lakh. Interest earned on VPF contributions above these limits will be taxed.

There is a fifth option: your home loan. It is one of the best ways to save large amounts of income tax. A home loan provides multiple, meaty deductions. You can save up to ₹1.5 lakh under 80C for principal repaid, ₹2 lakh for interest paid under Section 24B and ₹1.5 lakh under Section 80EEA for interest paid as a qualified borrower.[14] The large deductions possible with a home loan reduce the need for other deductions under 80C or other sections.

We have a sixth option, applicable to any family with a girl child: the Sukanya Samriddhi Scheme (SSY), which typically provides higher returns than PPF, but lower than EPF.[15] In 2021, it provided 7.6 per cent, also completely tax-free, returns.

There is one last and seventh option: Senior Citizens Savings Scheme (SCSS).[16] This can be availed by risk-averse senior citizens as well as those who opted for voluntary retirement.

PPF, SSY and SCSS are part of the postal savings universe that also gives you postal savings account, RDs and FDs, Kisan Vikas Patra and National Savings Certificate (NSC), which is also an 80C tax-saving investment—a five-year deposit. NSC, PPF, SSY and SCSS can be availed via an authorized bank or post office. Backed by the Indian government, these schemes are 100 per cent safe and provide assured returns.

However, they are only for the risk-averse. In that sense, anything these schemes can do, even an average ELSS could potentially do better. By doing better, we typically look at returns. And that is where ELSS funds score over other options.

Why ELSS?

ELSS are diversified equity MFs. It means if you invest in an ELSS, your money will be distributed into stocks of many companies of various sizes and sectors.

For example, one large ELSS fund worth over a billion dollars invests 31 per cent of its holdings in financial companies, such as banks and non-banking financial corporations. It invests 12 per cent in technology companies, 9 per cent in chemicals, 8 per cent in healthcare, and so on.

Among these sectors, it bets heavily on some companies. For example, 9.8 per cent of its holdings are with a supermarket chain. Another 9 per cent are with a large non-banking financial company. It has 8.3 per cent in a large technology company. In this manner, it creates a portfolio of stocks from 25 companies. They are mostly corporate behemoths. But some are also upcoming businesses. They have been picked by the fund manager for their ability to do good business and deliver value to shareholders over the long term.

Since ELSS are diversified funds, they minimize sectoral or company risk. So for example, if the technology sector is doing badly in a month, the banking sector may be doing well at the same time. One sector's bad performance gets cancelled by another's good performance. This stabilizes risks and returns.

You must be wondering why I am advising to opt for ELSS, a stock market-linked instrument fraught with risks. There are many reasons why ELSS is the best tax-saving investment for the young. Here are my reasons.

1. You can get high returns. This accelerates wealth creation. With a good ELSS, you may not need to look elsewhere for returns. As of December 2021, the Association of Mutual Funds India (AMFI) listed 26 ELSS funds operational since 2011.[17] Every single one of them had delivered returns of 13.9 per cent or more per annum for the last 10 years.

   Read that again. Even the lowest-ranked ELSS delivered nearly 14 per cent per annum over 10 years. These returns were a good 5–8 per centage points higher than the best debt investment schemes in the same time-frame—numbers you cannot scoff at.

   Of those 26 schemes on AMFI, 22 had delivered returns of 15 per cent or more. AMFI listed a total of 38 ELSS funds, some of whom were launched recently. Of those, 34 had delivered double-digit returns since their launch.

   ELSS and PF are both excellent long-term investment tools. But the extra returns matter when you remain invested in them for decades. Everything compounds with time—even bad returns—and you do not want to back the wrong investment for that long.

   If you invest ₹5,000 a month for 30 years in an ELSS that returns an average of 15 per cent per annum, you could save ₹3.5 crore. But if you applied the same plan to PF expecting 8 per cent per annum, you would only save ₹75 lakh in 30 years.

There is, of course, a recency bias in the returns data. We are looking at these numbers at a time when the stock markets are at an all-time high. The long-term returns are lower when the markets dip. Equity returns are never assured and are frequently volatile.

What is the antidote to volatility and negative returns? Long-term investment for at least three years. BankBazaar looked at the rolling three-year returns for the five largest ELSS funds with a 10-year track record as of December 2021.[18] These rolling returns are the profits generated by these funds between a moving period of three years—for example, 1 July 2015 to 30 June 2018, or 14 November 2017 to 13 November 2020.

Rolling returns reveal the per centage of times during the last 10 years when these five funds had positive three-year returns. They, therefore, provide a much deeper look at an asset's performance on a day-to-day basis.

Starting 1 January 2012, of the hundreds of three-year returns data points, the average returns from these five funds varied between 12.31 per cent and 18.3 per cent per annum. Of the data points, one fund had positive returns for 100 per cent of the period under review. For the other three, it varied between 98.41 and 94.14 per cent. The fifth had a relatively lower 83.71 per cent. But the ELSS category itself was positive for a whopping 91.59 per cent of the time.

Most equity funds took a dip into the red. No dip was bigger than the crash of 2020. Despite these short jaunts into the sub-zero territory, all these funds bounced back hard. This data, therefore, validates the idea that long-term investing in equity funds gives investors a good chance of beating market volatility to earn high returns.

2. ELSS has the shortest lock-in period for any tax-saving investment. With PF, NSC, SCSS or other options, your money could be locked in for a minimum of five to six years. PPF matures in 15 years. SSY matures in 21 years.

   Only partial withdrawals are allowed in these government schemes, and only under a defined set of circumstances such as child's education or buying a home. However, you could completely exit an ELSS in three years if you needed to.

   Risk-averse investors are concerned by daily market volatility. However, by definition, an ELSS is a long-term investment. Your money is locked-in for three years. Because of this, there is no point panicking about short-term price fluctuations. All you need to do is sit tight and wait out the turbulence.

3. ELSS provides convenience. You can start investing with as little as ₹500 a month. You can invest as much as you want. You can pause or stop investing any moment you want. When it is time for redemption, you can sell your investment and receive your funds in your bank account in three to four days.

   This is often not the case with PF, where redemption could take much longer. With ELSS, you can do all this sitting at home. You can register your investment account with your preferred fund house or fund aggregator. You can also manage, calibrate or sell your investment without getting up from your chair.

4. Do not like your fund? Just switch. There were at least 38 ELSS funds as of December 2021. Do your research, ask some experts, look at the ratings of any fund and buy the one that fits your investment agenda.

    One thing I would like to add here is that sometimes with an equity investment such as ELSS, the best thing to do is nothing. History shows us that the longer your time spent in the stock market, the better may be the returns.

5. The ELSS pricing is transparent. Every MF applies two charges: a total expense ratio and an exit load. The fund you buy will clearly advertise these. Expense ratio is the fund house and the aggregator's commission for managing and marketing the fund. The exit load applies if you cash out prematurely—within a year, for example. But it does not apply to ELSS funds. This is because the three-year lock-in prevents premature liquidation.

    The daily unit price of your fund is public information. At any moment, you can check what your investment is worth. When you cash out, you will be paid the latest applicable price.

6. ELSS attracts a very low rate of tax. It is not tax-free, like EPF, PPF or SSY. However, you pay only a 10 per cent tax on equity gains above ₹1 lakh in a year. This means your gains from ELSS are normally taxed at rate well under 10 per cent.

    Let us understand this with an example. Assume you have invested ₹2 lakh in an ELSS and you have held the investment for three years. In the fourth year, your investment is worth ₹3.25 lakh, implying gains of ₹1.25 lakh. Since these gains are on an equity asset held for longer than one year, under the current taxation rules, you pay no tax on the first ₹1 lakh. But you need to pay a 10 per cent tax on the rest, which, in this case, is 10 per cent of ₹25,000 or ₹2500. Therefore, the effective rate of taxation, in this example, on gains of ₹1.25 lakh is just 2 per cent.

Sure, ELSS is not as tax-efficient as debt investments, such as PF, but in an ideal scenario, would you rather pay zero taxes on 8 per cent returns or a 10 per cent tax on 12–15 per cent returns?

Consider the investment plan quoted in the first point about ELSS returns. An investment of ₹5,000 per month for 30 years (a total of ₹18 lakh) grows to ₹3.5 crore with the ELSS, and ₹75 lakh with PF. Your gains are approximately ₹3.32 crore and ₹57 lakh, respectively.

In the current taxation rules, you could get approximately ₹2.9 crore from ELSS after paying tax, or ₹75 lakh tax-free from PPF. What would you choose? The answer will depend on your capacity for risk.

Sure, there are market risks, and returns from equity are never guaranteed. This is important for us to understand and accept. But if you do not take your shot at the goal, you will not score.

Embracing Risk in Its Many Forms

So we shall let the reader answer this question for himself: who is the happier man, he who has braved the storm of life and lived or he who has stayed securely on shore and merely existed?

—Hunter S. Thompson, author and journalist

Every investment decision carries a degree of risk, even if you do not see it. Higher risks lead to higher rewards. Lower risks lead to lower rewards. Every investor must assess the degree of risk acceptable to them.

Why do we invest? We invest for the fulfilment of aspirations, for financial security and because we want greater control over our lives. We invest because we have to reach Serenity. A large, life-altering inheritance or a winning lottery ticket may not be awaiting us. We must shape our lives ourselves, the hard way—going boldly to where risks and rewards lie.

Investment risks exist in many forms. Assessing risk is a never-ending process. Risk is the known unknown. It constantly shapes and reshapes fortunes. One must understand risk in its various forms.

Early Jobber Sharda, an interior designer and a part-time stock trader, is investing in the stocks of an adhesive manufacturer poised for a bright future. She faces price risks. The price of her stock goes up and down every day. Sharda has been tracking the company's activities and its stock price. She wants to buy low and sell high to earn her profit. If she buys high and sells low, she will suffer losses.

Typically, investors concern themselves with price risks. Countless factors shape the price of any investment. Price risk can shape investment returns immediately. So investors feel compelled to act on it. But there are other risks that shape returns slowly, invisibly and in an unnoticed way.

Shubam, a Moneymooner, and a private hospital employee, is a hyper-conservative investor. She saves only through FDs. Despite being a diligent saver, her FDs are unfortunately returning only 4 per cent after tax deductions. This return is not enough to beat inflation, currently hovering around the 6 per cent mark. Shubam has not factored inflation risk in her investment style. It is actively destroying her returns. She needs to seek higher returns if she has to meet her financial goals. Inflation risk is an example of the invisible risk. Inflation does not affect the absolute price of an investment. Therefore, its effects are felt less than price risks. Inflation risks work slowly, like a waterfall eroding a rock face over many years. Its effects become visible only with the passage of time. Investors who do not understand inflation risk will suffer wealth erosion and fall short of their financial goals.

Moneymooner Narain, who runs an online business, invested in bonds in 2019. He believed his investments were going to appreciate because interest rates were due for a fall. In 2020, the RBI started slashing interest rates in the wake of the pandemic. Narain's bond investments soared, giving him double-digit returns, even as the stock market plunged dramatically. Narain understood the inverted relationship between interest rates and bond prices.[19] When interest rates rise, bond prices fall, and vice versa. This is called interest rate risk.

Prakhar, a Wealth Warrior and a medical representative, invested in a piece of land near his village. A colossal dumping ground was soon formed near the plot, leading to a fall in its resale value. The real estate market was slow. Prakhar found it challenging to sell the land to fund his son's higher education. It became an illiquid asset. It did not offer him liquidity to meet an emergency. This is because his investment—like most real estate investments—had high liquidity risk.

Wealth Warrior Suresh's risk appetite is poor and so was his investment diversification. In the wake of the 2008 financial crisis, he started focussing on just one asset class: gold.

Gold is one of the most accessible stores of wealth. It does well during periods of economic uncertainty. Between 2007 and 2012, as the global economy went through multiple crises, gold performed exceedingly well for Suresh.

The price of 10 g of 24-karat gold was around ₹4,800 in 2007. It shot up explosively to around ₹31,000 by 2012. And then it flattened out nearly for a decade, giving Suresh low or negative returns. Then, in 2019, gold price started rising again, soaring past the ₹50,000 mark before moderating again. By investing in just gold, Suresh had concentration risk. Though gold kept his finances safe in turbulent periods, it gave him poor returns through prolonged stretches of time. He needs to diversify and create an all-weather investment portfolio containing other options that provide better returns.

There exist various other forms of risk. If war breaks out in the Middle East, and the stock market plunges 10 per cent, you are facing geopolitical risk. If you have invested in a corporate bond from a company struggling to run its business, you may not be able to get your money back on time. This is called credit risk. If there is wild fluctuation in currency exchange rates and you have investments in an affected country, you will be facing currency risks.

Have you taken stock of risks in your investments? What are those risks? And what are you doing to protect your finances against them?

Risk Appetite versus Risk Tolerance

Beavers are preyed upon by wolves, bears, foxes, coyotes and even owls. Humans, too, exploit them for skin and fur.

Despite this, the rodent cannot hide in water to minimize contact with predators. Surviving is not enough. It must also proliferate. It must calm the flow of rivers by damming them—a difficult job laced with dangers. The size of a small dog, the beaver sometimes lifts and moves as much as three tons of wood with its tiny hands to build its dams and lodges. As it chips through trees along the waterline, it risks contact with predators. But it must take this risk. How else will it satisfy its need to build? This is the beaver's risk appetite. It is committed to the idea that it must go into the woods to gnaw down a tree. It must do so even if it means a face-off with a bear that has not eaten in a week.

'Busy as a beaver' goes the phrase. The beaver must engineer its dam lodge by winter and procreate to ensure the survival of its species.

Strengthening our finances via investment is tied to our ability to take risks. To achieve our goals, we will have to step into the financial jungle. Occasionally, we will cross paths with a grizzly bear. How we react to the grizzly bear's presence is defined by our risk tolerance. Some risks are acceptable, others can destroy us. Our capacity for investment risk is limited. Therefore, our interaction with risks should be kept at acceptable levels.

Time in Market versus Timing the Market

Let us talk about the Infosys example. The math goes something like this.

The tech giant had its initial public offering in 1993. You could apply for a share in the company at ₹95. When the company listed on the stock exchange, the price immediately shot up to ₹145—52 per cent above the offer price.

Let us say you had applied to buy 100 Infosys shares for ₹9,500. When the company listed, your investment was already worth ₹14,500. In 1993, this was a pretty penny. It could get you a colour television, a two-wheeler or even a plot of land.

But consider the alternative: you avoided the urge to cash out. You held on to your shares for a year. In 1994, the company announced bonus shares at a ratio of 1:1. It meant that for every Infosys share you had, you would get a bonus share at no cost to you.

The company experienced tremendous growth through the years. It went on to announce bonuses in 1997, 1999, 2004, 2006, 2014, 2015 and 2018. Its 2004 bonus ratio was 3:1, meaning it gave three bonus shares against per share owned.[20] All these bonuses meant that your 100 shares from 1993 multiplied to a whopping 102,400 shares by 2018.[21] As of December 2021, the Infosys share price was trading around ₹1,880. In short, the company had turned your ₹9,500 investment into ₹19.25 crore in 28 years, implying a rate of return of 42 per cent per year.

If you consider the dividends distributed by the company every year, your returns would be higher.[22] Dividends are part of the company's profits paid to qualified shareholders. In April 2021, the company declared dividends of ₹15 per share. It then declared interim dividends at the same rate in October 2021. If you had still been holding on to your 102,400 shares, your earnings from Infosys dividends alone would have been ₹30.72 lakh in 2021.

Now, here is the important question. How many investors would have held on to all their shares for 28 years, resisting the urge to cash out at various points of that investment journey? There can be many compelling reasons to liquidate an investment. The stock market crashes of 2000, 2008 and 2020, for example, would have seen huge chunks of the stock's value being wiped out, driving fear into the hearts of shareholders. In those 28 years, investors would have also had other compelling reasons to sell their investment, such as wanting to raise cash to buy property, finance a business or educate their children.

If the investors did hold on to most of their shares, they would have become ultra-rich by a small-sized investment in the early '90s. This is the value of time spent in the market.

Investment experts, who have seen many market cycles of ups and downs, often say it is best to buy high-quality investments and forget about them. Just as you would not do a daily check of the price of the house you live in, you should not bother yourself with the daily price volatility of stocks in good companies. If their business fundamentals are strong and they are generating increasing amounts of revenue, you do not need to worry about short-term risks and price fluctuations. You only need to hold your hand. Compounded returns would do the rest. That only happens with considerable time spent in the market.

Conversely, there is the strategy of timing the market. For every Infosys, there are a 100 other companies that, rightly or wrongly, failed to take off. Holding on to their stock may not have aided wealth creation. But it may have been profitable to make short-term trades with them instead of holding them.

Timing the market involves the use of predictive tools such as fundamental and technical analysis to study the direction of prices. Using the predictions, you can devise a plan to buy when prices are low and cash out when prices have peaked.

But timing the market is a near-impossible task. It is not an exact science. Nobody can confidently say where the troughs and peaks of a market lie. Trying to find them to time your investments could lead to losses.

On the other hand, what if you understood the financial securities markets well? You could improve your understanding of the markets by receiving investment advice from analysts and experts. If you were an expert yourself, you could do your own research. You could use that information to trade securities profitably.

Investment learnings are never-ending. For those who have neither the time nor the inclination to roll up their sleeves and get into the financial jungle themselves, there is the option of MFs.

Lessons in Compounding

One of the most important lessons in investment is that of the power of compounding. Infosys is a great example. Spending time in the market allowed a small investment to grow exponentially with time, creating returns that are normally unthinkable over such a long period of time. The power of compounding can be easily understood. For beginners, it might not be easy to comprehend. So let us look at another example.

Suppose you invest ₹10,000 a month in an investment plan that gives you an average of 12 per cent returns for 10 years. You invest ₹12 lakh this way. Thanks to the returns, you end up with a purse of ₹23.23 lakh after 10 years.

Here is the trick question: if you ran this investment plan for 20 years instead of 10, what would the amount be at the end? People who are not familiar with the concept of compounding say they would save double the amount, which is ₹46.46 lakh.

In reality, and thanks to the power of compounding, this investment plan would have generated ₹99.91 lakh after 20 years. How does this happen? Compounded growth is your returns generating their own returns with time.

In the first year, you invested ₹1.2 lakh. The plan generated returns of ₹8,093. You have a sum of ₹1.28 lakh after the first year. Next year, you invested another ₹1.2 lakh and earned ₹8,093 again. But what about the money you had already saved up? That ₹1.28 lakh from the previous year will also generate 12 per cent returns amounting to ₹15,371.

These returns get bigger in absolute terms as time passes. The longer you remain invested, the greater the compounding. After 20 years, if you remain invested for just five more years, your purse would nearly double to ₹1.89 crore. In another five years, it would nearly double again to ₹3.52 crore.

Yes, achieving tough goals with investing is *really* that simple. All it takes is small steps that must be repeated for years.

Mistakes Also Compound

1.00^{365}	=	1.00
1.01^{365}	=	37.8
0.99^{365}	=	0.03

The Power of Compounding

I want to share this viral image that speaks about the compounding power of small steps over long periods. It says one raised to the power of 365 still gives us one. However, one increased by just 1 per cent and raised to 365 gives us 37.8.

It is an infinitesimally small change compounded many times. It produces a dramatically and exponentially different result. Similarly, decreasing returns can also compound. One reduced by just 1 per cent and raised to 365 gives us 0.03. Let us look at this as a lesson in investment and opportunity risks.

Early Jobber Shamsuddin, a newly recruited computer science graduate, is looking to kick-start an investment plan. He is 25; he thinks he will retire at 60. He has a 35-year runway.

He has been provided two options. He could either commit to an investment plan which could provide 11.5 per cent returns per annum, or he could commit to another investment plan returning 12.5 per cent per annum.

Graph 2

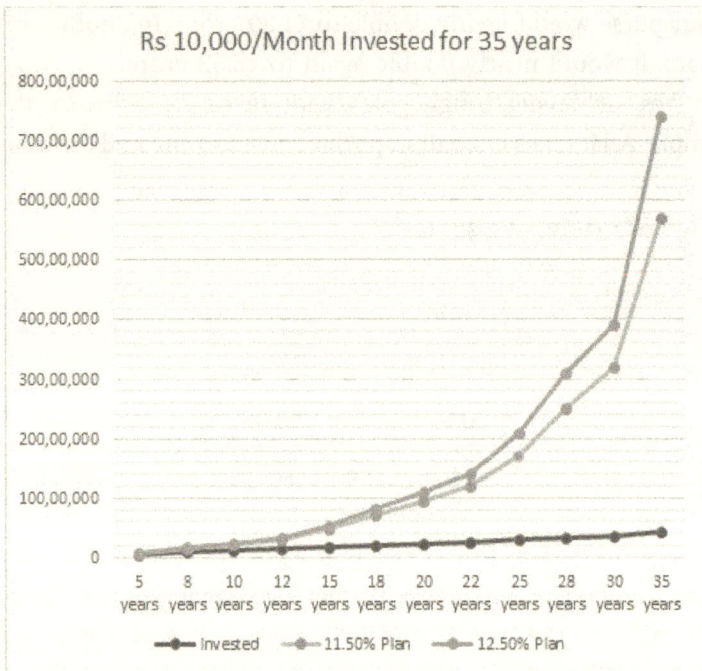

Young Shamsuddin wants to understand what the 1 per cent difference could do to him in the long term.

As these investments progress, there is not much difference between the amount saved over the first five years: the black plan gives us ₹8.1 lakh and the grey plan gives us ₹8.4 lakh. The latter is obviously doing better. But the difference is insignificant.

As the tenth year passes, the difference increases to six figures. The black plan gives us ₹22.6 lakh. The grey plan is comfortably ahead at ₹23.9 lakh. This gap will now start to dramatically widen as the years pass.

As the fifteenth year ends, the grey plan at ₹52.9 lakh is nearly ₹5 lakh ahead. By the nineteenth year, the difference goes over ₹10 lakh. The gap widens exponentially as seen from the diverging graph lines.

At some point after the twenty-fifth year, the gap is past ₹5 lakh. By the end of the 35-year plan, the grey plan has delivered ₹7.4 crore, which is ₹1.7 crore more than the black plan. This is the difference just 1 per cent additional returns make.

Short-term investment errors can be corrected. However, we have limited time. If we commit an investment error that spans 35 years, which could be most of our working lives, there is no coming back from there.

Look at this calculation to understand how wealth erodes through fixed-returns investments that cannot beat inflation.If Shamsuddin had attempted to invest only via a fixed deposit offering a 5 per cent return, and if inflation is 6 per cent, his real returns are negative 1 per cent. Despite the capital safety offered by the FD, it returns ₹1.1 crore, which is a paltry 14 per cent of what the grey plan offers.

You could play safe with an FD, but face extreme inflation risk, which provides low returns, or you can enter the securities market where you have rewarding options.

Wealth Creation and Financial Investments

Let us take a quick stock of our progress in the chapter so far. We have assessed our aspirations. We are using them as the guiding light for our investment goals. We have seen a smart and streamlined tax-saving plan. We have assessed risks and rewards. Now, we want to progress to wealth creation to strengthen our finances for the long term.

You may have sensed by now that for the purpose of wealth creation, this book will be focussing primarily on financial investments: MF, PF and even gold. They are easy to buy and sell, and the most transparent in terms of costs and returns. With them, what you see is what you get.

Finally, we will top off this section with the most important of all financial goals: home ownership.

Now, let us move to the one of the building blocks of financial wealth creation: index funds.

Buying the Haystack

Don't look for the needle in the haystack.
Just buy the haystack!

—John C. Bogle, pioneer of index funds

Everyone needs a life-altering investment decision: an Infosys allotment in 1993; a plot of land in a part of the city where demand is about to spike; the decision to start a business that is about to take off for the moon. For anyone who does not have these options, there are index funds.

An index is a measure of a securities market, and typically a subset of that market. The securities are typically stocks or bonds. Sensex and Nifty50, for example, are India's most important stock indices.

Sensex is often seen as an indicator of India's economic health. It is an index comprising publicly held stocks from

30 Indian companies. The Nifty50, also quite the economic weathervane, tracks 50 companies across 13 sectors.

The companies on these indices are large, well-capitalized, profit-generating businesses essential to our economy. Their share prices have appreciated considerably over time. They are what John C. Bogle called the haystack.

A typical index fund tries to copy the composition of an index. Bogle was the inventor and pioneer of index funds. Through his company, The Vanguard Group, Bogle championed the idea of low-cost MFs. Vanguard's index funds mimicked the stock market indices and liberated small investors from the need to find individual winners.

With the index fund, they could buy a whole index made up of the top companies. This gave them a cheap and easy way to generate market-linked returns necessary to build robust retirement savings.

Index funds exist in two forms: one, as MFs that you buy and sell via a fund house. These are also called fund-of-funds. Or two, as exchange traded funds (ETFs), which you buy and sell off the stock market exchanges as you would for a share in a company.

MFs can be active or passive. In an active fund, the fund manager must constantly take decisions to buy, hold or sell the fund's securities to generate optimal returns higher than the index. But in a passive fund, there is no need for a fund manager's expertise. Passive funds—which is what index funds are—are designed to replicate their chosen index. For example, a Nifty50 index fund would mimic the composition and returns of that index.

This gives investors the returns created by any index. And often, the long-term returns of stock indices are better than those of any asset class—much, much better.

In 2020, Deutsche Bank studied 200 years of returns from various asset classes in countries around the world. Their report, 'The Age of Disorder', reveals that long-term real returns from equity outperform those from bonds and commodities.[23] Nominal returns indicate actual returns. Real returns indicate nominal returns minus inflation, taxes and costs of investment.

In India, in the 1980–2020 period, equity delivered real returns of 9.6 per cent per annum, comfortably ahead of bond at just 0.9 per cent and gold at an even lower 0.3 per cent. Essentially, equity delivered 10.6 times the real returns from bonds and 32 times those from gold. In terms of per centage, these numbers are 1,060 per cent and 3,200 per cent, respectively.

Summarizing real returns from asset classes in USA, the report reveals the overwhelming margins by which equity outperforms the others. 'Over the entire sample period, US equities have outperformed corporate bonds, which have outperformed government bonds, which have outperformed cash, which interestingly has generally outperformed the commodity index analysed in this section,' the report states.[24]

The report adds that since 1920, equities have generated real returns of 7.65 per cent. It beats the 10-year and 30-year government bonds by more than 4.5 per cent points per annum, corporate bonds by 3.7 per cent points and treasury bills by 6.8 per cent points. Equities also outperformed gold by 5.6 per cent points per annum, oil by 8.4 per cent points and USA housing market (prices only) by 6.6 per cent points.

The report states that commodities over 100 years largely generated negative returns, except gold (2 per cent per annum) and copper (0.5 per cent per annum).

In summary, the long-term performance of India's stock indices compares favourably to other asset classes. This makes

Table 12

Global Equity, Bond and Commodity Performance History

	Nominal Returns					Real Returns				
	1860–1913	1914–1945	1946–1971	1972–1979	1980–2020	1860–1914	1915–1945	1946–1971	1972–1979	1980–2020
Equity (in per cent)										
India	7.50	5.10	6.20	20.20	17.90	NA	2.10	2.10	10.90	9.60
UK	3.50	6.10	11.70	8.00	10.90	3.40	4.10	7.30	-5.50	7.10
US	8.50	8.10	11.60	5.00	11.60	7.20	6.40	8.20	-2.90	8.30
Bonds (in per cent)										
India	3.50	5.50	3.40	5.40	8.50	-	2.70	-0.60	-2.80	0.90
UK	2.50	4.40	1.50	7.30	9.00	2.20	2.50	-2.50	-6.10	5.30
US	4.60	4.00	2.40	4.00	7.90	3.50	2.10	-0.80	-3.90	4.80
Commodities (in per cent)										
Gold	0.00	1.90	0.60	36.00	3.30	-0.90	0.00	-2.50	25.80	0.30
Oil	-3.80	0.00	1.20	35.20	0.10	-4.70	-1.90	-1.90	25.00	-2.80

Source: 'The Age of Disorder', Deutsche Bank's Global Fund Derivatives, 8 September 2020.

it a compelling investment option—even if through a plain vanilla index fund.

Why Index Funds?

Whether it is for my long-term investment needs or my daughter's education fund, I prefer index funds. They are low-cost and provide me the optimum risk-reward balance.

The returns history backs the idea that there is little chance of going wrong with a diversified index, such as Nifty50. This is a better option than trying to guess which individual stocks may succeed. It takes considerable time, money and effort to find the right stock pick. In the short term, the rate of success in the stock market is low.

Investors—whether seasoned or amateurs—are going to bet wrong and lose several times before they bet right and win. The yardstick for success is an investor generating better returns than the index. If you fail to beat the index, why not settle for the index?

It has been repeatedly seen that lack of information in the stock markets can have disastrous results for inexperienced investors. Short-term profit chasing, trying to time the market and not being patient with one's investments can lead to heavy losses. Most importantly, such investors underperform compared to an index.

Consider what securities research firm, Dalbar, said about investor trends in 2018: It revealed that while the S&P 500 index retreated only by 4.38 per cent, the average investor lost by over twice that margin at 9.42 per cent.[25] It said:

> In 2018 the average investor underperformed the S&P 500 in both good times and bad, lagging behind the S&P

by more than 100 basis points in two different months. In October, a bad month for the market (-6.84 per cent S&P 500 return vs. -7.97 per cent Avg. Equity Investor Return) the investor lagged by 113 basis points, while in August, a strong month for the market (+3.26 per cent S&P 500 return vs. 1.80 per cent Avg. Equity Investor Return) the Average Investor lagged by 146 basis points.

Investing in the markets is a series of decisions few are trained to make. For the average investor, the difficulty is not just in finding a winning bet, it is also in deciding how long to hold one's hand, when to sell and when to buy again. This difficult process of finding one winner in a sea of dozens of potential winners is akin to finding a needle in a haystack. Bogle's recommendation? Stop wasting time finding the needle. Buy the whole haystack. The haystack is essentially the whole market, or your preferred subset of it, in a single fund.

The average investor cannot hope to beat the index over the long term. This is what Bogle, too, believed in. 'Owning the stock market over the long term is a winner's game but attempting to beat the market is a loser's game,' he once said. And, therefore, buying the whole market may be a safer and better option.

The price of Nifty50, for example, has grown around 12.5 times since 1 January 2000, growing at a rate of 12 per cent per annum. In the same period, Sensex has multiplied 11.5 times, growing at a rate of around 11 per cent per annum. The price does not include dividend earnings, which would drive the returns even higher.

Every MF is benchmarked to an index. In an actively managed MF, such as an ELSS, the fund manager must constantly take decisions regarding the buying, holding and selling of the fund's underlying securities. Active MFs rely on the fund manager's expertise in making these decisions. They, therefore, cost more.

Equity MFs today have expense ratios ranging between approximately 0.25 and 2.8 per cent. On the other hand, you have index funds. They are extremely cheap, with most having expense ratios in the 0.01–0.3 per cent range. This is what we mean when we say index funds are low cost. They are passive funds. There is no constant stock-picking; they only need to mimic an index.

Index funds mimicking Sensex and Nifty50 have helped investors generate 11–12 per cent per annum without sweat, with limited market risk, at nearly no cost and with none of the difficult decision-making that individual investors face. These make them a compelling option for new investors looking to start their investment journeys.

The disclaimer that I want to add here is that an index fund or an MF delivering a certain level of performance in the past is not a guarantee of the same performance in the future. It may perform better or worse or the same way.

The Rise of Index Funds

The Securities Exchange Board of India (SEBI) regulates the trade of securities and commodities in India. Among its duties is the regulation of MFs in India. In 2017, SEBI decided to streamline the categorization of MFs in India. It said in a circular:

> It is desirable that different schemes launched by a mutual fund are clearly distinct in terms of asset allocation, investment strategy etc. Further, there is a need to bring in uniformity in the characteristics of similar type of schemes launched by different MFs. This would ensure

that an investor of MFs is able to evaluate the different options available, before taking an informed decision to invest in a scheme.[26]

SEBI's concern stemmed from the categorization and portfolio composition of funds. For example, some fund houses had multiple ELSS funds, each with own unique investment style. This could confuse a novice investor as to which option is best for him. In a market full of hundreds of attractive fund options, it is hard to compare funds within the same category. For instance, one fund house's large-cap fund could be dramatically different in composition compared to another fund house's scheme in the same category.

SEBI wanted greater standardization to help small investors evaluate and compare funds. To begin with, it dictated how a publicly traded company's market capitalization was to be defined. Market capitalization, to simplify, refers to a company's value on the stock market. It is calculated as the share price multiplied by the number of its shares. So when someone says that Amazon, Tesla or Apple are trillion-dollar companies[27], they are referring to the market capitalization of these businesses. Similarly, Reliance and TCS surpassed market capitalization of $100 billion in recent years.[28]

For the composition of MFs, SEBI said that only India's top 100 companies by market capitalization would be called large-cap. Mid-cap companies would now be those ranked from 101 to 250. And small-cap companies would be any company ranked 251 onwards.

Large-cap companies are India's corporate titans—large, stable businesses with a legacy of growth and excellence. Mid-cap companies are getting there. And small-cap companies are yet to see their growth unfold. Therefore, the smaller a company's market cap, the greater its potential for growth and value creation for shareholders.

Bear in mind that there is not much of a difference between the market caps of, for example, the ninety-fifth ranked company and the one hundred-and-fifth ranked company. But a line had to be drawn to minimize confusions caused to small investors. SEBI's action had an impact on the markets. Among the many things this recategorization did was trigger a rush for index funds.

Risks, Rewards and the Rush to Index Funds

The adoption of index funds, especially in the large-cap category, has been widely noticed in the past few years. In 2021, we saw over a 100 funds being launched by November.[29] Of these, 36 were ETFs and index funds. More were launched in 2022.

Why did this rush to the index happen, particularly in the large-cap segment? SEBI's shake-up reduced the large-cap space to the top 100 companies. Earlier, a large-cap fund could generate better returns by adding more mid- and small-cap stocks to its mix. But now, large-cap fund managers had to compulsorily pick 80 per cent of their holdings from the top-100 companies.

As of December 2021, the large-cap MF category had delivered 10-year returns of 15 per cent. The mid-cap category had delivered nearly 21 per cent for the same period. And the small-cap category had done even better at 22 per cent. Conversely, in a market crash, you could also see a small-cap fund falling much further than a large-cap fund.

In the weeks between February and April 2020 as the pandemic took hold, the BSE 100 Index fell around 24 per cent. The BSE MidCap Index fell more at 35 per cent. And the BSE SmallCap Index fell the most—by 37 per cent.

But let me come back to large-cap funds. As I mentioned earlier, every fund is tied to a benchmark. Several large-cap funds are benchmarked to the BSE 100 or the Nifty 100 indices. If you are investing in an active fund where the fund manager takes decisions to improve fund performance, you want the fund to, at the very least, deliver better returns than its benchmark. Therefore, you pay a higher commission for active funds to get higher returns than the benchmark. As it turns out, 2020 and 2021 were years in which a large per centage of active funds underperformed their benchmarks.

In April 2021, 'S&P Dow Jones Indices versus Active'[30] India report stated that a staggering 100 per cent of active large-cap funds had failed to beat the index in the second half of 2020.[31] The report states:

> Over the one-year period ending in June 2021, the S&P BSE 100 was up 55.96 per cent, with 86.21 per cent of funds underperforming the benchmark. Over H1 2021, 53.13 per cent of the funds underperformed the S&P BSE 100. Over longer horizons, the majority of the actively managed large-cap equity funds in India underperformed the large-cap benchmark, with 65.93 per cent of large-cap funds underperforming over the 10-year period ending in June 2021.[32]

It had similar bad news for ELSS funds. Nearly 49 per cent had been beaten by the benchmark over the 10-year period ending June 2021. Over a three-year period, the number was even worse at 76 per cent. The proposition before the small investor was, therefore, simple: if he is going to pay a high expense ratio of as much as 2.8 per cent and get less returns than the index, he is better off buying the index. Index funds cost a tenth of an active fund but delivered higher returns.

And thus they started becoming popular.

Suddenly, in the Indian markets, there is a glut of not just index funds but also the number of indices available to small investors. Nifty and Sensex index funds have existed for long. But now you can also invest in a mid-cap or a small-cap index. You can even buy the whole market of the top-500 companies through a single index fund. You can buy a bank index, a technology index, a government-owned business index or even a foreign index, such as Nasdaq100 or FAANG.[33]

If you do not like how your Nifty50 fund is skewed towards the top-10 companies accounting for nearly 70 per cent of the fund's portfolio, you can buy a Nifty50 equal weight index[34], which gives equal weightage to all 50 companies on the index. This is a good time to be an Indian equity investor. You can create an entire low-cost, high returns portfolio out of index funds to achieve your financial goals.

To quote Bogle again, 'The winning formula for success in investing is owning the entire stock market through an index fund, and then doing nothing. Just stay the course.'

Alpha and Risk

Let us come back to risk and rewards. Index funds offer you the bare minimum returns the markets offer. These returns are great, ordinarily. But what if you wanted more?

This is where active funds and the fund manager's stock-picking ability come in. The large-cap space has been run over by index funds. But fund managers have made an impact on the mid-cap and small-cap segments. The SPIVA India report confirmed this. 'Among all the categories evaluated in the SPIVA India Scorecard, the Indian Equity Mid-/Small-Cap category fared the best for active funds, with the majority of them managing to beat the S&P BSE 400 Mid SmallCap Index over the 10-year period ending in June 2021,' the report said.[35] As per the report, nearly 60 per cent of funds in this category beat the index over a 10-year period ending June 2021, as compared to nearly 34 per cent in the large-cap category and 51 per cent in the ELSS category.[36]

These funds generated returns over and above index returns. This excess return is known as alpha.[37] It is what intrepid investors are after. They cannot be satiated by index returns. They want more.

The mid-cap and small-cap categories, incidentally, are among the best long-term performers. There are also multi-cap and flexi-cap funds that invest across weight categories. Though they are riskier, they have rewarded investors handsomely over the decades. Thrown into your investment mix, they can be the sprinkles on your plain vanilla index fund returns—the alpha you seek. For example, if the large-cap index is returning 12 per cent, the others could potentially return 15 per cent to improve your portfolio gains.

You can evaluate active funds by parameters such as their long-term performance, independent ratings, ranking within the category and the margin by which they are able to beat their index. The difference in returns could be significant. For example, as of December 2021, the small-cap MF category delivered 10-year returns of over 22 per cent per annum. The S&P BSE SmallCap Total Returns Index returned a much lower 16 per cent in the same period.

However, the largest fund in the small-cap category, with assets worth over ₹17,500 crore, has delivered a whopping 27 per cent per annum in that period. The fund has delivered an alpha of a mind-boggling 11 per cent over the index. ₹1 lakh invested 10 years ago would have become ₹7.30 lakh in the small-cap category, ₹4.41 lakh in the small-cap index and ₹10.91 lakh in the active fund.

This level of performance is rare, but it does happen. And investors can make use of these opportunities to pad up their overall returns. Your MF choices will rely on considerations such as active or passive, long-term or short-term investing, or big or small companies. But the core of your portfolio should ideally be formed by the best-performing companies in India. This can be done via large-cap index funds, such as Nifty50 and Nifty Next 50. These are your blue chips, upcoming blue chips and large-cap companies. The term 'blue chip' refers to a well-capitalized, recognized, profitable business and is often interchangeably used with a large-cap company.

Let us also not forget that you could simply get your alpha from high-performing ELSS funds. These tax-saving funds, too, have a large-cap tilt. But given their long-term nature, they also consist of high-returns-generating smaller companies. The difficulty you may face with ELSS funds is their lock-ins.

Making Sense of Debt Funds

On the other side of the financial securities spectrum, we have debt instruments such as debt MFs, government and corporate bonds, debentures and corporate deposits. Their benefit is assured returns and above-average capital gains due to any prevalent credit risk and interest rate risk. You also pay a lower rate of tax on your returns if you hold your debt funds for three years or more.

Typically, debt MFs are defined by the average maturity period of their underlying instruments. A debt could mature overnight, in a week, in a month or a few months, in a year or a few years, in several decades or not mature at all.

As of 2021, as per SEBI's last classification of MFs, there are as many as 16 kinds of debt funds, along with 10 kinds of equity funds. These debt securities are bonds, bills and commercial papers. They are issued by central and state governments as well as corporates that need small loans for periods ranging from a day to several years. There are also perpetual bonds that never reach maturity.

To the investor, interest is serviced as mentioned in the bond contract given by the issuer. When the bond matures, the principal is repaid to the investor. The shorter the maturity period, the lower its risks and, therefore, the lower the returns. On the other hand, the longer the duration, the higher could be the returns.

The high returns are primarily from interest rate risks. When interest rates fall, long-duration bond yields increase, thus pumping up the returns of debt MFs that contain those bonds. The opposite is also true: when interest rates rise, long-duration bond yields fall.

For example, in 2019 and 2020, when interest rates softened, long-duration debt MFs returned category averages of over 12 per cent a year. But earlier in 2017 and 2018 when interest rates were hardening, they had returned just 3–5 per cent.

Therefore, the assumption that debt funds are absolutely safe is not correct. They, too, have daily price volatility, which could drive returns up or down. We earlier saw that LMFs have the lowest risk among debt funds. But as the returns increase, so do the risks. Despite the risks, their long-term returns are lower than what you could get from a plain vanilla large-cap equity index MF. This brings us to the all-important question: if they are so risky, what are debt funds good for?

The Best Use for Debt Funds

It is important to understand what a debt MF can give you that no other kind of MF can.

Debt MFs give you an easy way to invest in government and corporate bonds. Investing in these has not been an option for the small investor traditionally. This is because the minimum investments required in these securities often ran into tens of lakhs or even crores of rupees. But with the right debt MF, you could expose yourself to this market with as little as ₹500 a month.

The exception that has now been created is that in 2021, the RBI launched the Retail Direct platform. This website allowed small investors to trade central and state government securities, such as bonds and treasury bills, with as little as ₹10,000.

Government securities are practically risk-free, interest-generating investments. These come with a sovereign rating, though state government bonds (also called state development loans) are considered a shade below sovereign. These are the highest credit ratings any bond can get, implying there is the least likelihood of a default. What has been borrowed by the governments will be repaid with interest in a timely manner to the investor.

Let us spend a moment understanding what credit ratings are. A small borrower is assigned a credit score ranging between 300 and 900. Similarly, governments, companies and even countries are assigned credit ratings denoted by letters such as A, B, C and D. The ratings are layered. For example, ratings between AAA, AA+, AA, A and A- denote the bond issuer's strong ability to meet its financial commitments. BBB to B- denote ongoing challenges to the business, which may hamper its ability to meet commitments. CCC to C denote serious vulnerabilities or even a looming bankruptcy. D denotes that the issuer has defaulted or is about to default on its commitments.

These ratings are produced by credit research companies, such as S&P, Moody's, Crisil and Fitch.[38] Rating methodologies and denominations differ from one company to another.

AAA-rated securities sit just below sovereign-rated ones and are, therefore, very low-risk. Risks increase as you go down the ratings ladder. The possibility of returns also increases with low ratings, up to a point. Hence, we see lower-rated bonds offer higher returns compared to sovereign and A-rated ones. For example, in 2022, an AAA-rated bond may offer you a 7.5 per cent per cent yield, while an A-minus-rated one might advertise even 13 per cent.

The Cs and the Ds are not considered investment grade. The term 'junk bonds' is often used to describe them.[39] They may attract investors through even higher yields. But they are also more likely to default on maturity. This risk, as mentioned earlier, is called credit risk. What has been borrowed from you may not be paid back.

You do not have to wade through this dense jungle by yourself. You can invest in these securities via a debt MF. You can select the risk and returns you are comfortable with and leave it to the fund manager to pick the best securities for your investment needs. This answers what bond funds allow you to do. But is what they are doing good enough for your investment needs? We also need to understand post-tax returns.

Better Post-Tax Returns than Bank Deposits

Debt funds give you an alternative to FDs, albeit a higher-risk one. The short-term duration funds (overnight, liquid, money market and other low-duration funds) might give you returns comparable to, or marginally higher than, bank deposits.

Bear in mind this is not an apples-to-apples comparison. Bank deposits, as we saw in the first section, advertise forward and guaranteed returns. MFs do not guarantee or advertise any return. You can judge them only on past returns which, in no way, guarantee future returns.

Bank deposits are also insured up to ₹5 lakh per depositor by the RBI's deposit insurance scheme. Debt MFs have no such safety net. A debt MF is composed of different debt securities picked by the fund manager. In an adverse scenario, some of those securities can go into default, impacting your overall returns. This is the risk you run for higher returns.

While the returns may be comparable to or better than bank deposits, your post-tax returns can be significantly higher. If you held your debt MF investment for three years or longer, it becomes a long-term investment and thus eligible for a lower rate of taxation. This lowering of taxes on long-term returns happens through indexation benefits.

Long-term debt MF returns are taxed with indexation benefits at 20.6 per cent. This rate would be significantly lower than being taxed at a flat rate of 30 per cent that you may end up paying on a bank deposit. Indexation benefits allow you to calculate an inflation-adjusted price for your investment based on the year of purchase.

The values of this index are produced annually through the Cost Inflation Index (CII) table.[40] Since the inflation-adjusted price of an asset is likely to be closer to the sale price, your returns become lower, as do your taxes. This is good for you.

For example, you purchased a debt MF of ₹1 lakh in the financial year 2014–15. The CII index for that year was 240. You sold the investment for ₹1.5 lakh in the period of 2020–21, whose CII index was 301. Ordinarily, the entire gains of ₹50,000 may be taxable. But since the returns are long-term by virtue of the investment being held for six years, only ₹25,854 of those gains will be taxable. This is because the inflation-adjusted or indexed value of the investment is higher, as calculated under:

(index for sale year ÷ index for purchase year) × purchase price, i.e.

$$(301 \div 240) \times ₹100,000$$
$$= 1.25416 \times ₹100,000$$
$$= ₹125,416$$

Your investment was purchased for ₹125,416 and sold for ₹150,000. Your long-term capital gains became ₹150,000 – ₹125,416 = ₹24,584. Your taxes on the above gains were calculated at 20.6 per cent, i.e. ₹5,064. This works out to a tax rate of just over 10 per cent of the overall gains. This rate is nearly three times lower compared to your fully taxable FD returns.

There is another key difference between taxation of bank deposits and MFs. Your deposit interest income is taxed even if you have not liquidated the deposit. Your bank reports your interest earnings to the Income Tax Department, taxes them at source, and you also pay pending taxes, if any, while filing your tax returns.

This is not the case with MFs. Your returns are taxed only when you redeem or switch the investment. You could theoretically hold your investment for decades without paying any income tax on them.

The critical question, however, remains: whatever be the returns, are they beating inflation? Are the real returns positive? The answer, in most cases, is no. And this will continue to be the case globally, as interest rates remain low, struggle to beat inflation and hurt debt investors.[41]

The 20-year returns on the best-performing debt MFs are in the 7–8 per cent range.[42] This is a lower rate of return than even EPF, which currently offers 8.50 per cent. It is nearly 33 per cent lower than the lowest-ranked equity MFs and index funds, which offer around 12 per cent a year over the same 20-year period. The only silver lining in these returns is that the long-term bond returns are propped up by periods of interest rate-linked gains. Periods of falling interest rates see double-digit returns from long-duration debt funds, which are far higher than bank deposits.

In summary, debt investments are suited for short to medium-term tenures. This could range from a few days to a few years. During this period, the returns on the investment may be low, but there will be greater safety of capital, subject to the type of debt MF you buy.

This is what the retired and the elderly prefer. But for young investors, the longer you hold your debt investment, the higher your opportunity cost. Your real returns, as demonstrated earlier, could be much higher with equity investing. You cannot hope to consistently beat inflation simply with debt investments.

Save the Commission, Improve Your Returns

Every MF scheme comes in many variants. There are primarily two streams of variance.

1. Who is selling the MF? You can buy them directly from the fund house or you can buy them from an intermediary, such as an online aggregator, an agent or your bank.

The variant sold by the fund house is called a direct plan. You can buy them off the fund house's website. The other is called the regular plan. The only difference between the two is the expense ratio. Regular plans may charge 50 to 150 basis points higher than direct plans. This is to account for intermediary costs. In both cases, you can transact online. All you need is a KYC-compliant bank account with netbanking facility.

If you are a beginner to MFs, you can also rely on the intermediary's expertise, data analytics and advisory to finalize your fund choice. In this sense, the trade-off is acceptable. However, once you are well-versed with the MF market and know how to pick funds yourself, buy the direct plan. An additional per cent or two could make a massive difference—potentially worth crores—to your investment in the long run.

2. You could buy a growth plan or a dividend plan. This is a straightforward choice. If you are a young investor starting out in your investment journey, take the growth plan.

    Dividend payouts in MFs are rare and largely insignificant to a small investor. You would need to accumulate bucket loads of units to earn the kind of dividend that helps you meet your living costs. Despite being the same MF, the prices of dividend plans move much slowly compared to growth plans because they divert part of their growth towards dividends. In the growth plan, dividends get reinvested into the scheme, thus driving your compounded returns higher.

    Let us take the example of a very large large-cap equity fund. In 2021, it declared a dividend of ₹1.55 per unit held.[43] As of December, its dividend plan had a unit price of ₹20.[44] Its direct growth plan had a price of ₹51.[45] If you owned, for example, one lakh units in this fund, your dividend income would be ₹1.55 lakh for 2021. However, most small investors will need time to accumulate these many units. Unless you have that number, the dividend will not make any material difference to your finances.

The underlying principles in both cases: think of growth, tightly control costs and find ways to get better returns.

Investing Systematically

We have gone over the term 'systematic investment' several times in this section. But what does it mean?

The beaver must chew through hundreds of trees in a single year, painstakingly dragging them into the river to build dams and lodges. It must repeat these steps several times to achieve its goal. Similarly, a systematic investment plan (SIP) means repeating small steps hundreds of times over the long-term, breaking down a tough investment goal into small, achievable monthly goals. It has several advantages.

Firstly, an SIP allows you to buy your chosen investment instrument at various price points. You buy regardless of the market position because you have determined this instrument to be the best choice for your goal. This not only reduces price risks, it also gives you better rupee-cost average. Let us understand this with an example.

Munna, an Early Jobber with an electronics business, decided to invest ₹5,000 a month into his chosen MF. In the first instalment, his fund's unit price was ₹55. This allowed him to buy 90.90 units of the fund.

The next month, the fund's price fell to ₹52. This allowed him to buy 96.15 units. The fall continued for the third month as the price went to ₹48. This allowed him to buy 104.16 units. In three months, he spent ₹15,000 and accumulated 291.21 units of this fund. As he bought his units at different price points, he got an average price for them, which is total money invested divided by units bought. This worked out to ₹51.50 per unit. This is lower than the price he had paid in the first and second months.

Now, the price of the MF only needs to recover to ₹51.51 for Munna's overall investment to become profitable again. Once it recovers to its original price of ₹55, the value of the investment would appreciate to ₹16,016 with a profit margin of ₹1,016. Therefore, despite the prices being flat over three months, he would still make profit.

An SIP, therefore, helps you make money even when markets are flat by allowing you to buy units at different points. When the markets are low, you get to accumulate units at discounted prices. When the markets are high, you get a profit.

Secondly, SIPs enforce financial discipline. The ideal SIP should be programmed into your netbanking. It will automatically deduct the fixed amount every month to be diverted into your chosen MF. This ensures that money is being systematically invested every month. Each month, it helps you get closer to fulfilling your aspirations. SIPs with MFs can be as little as ₹500 a month. You can programme your SIP to create an annual step-up (for example, 10 per cent each year) to increase your contributions as the years roll by.

Thirdly, SIPs also reduce the need to track markets closely. For this, you need to be confident in your investment choice. If you have chosen well, the SIP will deliver. You need not concern yourself with the daily ups and downs of the market.

All That Glitters

Admittedly, when people a century from now are fearful,
it's like many will still rush to gold.

—Warren Buffett, in his 2011 letter to shareholders of
Berkshire Hathaway Inc.

No talk of wealth creation is complete without discussing gold. Indians have loved gold for millennia. It is a sign of wealth and prosperity. It is connected deeply to our culture. We buy it for weddings, festivals and even at the turn of seasons.

India and China are the biggest gold consumers in the world. As per the January 2020 update of the GFMS Gold Survey, India purchased 136.6 tonnes of gold in the fourth quarter of 2019.[46] China was just behind at 132.1 tonnes. One tonne equals 1,000 kg.

In 2021, India spent a record $55.7 billion on gold imports, more than double of the $22 billion it had spent in 2020.[47] It was also higher than the previous record of $53.9 billion in 2011, when demand for gold had peaked following economic and political unrest in different parts of the world.

Gold and silver were the only two precious metals used as a store for value and traded as a medium of exchange back in 600 BC. Gold is scarce, difficult to find, and laborious and expensive to mine. Filtering out specks of gold from dirt, refining it and shaping it into marketable form is another task. Gold has stood the test of time as a store of value—it does not corrode, lasts for centuries and is passed down as generational wealth. The yellow metal is malleable. It can be worn as jewellery or used as a decoration item. It is an all-season investment. It is one of the most-used collaterals for loans.[48] It is rare and its value only goes up with time.

This glittery thing has been relentlessly pursued by man. It has shaped history, economics and destinies. But as an investment option, it is fraught with risks. The risks are tied to the purity of the metal, its fluctuating prices, its safe storage and liquidity. Yet it may be good to have it as a part of your investment plan.

So let us quickly explore gold from two angles: as an item of utility and as an investment avenue.

Gold

Utility versus Investment

Gold can be bought as coins, bars, jewellery, artefacts, antique, household or personal items, bonds, exchange-traded funds and even MFs. No other form of wealth exists in such diverse forms. The purest form of gold is 24 karat gold, which is considered 99.999 per cent pure. The purity of gold used in jewellery typically varies from 22 karat to 10 karat. Karat is a measure of gold's purity measured in parts of 24. It can also reveal the per centage of the gold's purity. For example, 22 karat gold is 91.67 per cent pure gold, calculated as $(22 \div 24) \times 100$.

The gold used in jewellery cannot be completely pure. As the metal is soft, it needs to be used with other metals for stability. But bars, coins and other simpler forms of gold can be 24 karat.

Gold is almost like an independent currency with active circulation in the global financial system. Governments worldwide store it in their central banking system or in safety vaults in secure locations. Earlier, you could buy gold mostly only from jewellers or banks. Now, you could even buy them off reputed e-commerce platforms. Besides the price of gold, you also need to pay making charges and taxes on your purchase.

Gold jewellery making charges may be applied at a flat rate or per gram. The norms vary from one jeweller to the other. Making charges also attract GST at 5 per cent, apart from the 3 per cent tax you pay on the gold itself. You will also incur costs on storage. Lockers are available with banks and private providers, and you can even buy one for your home. These costs, however, eat into your returns. You must factor these costs if you intend to sell your gold in the future.

Physical gold is easy to buy, but not so easy to sell. You could still sell it for cash to certain jewellers at prevalent market prices. But finding such jewellers and going through the verification of the gold's purity can be tedious. You may also need to preserve the gold's invoice. Without it, retailers may refuse to buy the gold. In other cases, they may not give you cash, but give gold worth an equal value in exchange.

Personally, my connection with gold is more sentimental and less as an investment. It is too volatile for my liking. And it is far less liquid than an MF or a bank deposit.

I buy gifts for my wife on our anniversary when I can. But I end up buying precious stones, which are even more illiquid and depreciating. Overall, my family buys gold purely for aesthetic and sentimental reasons.

This covers gold in physical form. But did you know you can also buy and sell gold digitally?

Gold provides utility as jewellery or personal items. Gold bullion provides a mode of investment. But gone are the days when you needed to buy gold in physical form. You can now buy gold in dematerialized (demat) form as ETFs, MFs or bonds. When considering gold purely as an investment, these options may be much better for you.

In 2015, to encourage digital gold investments, the RBI

launched the Sovereign Gold Bond Scheme. It gave gold investors several advantages over physical gold. As per the scheme, you can buy gold bonds in units of 1 g going up to 4 kg. The unit price is linked to the average price of 24 karat gold. The bonds are stored in your digital investment storage—your demat account, which you can open via your bank or online trading platforms. The bond is linked to your PAN, your tax identity in India. It, therefore, cannot be stolen.

Gold bonds give you an interest income. Currently this is 2.5 per cent per annum, credited twice a year to your bank account. Physical gold does not provide you an additional income stream this way.

Gold bonds mature in eight years. Your returns, if any, are tax-free on maturity. This, however, is a double-edged sword. After all, gold is a speculative investment. Its returns could go either way for you. It is within the realms of possibility that gold prices will not move at all for several years and may even drop.

The RBI releases gold bonds in several tranches each year. You can buy them via an authorized bank, a stock exchange or even an online trading platform. If you buy it online, you will get a discount. You can also buy older second-hand tranches from investors selling them on stock exchanges.

Apart from gold bonds, you have gold funds—both ETFs and MFs—sold by most fund houses in the country. You can trade them off the fund house or on a stock exchange. They, too, are linked to the prices of 24 karat gold and provide you all the benefits of dematerialized gold just as the gold bond does. What you cannot do, however, is turn demat gold into physical gold.

Risks and Rewards

In any speculative investment, you are less concerned with what the investment does in terms of providing utility and more concerned about its price. You invest in it believing that its price will be higher the day you sell. Someone must pay a higher price for it than you, thereby allowing you to make a profit.

This expectation of profit creates difficulties with gold. Gold appreciates when there is economic uncertainty in the world. When all is well, it flatlines—sometimes for years. In this regard, over the long term, gold acts as a form of saving and not an investment. For example, between 1992 and 2003, average prices remained largely in the ₹4,300–₹5,000 range.[49] Gold returns in this period was lower than those from a savings account or PF.

From around 2003, gold started a decade-long rally, peaking around ₹31,000 by 2012.[50] This period saw wars, a global recession, inflation and civil unrest in many parts of the world. After that, gold remained flat for nearly a decade again. As fears of economic recession followed by a global pandemic took hold, gold started another rally going past ₹50,000. In the rally between 2003 and 2012, it appreciated nearly six to seven times. But in the latest rally fuelled by the pandemic, it appreciated less than one time. Now, compounded returns from gold are not what they used to be.

In the 10 years ending December 2021, returns from gold MFs and ETFs have been in the range of 3.4–4.8 per cent per annum.[51] This, along with the Deutsche Bank report mentioned earlier, tells us that gold is an option for conservative investors. There is little investment risk and, hence, little reward.

This is not to say that there will not be a series of events in the future that will trigger another gold rally. It remains to be seen.

But on the basis of recent performance, we can infer that the more gold you have in your portfolio, the lower your portfolio's overall returns might be. Those returns might merely track the rate of inflation. Therefore, they will be counterproductive to long-term wealth creation plans.

However, during times of economic uncertainty, as the returns from other parts of your portfolio drop, gold will appreciate. Hence, gold is considered a hedge against uncertainty. For example, consider you have a diversified investment portfolio. Assume that as of today, out of every ₹100 you have invested, ₹70 has gone in equity, ₹20 in bonds and ₹10 in gold. Now, there is a stock market pull-back by 10 per cent. You lose ₹7 in your equity holdings. However, due to the economic uncertainty that led to the crash, your gold holdings nudged up 20 per cent, increasing in absolute value by ₹2. Therefore, your net portfolio loss due to the falling stock market would have been softened by gains from gold.

But the higher the concentration of gold in your portfolio, the softer will be its growth through the long term. So how much gold do you want in your investment portfolio? You must decide this on the basis of your risk appetite, your financial goals and the time you want to remain invested for.

What you should not do is let sentiment dictate your investment choices—something we often see with gold.

The Dam and the Lodge

We now come to the final leg of the chapter: building the dam and lodge, without which a beaver's life purpose is not fulfilled.

Investing is the key to Strengthening. It is the big step we take as we reach to the apex of our 5S Pyramid. I, however, admittedly started investing late. But once I got started with my SIPs, it was soon time to take a loan and buy a house. Nothing compares to the security of a roof over your head. My parents had drilled this need in me. A loan helped me fulfil that dream.

After I got married, I bought my house. That, in its own way, is the biggest savings for most Indian households. For my parents' generation at least, this was the principal savings. Owning a house required hard work.

Is this the best returns on investment? Probably not—as we are about to find out shortly. We also have the 'rent versus buy' arguments. For me, owning a property is about the charm of building your own home from the floor up.

My wife and I moved into our first home with only one piece of furniture. Every time we travelled or went out on weekends, we would visit these cool boutique stores and pick up pieces. There is a story behind every piece in our apartment: the old, carved wooden horses bought from Jodhpur, from when we went to enjoy the Rajasthan International Folk Festival; the colourful, printed, red and yellow footstools bought from Jaipur, from when we went for the Jaipur Literature Festival; the metal owl bought in Mission in San Francisco; a finely carved antique mirror bought from Kolkata's Chor Bazaar; a fish made of recycled metal scraps bought right before our wedding at Chatukchak Weekend Market in Bangkok. Our home has become a store of these happy memories.

Housing, as we have seen through the eyes of the BankBazaar Aspiration Index survey, is one of the two most important life goals for Indians, the other being educating their children. The ideal purpose of a property is self-occupation. The less-than-ideal purpose is investment. Why is this so?

For starters, the cost of house ownership can be enormous for most Indians. An average-sized two-bedroom apartment can cost tens of lakhs, or even crores in metro cities. In a country with a nominal GDP per person barely around ₹1.5 lakh, home ownership can often shock a household's finances, and that might open the door to other potential risks. For example, many Indians dip into their PF savings for house purchases. They, thus, reduce their retirement savings.

Housing costs are extreme. Worse, returns from it are falling. Therefore, locking a lot of value in a low-returns-generating investment avenue can be harmful for your wealth-creation efforts.

As per the RBI's House Price Index, annual returns from real estate have declined precipitously after the heady growth seen in the previous two decades.[52]

Graph 3

Falling House Price Returns Since 2011

It was common to see property purchased at low costs in the 1990s and 2000s to be flipped for huge gains. Those were the years in which home ownership was encouraged—not just for one's security but also for the great returns. However, this is not the case anymore. Housing purchases in the last 10 years have been generating lower and lower returns each passing year, as the RBI data shows in Graph 2.

The House Price Index looks at prices in Mumbai, Delhi,

Bengaluru, Ahmedabad, Lucknow, Kolkata, Chennai, Jaipur, Kanpur and Kochi. In years gone by, the index saw annual jumps of 30–50 per cent in cities such as Bengaluru and Kolkata. But in the last few years, the returns fell to single digits.

Between the first quarters of 2020–21 and 2021–22, the returns on the all-India index were just 1.99 per cent. They had fallen nearly a third from the previous year's 2.81 per cent. These returns are lower than a savings account. The decline in house-price returns precedes the pandemic, and the latter only accelerated it. The poor returns do not justify the extreme costs of investing in real estate.

The situation is not likely to change dramatically in the coming years. Inflation in materials such as cement may drive up prices marginally. But there is not enough demand for the glut of unsold housing inventory in most large cities. This may keep prices subdued in the immediate future, though short-term spikes may be seen.

This is not the only reason why housing is not a good investment. Housing is also illiquid. You can liquidate an FD at a moment's notice. You can even part-liquidate it if so needed. But you cannot do that for a house. You must sell it as a whole. Even if you decide to, it can take months or years to find the right buyer. The process of negotiating the price, going through legal wrangles and completing the paperwork is not easy.

Besides, housing also has maintenance costs and property taxes. These eat into your capital gains—which are already low—and your peace of mind. If you thought that rent from the house could give you better returns, then think again.

In 2019, property consultant Knight Frank and law firm Khaitan & Co. in a report said that rental yields in India are among the worst in the world.[53] After the pandemic, scattered data shows that rental yields reduced some more as even upscale locations had to slash rent to maintain or attract occupancy.[54]

Rental yield is the per centage of your property cost that you can earn as rent. For example, if the property costs ₹1 crore and your annual rent from it is ₹3.6 lakh, the yield is 3.6 per cent. Net rental yield can be calculated as yield after costs of house ownership.

The report said:

> After deducting all the annual expenses from annual rent, such as property taxes, maintenance charges, agent fee and non-occupancy costs, the net rental yield is currently hovering in the range of 2-3 per cent across most Indian cities, which is one of the lowest across the world. And they have remained static over the past few years. With better interest rates and returns available in bank fixed deposits, public PFs and other instruments such as stocks and MFs, the lucrativeness of residential real estate as an investment class has lost its sheen.[55]

Spoon-Sized Real Estate Investment

There is the alternative of investing in real estate via Real Estate Investment Trusts (REIT).[56] They are doing to real estate investment what MFs have done for equity and bond investment: make them affordable.

Launched in India in 2017, REITs are a relatively new arrival. In 2022, only a few REITs existed from large realty groups. They allow small investors to make micro-investments in premium commercial real estate such as corporate offices generating high rental yields.

Just as index funds and MFs, REITs are unitized. They are

bought and sold in the stock markets, just as an ETF would be. With a few thousand rupees, you can buy a fraction in real estate—a Bengaluru tech park, for example—that would ordinarily cost hundreds of crores of rupees. REITs provide rental income apart from capital appreciation. REIT unit holders are like shareholders in a real estate trust. They are entitled to the rent generated by properties owned by the trust.

Beyond the enormous costs, real estate investing requires tonnes of paperwork, due diligence and an assortment of challenges involved with large real estate transactions. Once you own property, you also need to think about maintenance, security and income generation. But an REIT simplifies all of this.

An REIT investment entitles you to a proportional share of the rental income generated by the trust. You are entitled to the income. But you are spared all the above-mentioned pain, which will be handled by the trust.

If you do not like your investment, you can simply sell it on a stock exchange. If you like it, you can buy more the same way.

Should one still buy an REIT? With any investment, you should have a clear line of sight into returns, liquidity and risks. On these three parameters, you need to compare REITs to other forms of investment. For example, if an REIT returns 10 per cent a year through a combination of rental yield and capital appreciation, it compares favourably to a debt investment, such as PF or an FD.

However, can it also regularly hit 12–15 per cent like the best MFs can? These are questions you must ask of yourself to set your own investment expectations. There is also a need to diversify your investment portfolio, and a portion of your portfolio linked to REITs can bring you above-average long-term returns and regular liquidity through rental yield.

As always, before entering an investment, you must consider your goals, returns expectations, liquidity needs and risk appetite.

Preparing Your Finances for Home Ownership

Housing as an investment is a high-risk and low-rewards game. Now, let us look at how it can help you in terms of self-occupation.

Experts in India advise to opt for renting, instead of buying. The costs do not justify the purchase, they say. But home ownership is a cherished goal. We know this. Year after year through BankBazaar's surveys, Indians have said home ownership is one of their most important goals.

To fulfil one of our most cherished goals, we must prepare our finances first.

When Shikha, a Wealth Warrior and a management consultant from Bengaluru, decided to buy a home, she wanted to take an informed call. She knew about the high costs and low returns. She understood she cannot burn through her savings for housing several times in her lifetime she had other goals too. She decided to buy one house, which would be perfect as per her needs.

Shikha wanted a three-bedroom apartment. The prices in Bengaluru were high. Through her savings and home loan eligibility, she could afford a property costing up to ₹60 lakh. But her preferred three-room house came with the starting price of ₹95 lakh. She decided to delay the purchase—buying a small house first and upgrading it to a larger one later did not seem like a good idea to her. She waited for three more years to save up the additional needed funds.

Her income doubled in this period, which increased her

home loan eligibility. With higher savings and a bigger loan, she would now be able to buy her dream home, even if it had gotten a little costlier—₹1 crore.

What was the first thing she did? She approached a property lawyer with a copy of the documents of the apartment she wanted to buy. She made sure the apartment had all necessary clearances from local authorities. She also had to look out for the deviations from the approved construction plan, if any—those needed to be within permissible limits. Very often, properties in large cities deviate from local regulations. This creates legal risks. For example, in Bengaluru, many apartments are constructed up to five floors despite having permission for only four. Such deviations, if ignored, may create legal issues for the buyer and lead to hassles if the property needs to be put on resale.

This legal exercise cost her ₹5,000. But once Shikha's lawyer green-lit the project, she had peace of mind knowing the property would not come under legal scrutiny. She then needed to save up to at least 40 per cent of the property cost to make the transaction. This is because a house purchase is rarely on the basis of the base price of the property alone—other costs also add on.

The three-bedroom apartment she wanted to buy cost ₹1 crore. Utilities such as electricity and water, land record updates, paperwork, amenities and the maintenance fund added ₹5 lakh to the cost. GST was at 5 per cent, which added another ₹5 lakh. The costs of registering the property cost about 6.5 per cent, which worked out to another ₹6.5 lakh. The cost of interiors as per her taste worked out to ₹8 lakh. Miscellaneous costs, such as home loan processing fees, legal fees, moving and packing, added another ₹1 lakh or so.

This brought the total cost of the property to around ₹1.26

crore. Out of this, what would the home loan cover? It typically covers the base price, GST and costs of utilities and amenities. In this case, these costs amounted to ₹1.10 crore. But as per RBI guidelines, this being a high-value property sale, the loan would cover only up to 75 per cent of that cost—or ₹82.5 lakh. Hence, she had to spend the remaining ₹43.5 lakh from her pocket.

In a low-value property transaction—for example, one under ₹20 lakh—the lender can even finance up to 90 per cent. This per centage is called the loan-to-value (LTV) ratio—the per centage of the property cost that the lender can finance. However, for high-value loans, the cap is 75 per cent. Lenders must follow the LTV guidelines set by the RBI. As per the guidelines, the LTV for small loans (up to ₹30 lakh) can go up to 90 per cent. For loans between ₹30 and ₹75 lakh, the LTV can be up to 80 per cent.[57]

Shikha had been saving for years for this moment. She had ₹50 lakh ready to spend towards this house. She borrowed the rest from her bank and thus fulfilled her goal of owning a house.

Preparing Yourself for Home Financing

Unless you have a large inheritance, a lottery-winning ticket or huge savings, you are going to need a loan to finance your home purchase. The process of buying a home and taking a home loan can be arduous. It is replete with paperwork and financial balancing. It is likely to be the biggest personal transaction of your life. Expect stress—both financial and emotional.

Incidentally, trying to land the right home loan is exactly how BankBazaar came into being. When Arjun and Rati wanted to buy a home in Chennai, they were baffled by how complex the loan-taking process can be.[58] It inspired them to simplify the process for the common man, leading to the origin of BankBazaar. Through the experience of selling loans, we have learnt a lot about the home-financing market and how homeowners can cut costs and fulfil their aspiration of securing a roof over their lead.

So let us get into those learnings.

Know Your Credit Score and Credit Health

Know where you stand with respect to your credit health. It can make a huge difference to how much your loan costs. Today, the best home loan offers—with the lowest interest rates and fees waivers—are reserved for borrowers with credit scores of 750 or above.

Often, borrowers know very little about their credit scores till the time they apply for a loan. A survey by BankBazaar in 2021 showed that 27 per cent of the salaried respondents between the age of 22 and 45 did not know how their credit score impacted their loan interest rate. The higher your score, the lower your interest rate because you are seen as more creditworthy by the lender. Some government banks consider 700 as the optimal score. Private lenders may have a higher benchmark at 800.

As I mentioned in the chapter titled 'Savour', you need to keep a monthly check on your credit score if you use any form of credit. If you know your score is healthy, you have little to worry about at the time of applying for a new loan. However, if you do not know your score, you may be in for a rude shock. What if at the time of applying you are told that your score is 650 for a reason you were not aware of?

Checking your credit report every month will help you determine the reasons for such a decline and give you an opportunity to improve it before you proceed for your home purchase. Your credit score—and therefore your home loan eligibility—can also improve if you pay off existing small loans such as credit card dues. No matter your capacity for repaying the new loan, those existing loans will lower your home loan eligibility.

The lender will make evaluations on the basis of your current income, not what you expect to earn in the future. So if an ongoing loan is reducing your disposable income, it will also reduce your ability to repay a new loan.

Margin Money and Documentation

As we saw in Shikha's case, you are going to need margin money for your home purchase—anywhere between 10 to 40 per cent of the base price of the house. The RBI has guidelines for how much a home loan can finance.[59]

You can only proceed for your home purchase if you have the margin money. Apply for your loan when you have worked out your LTV math.

Next, the lender is going to need your documents: proof of identity, address, income earned and taxes paid. The rules regarding the documents you need to furnish vary on the basis of your source of income or residency status. So if you are salaried, one set of rules apply on you. If you are self-employed or a non-resident Indian, another set of rules apply.[60]

Ensure you have your papers in place. Unlike a credit card or personal loan, a home loan still requires a lot of paperwork. This is not likely to change soon.

Make sure that your proofs are up to date; your tax statements are ready; your Aadhaar and PAN should be at hand. Putting together all these documents at the last minute can be a hassle.

Once your paperwork is in place, you can start your loan hunt.

Compare, Compare, Compare

Interest Rates

Home loans are a long-term relationship with your lender. People often borrow for multiple decades—sometimes, 20 or 30 years. Often, such loans are paid off before their term as the borrower's income increases with time. That said, this relationship should be as frictionless as possible. It needs to be optimized for costs, ease of account operation through digitization and customer service, and proximity to the lender's branch office.

Let us first look at the most important thing: interest rates. The subject of interest rates can fill up a book. But, for now, we will focus only on home loan rates. The largest expense in home ownership comes from the loan itself. Sure, you have bought a house. But the loan might be costlier than the house in the long term. This needs attention.

By 2022, home loan rates had fallen to historic lows within a span of two years. We will go back in time to understand why this happened.

Today, most bank-disbursed home loans are linked to the RBI's repo rate. What does this mean? The repo rate is the rate at which the RBI, as the country's central bank, lends to commercial banks. This rate is subject to revision every two months. In August 2018, the repo rate stood at 6.5 per cent. By May 2020, it had fallen to 4 per cent and remained so till May 2022.[61]

To simplify, a rising repo rate indicates rising inflation. This necessitates for the RBI to increase interest rates to slow down borrowing, consumption and, thus, inflation. In economic theory, if the costs of borrowing are high, people are discouraged from borrowing for business or personal consumption. Thus, it slows down demand for goods and services. When demand falls, prices fall and, thus, inflation softens.

Similarly, if interest rates fall, people are encouraged to borrow more. Hence, a falling repo rate indicates that economic activity is subdued, inflation is under control and, therefore, lowering the rate helps people borrow more to stimulate the economic pulse of the nation.

Between 2019 and 2020, the repo rate fell by 250 basis points. It was slowly at first, as the RBI responded to slowing economic activity. Then the pandemic hit and the central bank had no option but to go nuclear.

Going further back, in 2019, the RBI said banks must link their floating interest rate loans to an external benchmark.[62] Every floating rate loan has a benchmark rate. That is the lowest rate at which a loan can be given. The interest rates of floating rate loans are periodically revised as per the prevalent macroeconomic scenario and the lender's business needs.

Upon the benchmark rate, the lender will apply a credit spread, which is the lender's own price for the loan charged to the borrower on the basis of his financial profile and loan needs. For example, if a large private bank says that its lowest home loan rate as of December 2021 was 6.7 per cent, it would mean it was charging a credit spread of 2.7 percentage points over the repo of 4 per cent.

Earlier, banks produced these benchmarks internally on the basis of the cost of funds and their business needs. Funds come to banks from the RBI as well as from depositors. The higher the costs of funds, the higher the loan rates.

As we examined in 'Save', your deposit is your loan to the bank. Bank deposits are the raw material of the lending industry. They are also liabilities for the bank, which need to be repaid with interest. Therefore, to earn revenues and profits, banks must lend at a rate higher than the rate they are being lent to. A bank can invite FDs at 5 per cent and provide a loan at 7 per cent. The difference of 200 basis points keeps the bank in business.

Now coming back to why home loan rates are linked to the repo rate. The RBI in 2019 said banks could no longer link home loan rates to internally produced benchmarks.[63] It gave banks the option of linking them to external benchmarks such as the repo rate, the three- or six-month treasury bill yield or any benchmark produced by Financial Benchmarks India Private Ltd.

The RBI did this because it wanted a better transmission of rate cuts from the central bank to the common man. It has been the central bank's refrain for years that it cuts policy lending rates to accommodate growth, but the cuts are not passed on by lenders to consumers who continue to pay higher rates.

For example, the RBI reported in 2016 that it had cut the repo rate by 150 basis points, but banks had reduced their lending rates by only 60 basis points.[64] This meant that at the policy level, rate cuts happen and banks get access to cheaper funds. But the policy cuts do not translate to proportionate cuts in retail lending rates. This keeps the costs of borrowing higher than they need to be, and so the central bank's policy creates less impact.

Loan benchmarks have been revisited many times over the decades. In 2019, the RBI raised the matter of poor transmissions again and said banks must benchmark all floating rate retail loans (such as home, car or personal loans) to one of the external benchmarks mentioned before. Of those, most banks chose to benchmark their home loans to the repo rate.

Shortly after the repo regime began in 2019, interest rates

fell precipitously to accommodate economic growth in the post-pandemic world. As home loan rates were linked to the repo rate, they, too, fell in a hurry.

Before 2019, it was unthinkable that home loan rates would go under 8 per cent. By around the start of 2020, one bank had slipped under that mark. Soon, the rest followed. By the end of 2020, at least a dozen banks and non-banking lenders had priced home loans under 7 per cent, with some going as low as 6.7 per cent. By the end of 2021, that list had increased to nearly two dozen, with the lowest rates reaching 6.4 per cent.

Getting back to our earlier point, why and how must you compare home loan interest rates?

Remember that only banks provide repo-linked loans today. Non-banking lenders and home finance companies are not obligated to link their loans to the repo rate.

Lenders want to remain competitive. All the large lenders have their lowest interest rates in a range spreading 30–50 basis points. You could still go to the large lenders—bank or otherwise—and expect a lowest-in-market rate. But there is a difference in how the floating rate is revised.

Repo-linked loans are floating rate loans. Their rates can be revised any time the repo rate is revised. For example, the repo rate is 4 per cent today and linked to a home loan priced at 6.7 per cent. If the repo rate went up by 25 basis points, this loan rate will rise by the same margin to 6.95 per cent.

Hence, with repo-linked rates, there is a degree of certainty as to when and by how much your loan rate would be revised. This is not yet the case with non-bank loan rates, which get revised at the lender's discretion their cost of funds. This may cause borrowers in a falling rate scenario to feel that their non-bank loan rate is higher than bank rates for similar loans. However, the loan market is competitive and all major lenders compete with others to provide the lowest possible rates to their consumers.

The last point I want to make about home loan rates is that you can get them as floating or fixed. Fixed rates seem attractive because the borrower is protected against rate hikes, which could make the loan pricier. Often, these loans have a fixed rate at the start of the tenure and then they switch to a floating rate for the remaining tenure.

The problem is that there already is a wide delta between the lowest floating rates and the lowest fixed rates. For example, in early 2022, one large private lender had their lowest floating rate at 6.7 per cent and their lowest fixed rate at 7.4 per cent.

This is a huge gap. Because of the higher costs, this loan is not a popular option. In fact, the pre-payment charges cause another escalation in the borrowing costs.

Choosing your home loan well would lead to potentially saving lakhs of rupees over the full course of the loan term.

How to Get the Lowest Interest Rates

Lenders typically advertise their lowest home loan rates. They are telling you how low their rates can go. But you also need to know how high their rates can go.

Several factors shape your credit spread, which is added to the loan benchmark rate. Each factor provides a graded scale. With the scale, your rate could go higher or lower based on how you answer the following questions.

1. Are you salaried or self-employed? To lenders, salaried borrowers are more attractive. The self-employed, even those with stable income, may have to pay a marginally higher rate.
2. Loan sizes are slabbed, and the higher slabs attract

higher interest rates. For example, one bank treats the lower slab as anything up to ₹50 lakh and the higher slab as anything over. The latter attracts a higher rate. The norms, however, vary from lender to lender. Many prefer to slab them as up to ₹30 lakh, ₹30 to ₹75 lakh and ₹75 lakh and above. The higher you go, the more you pay.

3. What is your LTV ratio? The lower you go, the lower your rate, and vice versa.

4. What is your gender? Women today get preferential rates to stimulate home ownership for them. Most lenders lend at marginally lower rates to women. We have seen year after year at BankBazaar that women take bigger home loans than men.

   In our 2021 findings, women borrowed an average of ₹29.65 lakh against ₹26.99 lakh by men. Lenders also encourage loan applicants to apply with a female co-borrower to get lower interest rates. Another advantage of a female co-borrower, such as your spouse or mother, is that income tax deductions from the loan can be claimed by all co-borrowers. This helps maximize your overall deductions, thus increasing the household disposable income.[65]

5. What is your credit score? This weighs heavily in your rate calculation. The higher your score, the lower your rate. Again, scores may be slabbed by the lender. For example, 800 and above may get the lowest rates; 725–799 and 675–724 may get progressively higher rates; and 674 and under may not get the loan at all. The norms vary from lender to lender.

6. Are you eligible for special schemes? Many banks provide lower rates to customers who have salary

accounts: the military, employees of chosen corporates, including the lender itself, people buying homes with premium developers or people looking to refinance their running home loans.

7. Lastly, are you borrowing from a large lender or a small one? The lowest rates come from the largest lenders. Typically, government banks have lower rates, though the rates from large private lenders are similar. If you borrow from a small lender, expect higher rates.

In a vibrant lending market, there are many attractions for customers. Use them to save your money.

Costs, Proximity, Customer Service

One of the first things you can do to help yourself in your home loan hunt is to check your pre-approved offers. Just as with credit cards and personal loans, your bank may have pre-approved a home loan offer for you on the basis of your relationship with it.

To check your pre-approved offers, you can go to an online financial services platform such as BankBazaar, or check your bank through netbanking. Compare those with the ongoing home loan offers across the market. A pre-approved offer can help you cut down a lot of the paperwork, but not all of it because of it being a home loan.

It can also help you save on processing fees, which are often waived off for priority customers. If you apply with a lender with whom you have no prior relationship, the costs may be higher.

Beyond loan application fees, you can also compare loan options for account management costs, such as late payment penalties, pre-payment charges, statutory costs and legal opinion on the property. These are minor costs and there may not be a huge difference in these charges from one lender to another. Still, these would be good to know about.

Secondly, ask yourself what kind of customer service you want. This is a deeply personal thing. We have seen on BankBazaar that young customers have a deep preference for digitization and fast service. Your home loan is a long-term relationship with the lender. To make it as frictionless as possible, you should seek the kind of customer service you want. This may mean paying a higher rate.

Some lenders still prefer business the old way: face-to-face meetings, paperwork and standing in queues. Others prefer easier and digitized banking. In a pandemic, you may want to avoid a lender that needs you to visit a crowded branch for every little thing.

Lastly, though lending services are digitized to a great degree, you may still need to visit the branch now and then to get help with your account. In this regard, borrowing from a lender with a branch in your proximity is useful. It will save you time and help you avoid the hassle of taking time off work to attend to your home loan problems.

Select Thoughtfully

Remember the point about 'hard' and 'soft' credit score checks?

The point of the exercise above is to help you thoughtfully select your best loan option from the dozens available in the market. This should keep you from making too many applications at the same time. Too many loan applications in a short span of time will lower your credit score, which would then need you to pay a higher interest rate, and that could translate into additional lakhs of rupees you might need to spend over the loan tenure.

When finalizing your loan, you will also be given the option to choose a loan tenure. The number of years you can take to repay your loan is typically decided by when you intend to retire. In retirement, your income-generating ability could be lower, thus lowering your ability to pay EMIs. Therefore, lenders would like for you to complete your payments while you are still working. An exception to this may be government employees, who are assured of a pension income and can, thus, continue to pay their EMIs even in retirement.

Home loan tenures can range from one to 40 years. There is no one-size-fits-all pick here. You must pick optimally on the basis of your ability to pay your EMIs. The longer your tenure, the smaller your EMIs—however, your interest will be higher.

If you borrow ₹50 lakh at 7 per cent for 20 years, your EMI is ₹38,765 and interest will be ₹43.03 lakh. If you pay this loan over 30 years, your EMI falls to ₹33,265, but your interest increases by more than 60 per cent to ₹69.75 lakh.

You can calculate these numbers with any online EMI calculator.[66]

Often, homeowners face low income as a constraint at the start of their loan. The smart thing to do in such a case is to start with a long tenure and smaller EMIs. And as your income increases, ask the lender to increase the EMI proportionately. You can also pre-pay the loan periodically. This would have a dramatic effect in reducing your loan interest as well as your loan tenure, allowing you to get out of debt sooner.

We will explore the subject of being debt-free in the next chapter.

Strength to Serenity

The purpose of this chapter has been to introduce you to common and not-so-common ways to approach investing to strengthen your finances. There is so much, though, that has not been touched upon: stock trading, futures and options, derivatives, commodities, real estate, foreign exchange and even cryptocurrencies. These may be subjects for another book, perhaps. There is much to talk about them. For example, look at the dramatic developments in the cryptocurrency space since the start of the pandemic.

At the time of writing this, it had been just months since an anonymous and ostensibly wealthy investor used cryptocurrency to make what is being called the greatest individual trade of all time.[67] The cryptocurrency in question, Shiba Inu, was launched in 2020. In August 2020, this anonymous investor purchased $8,000 worth of tokens in this currency.

The crypto market was going through a major boom. And this coin—to quote Reddit—took off for the moon. As the months rolled by, Shiba Inu became the best performing investment of any kind on the planet as of 2021. It registered 7 million per cent growth since its launch.

This outrageous rally turned the anonymous investor's $8,000 into $5.7 billion by October, in just over 400 days![68] There is no precedent to such returns in the history of investment.

Each of these market-linked investment options contains a multitude of risks and rewards. We know that for anything that can be legally traded, if there are enough buyers and sellers, you can make a profit. But one must take the time to learn the trade. I emphasize on the words 'legally traded'. As of 2022, the Government of India has recognized cryptocurrencies as 'digital assets', but refused to confirm these assets as legal.

India now has a tax on cryptocurrency profits at a flat rate of 30 per cent.[69] The tax announcement came after years of speculation about whether India would ban cryptocurrencies. The tax has created the impression that these digital assets now have legal validity. The reality, however, is more complex.

Days after the new tax, Finance Minister Nirmala Sitharaman said that the tax does not mean cryptocurrencies are legal. 'I am not doing anything to legalise it or ban it or not legalise it, anything at this stage,' she told the Rajya Sabha. 'Banning or not banning will come subsequently when the consultations give me inputs.'[70]

These complexities and ambiguities will keep the crypto pot on the boil. The crypto market has also undergone a meltdown in 2022. Even Shiba Inu fell over 90 per cent from its peak.

What will also interest industry watchers is the arrival of digital coins issued by central banks themselves—a development that may transform commercial banking. As of 2021, China was experimenting with a digital yuan. In February, India announced its intent to launch a digital rupee. The RBI had said it may be launched at some point in 2022.[71]

Let us understand the transformation unfolding before our eyes. Central banks print currency notes. For centuries, central banks have relied on commercial banks for the movement, storage and distribution of currency notes. These are time-consuming and costly activities fraught with risk.

On the other hand, a central bank digital coin (CBDC) would solve these problems. Digital currency can be willed into existence on the distributed ledger technology that is blockchain. With this, digital money can potentially go from the central bank to the markets without commercial banks acting as intermediaries. If so is to happen, how would the role of commercial banks be redefined?

Also consider the conflicting ideas at play. Cryptocurrencies stand for decentralized finance. Blockchains are decentralized records maintained by a large network of computers around the world. Bitcoin is the most famous implementation of blockchain technology. Nobody is in charge of some of these blockchains. On the other hand, central banks stand for centralization and control. Their job is to singularly manage the creation and flow of money in an economy. We are witnessing the convergence of two opposing worldviews on the flow of money.

Hence, uncertainty looms over how CBDCs will transform the global economy. Their impact on commercial banking is yet to be understood. Meanwhile, there are also question marks over cryptocurrencies like Bitcoin—their legal validity, utility, underlying value and their ability to stably store value. They are in a speculative bubble—one of the biggest in history.

In the stock markets, a 20 per cent movement is considered sizeable. On the crypto markets, such movements happen every other week. The extreme volatility makes them unreliable as currencies. In any speculative investment, investors hope someone will pay more for their investment than they did. It is the same with cryptocurrencies.

The underlying blockchain technology has real-world use cases—decentralized record keeping, payments, internet-of-things solutions, smart contracts, e-voting or gaming. But as currencies, they have a long way to go.

Talking about the first principles of any style of investment, do your research first. In the crypto space, tens of thousands of coins exist now. Each claims to be unique. The space is steeped in jargon and obfuscation. If you wish to invest in a coin, understand it to the best of your ability because the risks are high.

Any investment portfolio should be a sensible mix of various options—real estate, gold, equity, MFs, small savings and, of course, liquidity in the bank. Life goals, risk tolerance and earning capacity should be taken into consideration.

If you want to start investing in a space you do not fully understand, control your exposure. For example, one per cent of one's investment portfolio is a safe enough starting point for most investors. The higher you go, the greater the risks. So if your investment portfolio is worth ₹50 lakh, start with 1 per cent or ₹50,000. In the worst-case scenario where you lose it all, you may easily earn that 1 per cent again from other investments. However, it could take years to recover from bigger losses.

Lastly, do not do anything you would not do with other investments, such as evading taxes or money laundering. Make your profits but pay your fair share of taxes. Exercised well, any investment option can strengthen your finances.

It takes weeks of hard work for the beaver to build its lodge. It will take you years to strengthen your finances through your chosen mode. There will be disappointments along the way and the markets may not always perform the way you want them to. But like the beaver, you must keep at it, plugging away in a focussed manner, gradually giving shape to the vision in your head.

The fulfilment of your life's purpose—your aspirations—depends on it.

V

SERENITY AND THE APEX

THE BOWHEAD WHALE AND
THE SECRET TO SERENITY

Bowhead whales are considered the longest living mammals. Their average lifespan is twice the average of those of humans. These residents of the arctic and subarctic floes are known to have lifespans of over 200 years.[1] These somewhat introverted, slow-moving whales can grow up to 60-ft long and weigh 100,000 kg. The weight does not stop them from leaping out of the water and flapping their flippers, much to the delight of whale watchers.

Bowheads are named so due to their massive bow-shaped triangular skulls. They use them to smash through thick ice to breathe. Their skin contains several inches of blubber, which keeps them warm in the icy waters.

Bowheads are one of the 16 kinds of baleen whales. Baleens are hundreds of bristly, comb teeth-like filters made of keratin in their mouths. These whales need a daily feed of about 2,000 kilos, mostly zooplanktons and krill. They fill their mouths with their prey, filter the water out through the baleens and keep the food trapped in.

The longevity of bowheads has been a matter of scientific curiosity. They are huge and their cell count is larger than that of any known mammal—something that should have hurt their longevity. The more cells you have, the higher is the chance of one of them mutating into cancer. Surprisingly, bowheads are cancer resistant. They have genes capable of repairing DNA, which slows down their ageing process, leads to creation of healthy cells and allows them to live for centuries.

The bowhead might someday unlock genetic secrets that would help increase human lifespan. Self-preservation, living an easy-paced life and filtering out the good from the bad are indeed some of the lessons we can learn from the bowhead and implement in our financial lives. These pursuits of the finer things in life become especially important as we approach the peak of our 5S Pyramid, at the end of which is Serenity.

By this stage, we aim to be debt-free and to have fulfilled our aspirations. We need that roof over our head. We need to have educated our children and we need to be able to retire from worldly cares after having secured a retirement purse.

Before we reach Serenity, there are a few more things to take care of with our finances.

Life Expectancy and Serenity

Globally, human life expectancy in 2020 was 73 years.[2] India, with 70, is just under the global average.[3] India's life expectancy had languished in the mid-to-low 20s after the first half of the twentieth century, dragged heavily by a very high child mortality rate in the high 300s.[4] This means that out of 1,000 children born, more than 300 did not live past the age of five. The situation was particularly bad around the years of the Spanish flu when India's life expectancy fell to the low 20s.

As India emerged from the shadows of colonialism in 1947, its life expectancy stood at a mere 32. The number was well under the global average—mid-40s. However, through the last few decades, the number has more than doubled. Another way of seeing this is that the average Indian today lives a full, additional life compared to his ancestors a century ago.

Globally, too, life expectancy has doubled over the last century. Surely, we are somewhere close to the peak of life expectancy? How can we go on adding to our lives? But life scientists believe that it may be possible to double our lifespans again. Some say—and it is hard to believe—that we may live to be 150.[5] At this rate, we will soon be competing with the bowheads.

It sounds insane. By the end of this century, it may be possible to have a lifespan four times as long as those of humans from the early twentieth century. This is expected to be achieved by advancements in medicine, diet, gene editing, age-reversing and the removal of risk factors such as cancer. Other risk factors such as road accident rates will plummet as automated cars will increasingly take to the streets.

There have been a rising number of centenarians in the developed world. There were around 451,000 of them in 2015, most of them in developed nations, such as Japan, Italy and Israel.[6] The United Nations believe there will be nearly 3.7 million centenarians by 2050, with every 12 Indians out of 100,000 living to be hundred.[7]

It seems that longer lifespans will have a profound impact on everything. As scientific advancements start giving us increasingly longer lives, we also need to think about how we are going to plan our finances to stay the course.

India's women especially need to think about this. They will outlive men. India's women had a life expectancy of about 71 years as compared to the 69 for men, as per World Bank data for 2020.

Serenity cannot be momentary. We need lasting financial security—right till the end of our lives.

THE 5S PYRAMID
BankBazaar

Serenity ← Credit score, Debt-free assets, Retirement → Finally!

Home, Assets, Investments → Strengthen

Savour ← Credit card, Personal loan, BNPL

Insurance: Health, Term, Vehicle, Property → Secure

Save ← Savings, Fixed deposits, Liquid mutual funds

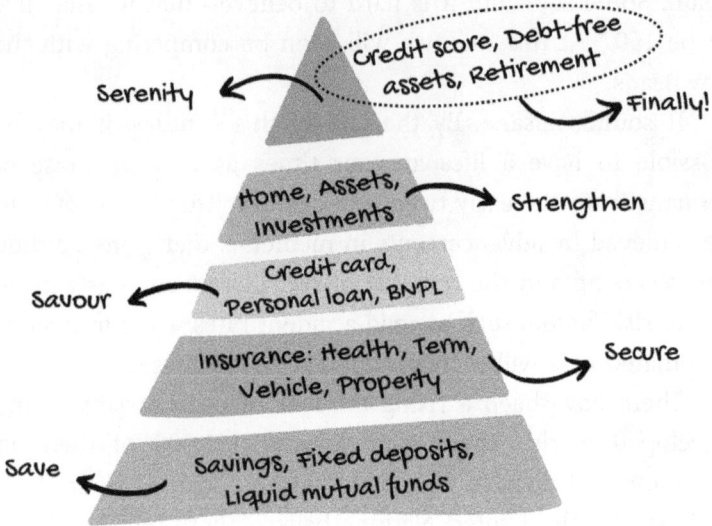

Review Your Finances Periodically

Serenity is easier to assure when you take stock of your finances periodically. You are passing through life stages. Your needs are evolving. Your responsibilities towards family increase with time. The money plan you had in your 20s might not work for you in your 40s. Hence, ensure your money management plans are up to date. They need to be relevant to work in your long-term interests.

Tweak your plans periodically for the best results. Your emergency fund should be revisited periodically. Your emergency income needs in the future will be larger than what you needed in your 20s and 30s. Consider topping up the fund periodically. It must match your most recent lifestyle, assuming it is a lifestyle you do not wish to downgrade during an emergency.

Your insurance—life and health coverage especially—needs to be looked at once in three years at the very least. Higher coverage can be bought to budget for greater risks.

Longer life spans may mean greater chances of diseases such as cancer.[8] These diseases are costly to treat. They pose a large threat to your finances. Thanks to medical inflation, the costs also keep rising each passing year.

Your health coverage may need padding every few years. Your family, too, may expand. They need to be brought into your coverage, which needs to increase with time. Your term coverage needs might also increase. With time, you assume greater responsibilities, such as becoming a parent, taking a home loan or becoming the caretaker of a parent. You must ensure your coverage factors in such needs.

Lastly, your investments should perform as expected. We have gone over the extreme need for goal-setting. Goals alone should dictate the investment costs, risks and returns expectations with the caveat that you will start applying the brakes on risk as you get closer to what you had aimed for.

This leaves us with one situation. What if the money saved for one goal is inadequate, and you need to dip into the funds saved for another goal? Returns and liquidity might not be uniform across those investments because no two investment goals can be alike.

For example, you had saved an FD for a car purchase, but the car's price exceeded your budget for it. You had to dip into your long-term retirement fund made of equity investments. However, the stock market had recently crashed. Dipping into your retirement fund would need you to book substantial losses—or selling off a chunk of your fund at a reduced cost. This would be detrimental to your retirement planning.

Is there a way to keep all investments at a level where risks and rewards are optimized? This brings us to the idea of asset allocation.

Asset Allocation and How It Helps

> *The most important key to successful investing can be summed up in just two words: asset allocation.*

—Michael LeBoeuf, American business author and former management professor at the University of New Orleans

Asset allocation refers to owning a mix of assets chosen on the basis of their risks and rewards. It creates an investment portfolio that meets your bar for risk tolerance and performs in all economic weather. Asset allocation can be aggressive when you are young, but as you age, you become more conservative. The fear of losing your capital becomes higher. So you gradually calibrate your portfolio for greater safety and lower returns.

To give you an example, a conservatively balanced portfolio consists of 50 per cent equity, 30 per cent bonds and 20 per cent gold. Now assume that on average, equity returns 12 per cent, bonds, 6 per cent, and gold, 4 per cent. For every ₹100 invested as per this asset allocation, this portfolio will, therefore, generate ₹6 on equity, ₹1.8 on bonds and ₹0.80 on gold. In all, it generates ₹8.2 per ₹100 invested or 8.2 per cent per annum.

Allocation strategies can vary from one investor to another. Consider Suresh, a Wealth Warrior, who has been investing since his 20s. The 55-year-old works as a vice president in a well-known consumer goods company. He has been reviewing his portfolio periodically for decades. He started off conservatively, saving with FDs, endowment plans and some gold till his late 30s. He soon realized he had an appetite for much higher risks.

Then, through his 40s and 50s, he followed a strict allocation of 80 per cent in equities, 15 per cent in debt investments and 5 per cent in gold. His strategy also incorporated the need to maintain the balance.

For example, the share of equities was frequently above or under the 80 per cent mark because of market volatility. To maintain his preferred ratio, Suresh rebalanced his portfolio once a year. He sold assets with excess allocation and bought assets whose allocations had shrunk.

For example, in a booming market, Suresh's equities would balloon to 90 per cent of the portfolio. Therefore, Suresh would secure his gains by selling some equity and restoring their proportion to 80 per cent. He can then reinvest the gains in bonds and gold in the ratio of 15:5.

Suresh also had plans of lowering his equity exposure in retirement, changing the split down to 60-30-10 as per his income needs. In this sense, asset allocation becomes an active style of investment. It needs regular decision-making with respect to portfolio composition. It can be messy, and involve booking profits or losses. It needs payment of redemption charges and taxes on gains. You also need to track whether the gains are long-term or short-term. The charges and taxes can reduce your returns potential, even if it shields you against risks.

Consider what Suresh's son Harit has done. The 26-year-old Early Jobber has taken a leaf out of his dad's book. But he has found a smarter way to achieve asset allocation. Harit has bought a dynamic asset allocation MF. It is a kind of hybrid fund. As the name suggests, a hybrid investment plan invests across asset classes: equity, debt and even gold.

Hybrid funds can be equity-oriented or debt-oriented. This decides the weight of either asset in the fund. For example, an aggressive equity-oriented fund may have 90 per cent equity exposure and 10 per cent debt.

A regular hybrid fund will stick to its allocation style with minimum deviation. But in a dynamic allocation fund, the allocations can change dramatically on the basis of the economic weather.

For example, when there is headroom for growth in equities, the fund can make a large 70–80 per cent exposure in the stock markets and deliver better returns to investor. But when the stock markets are overpriced and ripe for a crash, the fund can secure its gains by exiting equities and polarizing towards debt securities. A dynamic allocation fund takes away the stress of decision-making, profit-booking, rebalancing and taxation. The decisions and rebalancing are done automatically by the fund.

The solutions exist in the market. You need to find the one that works for you.

Be Smart about Retirement Planning and Educating Your Children

There exist many solution-oriented investment plans in the market. Some plans aim to assist you after you retire. Others aim to fund your children's education. These two are the most critical goals in terms of your finances apart from buying a house.

Investment plans should be made keeping in mind the goals they have to cater to. Time being of the essence, you cannot afford to back the wrong plan.

Often, child education and retirement savings plans mix investing benefits with insurance. They provide an assured return. The returns look attractive on paper, but you must look beyond the labels. Ask some basic questions.

For example, what would be the annual rate of return? Do the returns beat inflation? Will the returns be taxed? Will you lose money if you had to liquidate the investment prematurely? Most importantly, if you passed away today, would the insurance coverage be enough for your family's income needs?

These are the questions investors often do not ask when it comes to assured returns plans. The key problem is that the returns are low. They underachieve as investment and life insurance cover. If you need liquidity for any reason, you cannot exit these plans without incurring substantial losses. The assurance of returns and cashback draw investors to such plans—and sometimes, it is the label. It should be remembered that if these investment plans are not beating inflation, they may not help you achieve your goal.

Let us analyse the benefit structure of a child plan being sold as of 2021. Assume that your plan needs an investment of ₹1 lakh per annum for 20 years. In the fifteenth and sixteenth year, you get a cashback of ₹2 lakh a year. In the next four years, the cashback becomes ₹3 lakh. The plan pays a total cashback of ₹16 lakh.

Cashback plans, also called moneyback plans, are life insurance-linked investment plans. They periodically pay back an assured sum of money. In a child plan, the cashback schedule may be linked to the various stages of a child's education, typically from high school to a master's degree.

In the twenty-first year, the policy matures, and you get ₹20 lakh plus accrued bonuses, apart from the ₹16 lakh already paid as cashback. If you passed away during the policy term, your family would receive the life insurance benefit of ₹20 lakh plus bonuses.

On a total investment of ₹20 lakh, the plan returns ₹36 lakh in multiple instalments, allowing you to finance the different stages of your child's education. Sounds good, right? But what about the annual rate of return on this investment?

Using the numbers above, let us calculate the benefits of another investment. But this time, we will benchmark the investment returns against the minimum returns provided by any equity MF. In a 20-year period ending on 1 November 2021, the minimum returns provided by any equity fund was 12.75 per cent per annum.

Assume you invested ₹1 lakh a year in this plan for 20 years. You also withdrew ₹2 lakh in the fifteenth and sixteenth years and ₹3 lakh in the next four years. Despite the withdrawals of ₹16 lakh in tranches and the bare minimum rate of return, you would still be left with around ₹67 lakh at the end of 20 years—more than three times of what the aforementioned child plan was returning.

On the child plan, the annual rate of return works out to approximately 6 per cent if you are left with just ₹20 lakh and bonuses. The returns are lower than that of EPF today, which would have left you with around ₹33 lakh in 20 years. So why would anyone chase assured returns when they are so low?

Assured returns, while reassuring, may prove too low for the goal that you are investing for. In the above case, your investment returns were approximately 6 per cent, while education inflation is in double digits.

A well-known business school charged ₹4 lakh for its two-year management programme in 2007. In 2021, it charged ₹27 lakh. This implies an annual inflation rate of 13.58 per cent in the course fees over 15 years.

Assuming that the rate remains constant, the course would cost ₹1.82 crore in another 15 years. Achieving this number with an investment with low returns would require you to pay a high investment cost. Remember our analogy of the trip from Mumbai to London?

For instance, you would have to invest ₹62,000 per month for 15 years to save ₹1.82 crore, given there is an assured rate of return of 6 per cent. But if the rate is a market-linked 12 per cent per annum, you can get there with just ₹36,000 a month, which would strain your finances lesser. Also, with a market-linked investment such as an MF you also have the flexibility of liquidation at any moment of your choosing. But when it comes to assured returns plans, a premature surrender would carry heavy charges and leave you with losses. Not only would you suffer financially but also lose precious time.

It is common to make such investment mistakes at the start of your professional life. It is, however, important to take corrective actions and not make those mistakes long-term. Else, the repercussions would be severe.

Assured return investments often draw a huge premium, but low returns. Over the long term, they will cause you to miss investment goals by a wide margin. When you miss your goal, you will need to take a loan to bridge the gap. This would again entail interest costs. This is detrimental to the formula for Serenity.

When investing for goals that are far away in the future—whether your child's education or your retirement—the data shows that equity MFs or index funds can perform much better. Over a span of 10-plus years, they should be able to provide double-digit returns, liquidation without penalties and the option to change your investing style if it is not working for you. And since the investment cost is low, you would have enough money left to buy yourself adequate life coverage. This is, of course, on the basis of historical data with the disclaimer that the past does not predict future MF returns.

Lastly, most child plans provide life insurance as well. The problem with these plans is the low life coverage. In the above example, a life cover of ₹20 lakh could prove inadequate—not just for your child's education needs but also for the income needs and sustenance of your surviving family members.

Therefore, to keep your family's financial goals from being derailed by death or disease, it is vital to insure oneself with an adequate term plan. Only this may sufficiently cover the family's life risks. Also, each member of the family should have a health cover of at least one time the annual income. This would ensure that a costly hospitalization does not force you to dip into the funds saved for your child. Your child's future is too important to take a bet on with opaque investment plans that may lead to disappointment.

Market-linked investing for the long term is almost always the smarter option. Therefore, I am saving for my daughter's education using index funds.

Preparing Your Pension

The matter of assured returns brings us to pension plans, also called annuity plans. These plans are simple. Here is how they work.

You need to pay the pension provider a sum of money. You can pay either a lump sum or instalments over the years. On retirement, the pension provider starts paying you a monthly income for the rest of your life. The pension providers—also called annuity service providers—are life insurance companies. For example, you invested ₹1 crore to make a lump sum purchase of an annuity plan. The annuity plan pays you ₹6 lakh a year as pension in monthly instalments of ₹50,000 for the rest of your life.

Government employees, to cite another example, make small, monthly contributions to their pension fund their entire careers. By retirement, this pot of money grows manifold. It then allows the retiring employee to receive a pension as per their station.

While government employees may have this option, others must take the matter of retirement planning in their own hands. Their pension is going to be based on what they save during their working lives.

Annuity plans help provide a stable income in retirement. This is the time when you would have stepped back from an active work life. This is the phase you worked hard for all your life. You put your money to work to ensure you will not be left wanting in your golden years.

The pension amount need not be very high. Pension planning assumes you have already taken care of financial responsibilities, like home ownership and your child's education. The pension needs to sustain your daily income needs to manage your household, health and leisure needs.

Leisure is important to Serenity. After all, the bowhead cannot spend all its time hiding in deep waters, avoiding predators and stuffing itself with plankton. It must break through the ice, do some flips, play with mates and sing its songs too.

With these annuity plans, you will not have to worry about an income till death. The plans also provide the option of your nominee getting the annuity purchase price on your death. This sounds attractive. This is why many elderly put their trust in these plans. They do not want market risks or having to worry about capital safety. They want the money to keep coming in.

However, the problem again is inflation and the inadequacy of assured returns. The yield in the example above is already a low 6 per cent—not enough to beat inflation in an Indian context. With taxes, the returns fall further. Sure, the money would keep coming, but once adjusted for inflation, it would get lesser each year.

We are going through a global phase wherein senior citizens relying on fixed income earnings are struggling to keep pace with inflation. Interest rates have declined, but inflation is up. The pension income is not what it used to be. You would not want to deal with the stress of falling income in the years you had earmarked for Serenity.

To quote Olivia S. Mitchell, an economics and public policy professor at Wharton University, 'Low returns from the markets are essentially a tax on retirees.'[9] By markets, Mitchell means debt investments such as bonds. 'In the good old days, people used to ladder their bonds, put a little bit of money in the market, and try to live off those returns. This is not feasible any longer. In fact, it is even worse, because those lower nominal returns are in many cases negative in real, or inflation-corrected, returns.'

Fixed income—bonds and bank deposits—were the go-to options for senior citizens. In a low-interest rate era, they no longer help.

Consider the Senior Citizen Savings Scheme, the government-backed investment option. It provides full capital safety, guaranteed returns and a quarterly income for eligible investors. The retired can invest up to ₹15 lakh in an SCSS account for five years, extendable up to eight years. You can open an SCSS via the post office or an authorized bank. The SCSS had an interest rate of 8.6 per cent in 2019. If you invested ₹15 lakh in it, it could generate a quarterly income of ₹32,250. The interest rate in 2022 was 7.4 per cent. So the SCSS generated ₹27,750 a quarter.

Moreover, pension income is fully taxable in the hands of the pensioner as per their income tax slab. The SCSS returns are lower now in absolute terms. They are worse adjusted for inflation and taxation.

There is a dearth of institutional data on how India's senior citizen investors are adjusting to falling interest rates. But judging by social media chatter, it seems many have had to invest in the equity market for higher returns. The joke goes that youngsters, armed with stocks trading apps, are becoming short-term traders, while the elderly are becoming long-term investors.

Considering the pandemic, the news is even more worrisome. As per the 2021 BankBazaar Aspiration Index survey, 51 per cent of respondents aging between 25 and 45 years said the pandemic set their retirement age back by one to five years. Further, 43 per cent said they were yet to have a retirement corpus. These findings correlate with similar surveys that revealed that Indians defer retirement planning till it's too late.

This is understandable in a country like ours. Maslow's physiological and security needs—food, shelter and health—are immediate for most Indians. It makes thinking about 40 years into the future difficult.

So what should investors do in their work lives to make sure they never run out of money in retirement? After all, there can be no Serenity without income stability. We will get to the solution shortly.

The National Pension System: Pros and Some Cons

Intrepid investors reading this may have noticed that this book has not yet recommended investing in the National Pension

System or NPS. We will take a look at why that has not been done. But first, for those who are new to NPS, let us get a primer on it.

NPS is one of the best ways to save for retirement. It collects contributions from workers aging between 18 and 70 years. The contributions also get tax deductions.

Under Section 80CCD (1), you can deduct up to ₹1.5 lakh through contributions to your NPS account. Further, under 80CCD (1B), you can deduct another ₹50,000. This way, you can claim deductions of up to ₹2 lakh a year through this option.[10]

The investment costs of NPS are very low and comparable to index funds.[11] Your money is split into equities (E), government bonds (G), corporate bonds (C) and alternative funds (A) such as REITs. The returns are similar to index funds. NPS also provides an active versus auto diversification choice. In the active choice, you have a greater handle over equity allocation.

Up to the age of 50, a maximum of 75 per cent of your portfolio can be equity, which could help you earn better returns. But as you reach 60, the equity allocation is reduced to 50 per cent to budget for your lower risk appetite. In the auto choice, you can pick between an aggressive, moderate or conservative style of investment. The more aggressive your style is, the deeper your equity exposure will be.[12]

Investors also have the choice of picking from a list of pension service providers, such as LIC, HDFC, UTI, and so on. The NPS website publishes their past performance. This data on returns can be the basis for your selection. Overall, a hybrid investment can give you better returns compared to a plain vanilla debt investment, such as PPF.

As of December 2021, NPS had 10-year returns of approximately 15 per cent for equities, 10 per cent for corporate debt and 9.5 per cent for government debt. So for every ₹100 invested with an aggressive split of 75-15-10 in the E-C-G funds, the returns could be approximately ₹10, implying 10 per cent returns over 10 years.

If you invest ₹1.5 lakh once in 12 months for 30 years in an investment returning 10 per cent, you will get a corpus of ₹2.71 crore. At 8 per cent, it will be ₹1.83 crore. At 6 per cent, it will be ₹1.25 crore. In comparison, a 15-year PPF returning 7.1 per cent can only give you ₹40.68 lakh under the current rules.

For conservative investors favouring corporate and government schemes, the returns are much lower in the current economic environment as a result of falling interest rates.

The NPS sounds fair up to now. It is also easy to sign up for it online. The NPS website makes it very convenient. Making contributions to your account via netbanking is also easy.

The problems rest in getting your money out.

Your NPS account matures when you reach the age of 60. At this point, you can withdraw your investment. However, under the current rules, you need to mandatorily spend at least 40 per cent of your NPS corpus for buying an annuity plan. You can redeem the rest—60 per cent of the corpus—as tax-free and use it the way you wish.

The NPS is managed by the Pension Fund Regulatory and Development Authority (PFRDA). Its vision is to promote and develop systems to serve the income needs of the elderly on a sustainable basis. This is achieved in part by ensuring that the retirement money is not misallocated or misused by other family members. With the annuity plan, the money keeps coming in.

You can prematurely withdraw your NPS corpus before your turn 60, but at least 80 per cent of your corpus needs to be used for purchasing annuity. However, if your corpus was less than ₹2 lakh, you can withdraw the whole amount without buying annuity.[13]

Under the current rules, the annuity requirement has created some problems. Annuity, as we have seen above, is a fixed income plan, and its returns do not beat inflation.

As long as you are invested in NPS with a high equity allocation, your corpus will keep growing at an above-average rate. The moment you need to take the money out and are forced to buy a low-returns annuity plan, your overall returns from your pension portfolio will fall.

The PFRDA understands the problem with the annuity requirement in a low-interest environment. It has, over the recent years, taken measures to ease withdrawal norms. This has helped NPS investors with small corpuses who do not wish to be stuck with meaningless pensions of a few hundred rupees a month.

There have also been suggestions that the 40 per cent annuity be done away with. In its place, a systematic pay-out method that returns the 40 per cent to the investor over a period of 15 years has been suggested.[14]

This, for now, remains an idea. So investors should get into NPS with their eyes open. Unless it comes to fruition, the annuity requirement exists with its pros and cons. Mind you, these are the options today. For all we know, there will be fewer cons by the time you turn 60.

Financial safety nets for the elderly form the need of the hour. May the markets provide solutions.

But in the current scenario, the better way to generate pension seems to be...

Systematic Withdrawal of Mutual Funds

Just as you systematically invest in MFs and index funds, you can also systematically withdraw from them. You can thus generate regular income for yourself. This solution is clean, simple and elegant. It also does not need you to lock in your money into schemes with withdrawal restrictions. You can use your money on your own terms.

Consider what Saba, a Wealth Warrior and a production designer, wants to do with her MFs. At 36 she plans to retire at 60. She has been aggressively investing in MFs since she was an Early Jobber. She is of the view that ₹10 crore by the age of 60 would be enough to sustain her bohemian lifestyle.

Saba started investing ₹5,000 a month in an equity MF when she was 25. She systematically stepped up the investment by 10 per cent each year. Assuming moderate 12–13 per cent returns a year, she believes she can get ₹9–₹10 crore by the time she retires.

She hopes the equity markets will outperform and deliver 15 per cent, with which she could save around ₹16 crore by the age of 60. But this remains to be seen. The extraordinary returns of the past may not necessarily repeat in the future. But if they do, and she hits her ₹10 crore milestone before time, she can be even ready to retire before the age of 60.

The key to Serenity is always having enough money at hand at the time of retirement. The money needs to last till the end of your life. For example, if you have saved up ₹10 crore, use it in a way that the money grows instead of depleting. If you withdraw 5 per cent, you are left with ₹9.5 crore. To take the savings back to ₹10 crore, you need to keep it in an instrument that generates at least 5.3 per cent returns. Our expectation, on the basis of historical data, is that the equity markets continue to grow at an average of 12 per cent per annum with the standard disclaimer that the past is not predictive of the future.

In retirement, you will need to maintain a balance between your withdrawal needs and your growth needs. Your rate of withdrawal should ideally be lower than the rate of growth. If you follow this, your money will keep growing. If you do not follow this, the money will start depleting.

Saba planned on withdrawing up to two years of living expenses at a time. The rest of her corpus will remain invested. This way, she would end up taking out only a small portion of her investment that would be necessary for her immediate needs. The rest could potentially double every five to six years at the same rate of return.

Saba must take care to time her withdrawals in a way that guards her against market volatility. If she withdraws when the markets are high, she would use a smaller portion of her portfolio compared to when the markets are low, but even a small withdrawal could mean a sizeable depletion. She also has the option of switching some of her equity investments for debt, so that she has better protection against volatility. Her rate of growth would be slower, but that should not matter much if the corpus is sizeable.

MF withdrawals can be lump sum or systematic. In a Systematic Withdrawal Plan (SWP), you can programme your MF account to liquidate a fixed amount of money or a fixed number of fund units into your bank account. It gives you cash when you need it. It also ensures that the rest of your investment keeps growing and you never run out of money.

The blubber around the bowhead whale's flesh protects it from the extreme arctic cold. Similarly, you, too, need to insulate yourself against inflation with wisely planned investments. Doing go will help you reach the final stage of the 5S Pyramid.

Pay Attention to Data Security

We are in the age of digitized finance. No wonder financial crimes today are also digitized. To achieve Serenity, you need to keep track of your digital safety.

Data security is important whether you are in your teens or in your 80s. It is also a moving goalpost. A safe digital habit today might become not so safe tomorrow. You must keep yourself updated about the safe use of technology and the Internet. There is a wide variety of scams and fraudulent activities you must guard yourself against. Take tech support scam, for example. In a 2021 report on tech support scams, Microsoft said 31 per cent of the Indians surveyed lost money in a scam, the highest for any country.[15]

The RBI recently said that 83,000 bank frauds were reported in 2020–21.[16] In these instances, ₹1.38 lakh crore was fraudulently withdrawn from accounts. Less than 1 per cent of this amount could be recovered.

I have been the target of sophisticated digital attacks too. In one case, the attacker sent an email in my name to BankBazaar's chief financial officer (CFO) instructing him to transfer funds to my bank account. Our alert CFO spotted the fakery. The email was from an unknown domain. The mail, too, was unusual.

In another sophisticated attempt, an attacker, posing as a member of our board, emailed me asking me to upload proofs of investment to the company. Again, the email was from an unknown domain. The key to identifying both attacks was a combination of looking at the sender's email address and not just the sender's name, which can be easily faked, and calling the sender when an unexpected mail is received.

You must educate yourself about the many digital risks that exist today. Knowledge alone can help you identify a trap and steer clear of it. It will prevent you from losing your hard-earned money through your bank account, credit card or a payment app.

Your ATM pin and netbanking passwords should be updated every few months. When setting them, steer clear of the obvious: your date of birth, birth year or child's birth year may be some of the easy guesses. Try something less obvious. For example, you are a Sachin Tendulkar fan, and your ATM pin is inspired by his batting average in Test cricket: 5378.

When setting passwords, be creative. Consider information security firm Nordpass's list of the top-200 most common passwords in 2021, so that you know what is to be avoided.[17] Some of the most used passwords in India were 'qwerty', 'password', '123456', 'india123', 'abc123' and 'sairam'. Using these passwords could invite financial nightmares into your life.

Create your passwords with mixed-cased letters, numbers and special characters, as these are harder to guess. Test them on password strength websites. For example, according to Security.org, it takes a password-cracking computer programme about seven milliseconds to guess that your password is 'sachin'.[18] It would become just a little more secure if the password is 'Sachin'. Notice the uppercasing. But it still takes only 400 milliseconds to guess it, so it is not enough.

It takes three days to guess 'Sachin123', five years to guess 'Sachin@123' and one sextillion years to guess 'Sach!n@ t3ndulkar@5378'. The more complex your password, the harder it will be to be guessed.

Password strength, along with regular updates, will give you enhanced security. This will, however, not protect you against a data server breach that leads to login credentials being exposed. For protection against this, set a unique password for each web service you sign up for. We tend to use the same password across web services. If so, avoid using the password you use for a sensitive account (such as a bank or email) on a low-tech and unsafe website. If that website gets hacked, it jeopardizes your sensitive data.

There are many ways fraudsters can steal your passwords. A common method is to send you a web link via text or email. The link is a website masquerading as a reputable website, such as that of your bank. This method is called phishing—an activity on the rise in India. An information security firm reported that 83 per cent of the surveyed Indian corporations reported a rise in phishing attempts on their employees.[19] Never click on these suspicious links.

Ensure that you are using your login credentials on the right web service. Look for the SSL certificate and check the link you are on. A secure link would have 'https' instead of 'http'. If you are using an updated web browser, pay attention to the security warnings it provides.

No bank or financial institution will ask you to disclose your login information, card CVV number or one-time passwords in any circumstance. Never ever disclose sensitive data through any other channel than the one explicitly meant for the use of that information. In case of phishing attempts, report to your bank to allow them to investigate the matter.

When it comes to ATMs and cards, be aware of your surroundings. Avoid unsafe ATMs. Look out for shoulder surfers—people who try to see your password as you type it. You are at higher shoulder-surfing risk in crowded places like grocery stores and petrol pumps. Conceal your typing the best way you can. If you feel you have been compromised, change the password immediately.

When using an ATM, give the swiper a shake to check for skimming devices. These are illegal attachments to the machine meant to collect your card information. Watch this video by a cybersecurity expert who explains why it pays to be paranoid: https://bit.ly/atm-skimmer.

When paying with your card, ensure the swipe machine is brought to you and the transaction is conducted in front of your eyes. If you lose sight of your card, especially in a strange place, there could be trouble. The card could get cloned or misused. The data procured through these unauthorized swipes can be used to make copies of your card, which can then be used for fraudulent transactions.

If you are browsing from a home computer, use up-to-date versions of internet browsers and operating systems. Older software present greater cybersecurity risks. They were not built to protect against modern crime technology. Make sure you have the latest anti-virus and malware support on your computer systems. These keep viruses, trojans, malware and ransomware, which can jeopardize the safety of your sensitive data, at bay. Ransomware is especially terrible. It is a software designed to hold your computer captive. It demands credit card or cryptocurrency payment as ransom through unsecure channels.

When you are browsing from a public computer, you may be better off not accessing your netbanking or other sensitive accounts. If you absolutely need to, use the virtual keyboard available on financial websites. This would thwart key loggers— unethical software that records keyboard inputs such as your password.

Dispose your data safely. Credit card bills, bank statements or MF statements in printed form carry sensitive information, such as your name, address, PAN number or partial credit card number. If someone means harm, they may dive into your trash to dig out these documents. Different aspects of your life may be pieced together by your digital and financial footprints. Shred these documents to prevent misuse.

It is not unusual to share things like credit cards with your children. But remember that they are not experienced enough to discern a real website from a phishing one. They will also tend to make downloads from unauthorized websites that are full of cybersecurity risks. They should first be taught about how to make safe online transactions.

Lastly, do keep yourself updated about the regulations around payments fraud. For example, a customer's liability will be zero if he is not at fault for an unauthorized transaction and has reported it to the bank within three working days.

Cybersecurity is financial security. And financial security is the key to Serenity.

Don't Miss Your Tax Returns

Being scrutinized by the Income Tax Department (ITD) can be detrimental to your peace of mind. This happens when the department believes one has not paid their fair share of taxes.

The taxman's grip on the informal economy and black money has been tightening. Tax evasions are being unearthed regularly. The department now has sophisticated analytics tools including machine learning at its disposal.[20] Using such technology, officials can analyse tonnes of tax records to make short work of tax evasions. Notices are sent immediately, leaving taxpayers scampering for remedy. These tools have also been used to detect discrepancies as little as ₹100 in tax filings.

The shortfall in your taxes paid may be wilful or accidental. Either way, you must exercise great care in filing your tax returns, which are a statement of the taxes paid. Your returns summarize income earned, taxes deducted at source by your employer or payee, pending taxes paid by you and excess taxes returned to you by the ITD.

The rules for filing tax depend on the size and source of income. For example, the salaried have different norms from the self-employed. The government has been trying to simplify its interaction with taxpayers through digitization and making those interactions seem less intimidating.

The truth is that taxation is a complicated matter. To rephrase physicist Richard Feynman talking on quantum physics, if you think you understand taxation, you probably do not understand taxation.

It is very easy to misunderstand our labyrinthine tax code and miss paying a tax or claiming a legitimate deduction. You have the right to manage your own tax plan, deductions and filing returns. The latter, along with pending taxes, can be taken care of online. But it would be advisable to avail the services of an expert who can help you make error-free filings. After all, if errors are detected many years later, you may have to pay pending taxes with interest at the rate of 1 per cent a month.[21]

Do not forget to file the returns on time. For the salaried, the deadline for tax returns is 31 July of the year following the financial year. For example, for financial year 2020–21 (April to March), the returns need to be filed by 31 July 2021. Late filings are penalized with anything from ₹1,000–₹10,000, depending on how big your income is and how late you are.

Tax filings are also important for availing loans, obtaining visas to certain countries, getting a refund of excess taxes and carrying forward your capital losses to reduce your taxable income. Late filings will mean that you will have to pay a penalty along with interest on back taxes, and you will not be allowed to carry forward your capital losses. Capital losses, such as losses from the stock market, can be reported for up to eight years in your tax returns. They can be offset against similar gains and reduce your taxes.

In short, we must all do the annual tax-filing exercise on time and with great care. Anything else may invite the taxman's scrutiny, which would impede our journey to Serenity.

New Regime, Old Regime and the 20 Per Cent Formula

While we are on the matter of taxation, there is now also the difficult choice of picking between two kinds of tax regimes.

The old income tax regime for individuals involved tax deductions through investments, insurances and qualified expenses. The deductions allowed you to reduce your taxable income and thus your tax liability.

From April 2020, a new alternate, optional tax regime was introduced. This regime provided none of the usual tax deductions. This meant your taxable income will be nearly equal to your total income. However, the new regime allowed you to pay a lower rate of tax on that income.

For example, if you earned ₹11 lakh for the year, the old regime needed you to pay a marginal tax rate of 30 per cent. But as per the new regime, the rate on that income became 20 per cent.

This creates the impression that the new regime is better, and not aiming for deductions may be the better option. So why get into the complications of creating a portfolio of tax-saving instruments?

The fact is that most of us are eligible for some deduction or the other. For example, rent paid, children's school tuition and PF contributions bring down our taxable income without any tax planning. Therefore, at the very least, we must compare our tax liabilities under each regime.

The simplest way to do this is by using an income tax calculator. Put in your income and deductions, and you should be able to see your taxes under each regime.[22] You should go with the regime that allows you to pay lower taxes.

At BankBazaar, we devised the '20 Per Cent Formula' for picking a tax regime. This is a simple yardstick to measure if you should stick to the old regime or take the new one. The formula will need you to check if all your tax deductions amount to 20 per cent of your total income. For example, if your total income is ₹10 lakh and you cobbled together ₹2 lakh in deductions, the old regime may be better for you. In the new regime, without the usual deductions, you will pay ₹78,000 as taxes. In the old one, you will pay ₹75,400, thus saving ₹2,600.

This is a highly simplified solution and may not work for all. Everyone must calculate their taxes on the basis of their income, life situation and capacity for tax-saving.

Table 13

The 20 per cent Formula				
Salary Income	Taxes Paid			Additional Taxes Saved by 20 per cent Deductions
	Old Regime, with No Deductions	New Regime, with No Deductions	Old Regime, with 20 per cent Deductions	
₹500,000	₹0	₹0	₹0	₹0
₹750,000	₹65,000	₹39,000	₹33,800	₹5,200
₹1,000,000	₹117,000	₹78,000	₹75,400	₹2,600
₹1,250,000	₹195,000	₹130,000	₹117,000	₹13,000
₹1,500,000	₹273,000	₹195,000	₹179,400	₹15,600
₹1,750,000	₹351,000	₹273,000	₹241,800	₹31,200
₹2,000,000	₹429,000	₹351,000	₹304,200	₹46,800

The formula may stop working at very high income levels. For example, if your salary income is ₹50 lakh, it would be difficult to cobble together deductions of ₹10 lakh.

Be Debt-Free

You can reach Serenity only when you are debt-free. It is a good idea to pay off your debts before retirement. You need to be able to enjoy the limited income you have without worrying about your liabilities eating into it.

Loan interest costs are huge over the long term. If you buy a ₹70-lakh house with ₹50 lakh as your home loan for 20 years at 7 per cent, your interest will be projected as ₹43.03 lakh. The interest is over 60 per cent of the house cost. Lenders and home finance companies set your loan tenure in a way that it is paid off before your projected retirement age. They can make relaxations for government employees with pension income. These pensioners can, to an extent, continue paying their EMIs in retirement.

But for others who do not want to carry this liability into retirement, it is best to settle your dues while you are working. Even a single pre-payment can have a huge impact on your loan tenure and benefit you.

For example, if you borrowed ₹50 lakh at 7 per cent for 20 years, your interest is going to be ₹43.03 lakh and your EMI, ₹38,765. If you pre-pay a single EMI right at the start of the loan, your loan tenure reduces by three months and your interest by ₹1.15 lakh.

An EMI factors both interest and principal payments. But a pre-payment is counted only against the principal. You can devise a pre-payment plan for yourself to pay off your loan quicker. You can pre-pay as much as you want, subject to the lender's conditions on the minimum pre-payment amount. The key is to find a sweet spot between getting out of debt and balancing your savings and investment needs.

Pre-payments to your loans can be done as and when you have liquidity. This can be through increasing income, annual bonuses, business windfall or any other income that helps reduce the loan balance. You can pre-pay in the form of a lump sum or by increasing your EMI. As your income rises with time, increasing your EMI provides you an easy way to pre-pay. The amount you pay over and above the normal EMI will be adjusted against the principal, thus accelerating your journey out of debt.

There are costs of pre-payment. For floating rate home loans, the cost is simple interest, normally a small sum. It can be minimized by making the pre-payment at the start of any month.

For fixed rate home loans, car loans and personal loans, pre-payment charges apply. This is normally a per centage of the loan balance—for example, 2 per cent of the loan balance before pre-payment. The impact of a pre-payment is higher when closer to the start of the loan. If you pre-pay aggressively in the first quarter of your loan tenure, it can shave years off the loan.

But money is precious and in limited supply. Is there an optimum way to pre-pay? Not all money can be thrown towards pre-paying a loan while ignoring one's savings needs.

The 5 per cent Method

Here is the answer: a systematic pre-payment plan (SPP). It allows you to maximize the impact of pre-payment while keeping the costs of pre-payment at an optimal level, and still helping you get out of debt.

Table 14

Plan	Pre-Payment Amount	Total Pre-Payment	No. of Pre-Payments	Average Pre-Payment	Loan Tenure in Months	Interest Paid	Savings over Original Loan Interest	Ratio of Loan Pre-Paid (in per cent)	Pre-Payments as Ratio of Interest Saved (in per cent)
No Pre-Payment	₹0	₹0	0	₹0	240	₹4,303,587	–	–	–
One Extra EMI	₹38,765	₹659,004	17	₹38,765	203	₹3,521,578	₹782,009	13	84
5 per cent of Loan	₹250,000	₹2,500,000	10	₹250,000	111	₹1,777,683	₹2,525,904	50	99
5 per cent of Loan Balance	₹38,765–₹250,000	₹1,666,002	12	₹138,833	140	₹2,085,613	₹2,217,974	33	75
10 per cent of Loan	₹500,000	₹3,272,215	7	₹467,459	73	₹1,102,056	₹3,201,531	65	102
10 per cent of Loan Balance	₹38,765–₹500,000	₹2,333,278	9	₹259,253	105	₹1,395,109	₹2,908,478	47	80

Loan: ₹50 lakh at 7 per cent for 20 years. Every pre-payment happens at the start of each loan year. Pre-payment amounts are theoretical; minimum payment rules may apply. Simple interest and pre-payment charges as applicable and not accounted for in above calculations. Pre-payment charges vary from one loan to another.

Girish, a finance news editor with a newspaper, was about to take a home loan that he intended to pay off quickly. The 34-year-old Moneymooner planned to borrow ₹50 lakh at 7 per cent for 20 years. The interest on this loan was projected to be ₹43.03 lakh, and that was a lot. Girish was curious to know if there was an ideal way to plan his pre-payments to minimize interest.

He had the following options:

1. Pre-paying one extra EMI every year
2. Pre-paying 5–10 per cent of the loan every year
3. Pre-paying 5–10 per cent of the loan balance every year

All pre-payments are planned at the start of each loan year—i.e., once every 12 months.

On the basis of this table, Girish calculated that the sweet spot for him would be pre-paying 5 per cent of the loan balance every year. In the first year, he will need to start off with ₹2.5 lakh—5 per cent of ₹50 lakh—and taper down the pre-payments as the loan gets smaller.

He learnt he would have to finish with a twelfth and final pre-payment of ₹38,765, which is the value of his EMI. It is the bare minimum his bank will need him to pre-pay.

Here is why the 5 per cent reducing balance option will work best for him.

Firstly, it will shave off his interest from ₹43.03 lakh to ₹20.85 lakh. This will save him ₹22.17 lakh. He can utilize the money for his son's college education fund.

Secondly, it will close the loan in 140 months instead of 240—eight years and four months will be reduced from his loan.

Thirdly, as a borrower, you want your EMIs to carry the maximum load of your loan. EMIs are a must. Pre-payments are optional. In the highlighted plan, pre-payments help pay only 33 per cent of the loan. This is excellent. It means the EMIs did the heavy lifting of paying two-thirds of the loan. This will help Girish pour less of his savings into pre-payments. He can thus simultaneously focus on investing for his child's education.

Fourthly, the pre-payments will add up to ₹16.66 lakh, which will be lower than three other plans, except the one extra EMI plan, which was too slow for Girish's liking. He wanted a more aggressive approach.

The ₹16.66 lakh pre-paid amount is just 75 per cent of the interest savings of ₹22.17 lakh. This is the lowest of the five pre-payment plans in the table. This, too, is excellent. It means that for every ₹0.75 pre-paid, Girish saved ₹1 in interest. In the other cases, he has to pre-pay between ₹0.80 and ₹1.02 to save the same rupee. The lower this ratio, the more he would save as interest through pre-payments. It means that your savings are larger than the pre-payments made.

Home loan interest is one of the biggest things you will pay for in life. It will be sensible to take an active approach in cutting it down. The more you save, the more you have left for a comfortable retirement and other life goals.

Refinancing Your Home

Sometimes, you can get stuck with a high-interest home loan. The costs of this can be huge. You need a handle on it. One of the ways to do this is by refinancing your home. Refinancing— also called a loan balance transfer—is paying off an old loan with a new one. The new loan is offered to you at better terms, such as a lower interest rate. Refinancing can be done either by your current lender or a new one. The choice is yours. You must pick the one that works the best for you.

A loan of ₹50 lakh at 8 per cent for 20 years attracts interest of ₹50.37 lakh. If this loan is refinanced at 7 per cent, the interest falls to ₹43.03 lakh. This provides savings of over ₹7 lakh, which can be used for investments and for achieving various aspirations. There are situations when refinancing helps. There are situations when it does not. How can you tell?

Refinancing early in your loan tenure—typically in the first half—makes the maximum sense. Similarly, when more than half your loan balance is left, it makes more sense. During such periods, your EMIs focus mostly on interest payments. Therefore, a refinanced loan at a lower interest rate when most of your loan is still left will lead to heavy savings. Refinancing late makes little difference, since most of your interest is already paid off.

When there is a sizeable difference in your existing loan rate and rates being offered in the market, consider refinancing. A loan cheaper by around 50 basis points or more could lead to a shorter loan tenure, lower EMIs, lower interest payments and large long-term savings.

Older loans linked to previous benchmarks tend to be more expensive than new loans. Bank loans taken after 1 April 2016 are linked to the marginal costs of funds-based lending rate (MCLR). Loans before that date are benchmarked to the base rate. Bank loans issued after October 2019 are linked to the repo rate. Repo loans are now the cheapest.

For example, in January 2022, the lowest repo-linked home loan rate from a large government bank was 6.7 per cent. Its lowest MCLR-linked home loan was 7 per cent. And the base rate is still at 7.45 per cent. It makes sense to move away from older benchmarks for higher savings.

The other point about interest rates? Your credit score may have improved since the time you took your loan. For example, your score might have been 700 when you were paying 8.5 per cent on the loan. But your score might improve to 850 eventually and you might become eligible for a 6.5 per cent loan.

Next, consider the costs. Refinancing has a cost. When the projected savings from refinancing exceed the costs, you should consider refinancing. When you refinance with your own lender, the costs are lower and the paperwork, minimal. In most cases, you can put in the request for the transfer, pay the fee and be done with it. But refinancing to a new lender has higher costs and paperwork—typically, 0.2 to 0.4 per cent of the loan.

The new lender needs to establish your income, identity, and the legality of the property and its documents. The biggest costs here will be the processing fees, legal fees and memorandum of deposit (MOD) charges. MOD is a statutory cost of registering your loan agreement. It varies from one state to another.

There is another set of costs, which is interest. For the loan you are pre-closing, there will be a simple interest charge. For the new loan, there may be a pre-EMI interest charge applicable for a few days or weeks. Add up these costs. Deduct them from any interest savings you can generate from the new loan. If the difference is sizeable and is saving you a huge sum of money over the long run, then go for refinancing.

Beyond the interest rate, there are other considerations, such as digitized services, quality of customer service and proximity to the lender's branch. Like I had mentioned in 'Strengthen', your relationship with your lender is going to be long-term and needs to be frictionless. If you are displeased with your lender's services, go to one that you like—even if that means paying a slightly higher rate.

The Switch Hit

Joel, a Wealth Warrior and a financial advisor, decided to refinance his home in 2021. He had a balance of ₹45 lakh left on the loan and 13 years left to repay. He was paying a steep 7.8 per cent on it.

Joel's own lender, a bank, offered him 7 per cent on a refinancing deal. The switch would cost him ₹5,000. All he needed to do was fill out a form.

He also received an invitation from a home finance company, which was offering him 6.8 per cent. That switch, accounting for processing fees and MOD charges, would cost him ₹25,000. The paperwork will be more intense.

Joel did the math. Refinancing with his own bank could reduce his EMI and save ₹3.02 lakh over the remaining 13 years. It would also save him paperwork. With the new lender, he could save ₹3.58 lakh factoring in the costs and paperwork. Beyond the additional interest, he felt this was a better deal. The new lender's branch was closer to his home and had better digitized services—an added benefit in a pandemic.

Joel then tweaked the new lender's plan to include the Switch Hit. He would take the new loan, but instead of paying a lower EMI of ₹43,527, he would pay his old EMI of ₹45,987. As a result of this, a micro pre-payment of ₹2,730 will be built into each EMI. This accelerates his repayment, shaving off a full year off his loan. This cut his tenure from 156 to 144 months. It increased his savings by ₹2.1 lakh. It boosted his interest savings to ₹5.68 lakh.

Often, we refinance for lower EMIs. However, if our finances permit, it is good to keep the EMI pressure on. If you opt for a lower EMI, the time taken to repay your loan extends. Refinancing with Switch Hit, therefore, saves you both time and money.

Table 15

Particulars	Ongoing Loan	Refinance at 7 per cent with Same Lender	Refinance to New Lender at 6.8 per cent	Refinance to New Lender with Switch Hit
		Home Refinancing Options with Switch Hit		
Loan Left	₹4,500,000	₹4,500,000	₹4,500,000	₹4,500,000
Tenure Left (Months)	156	156	156	144
Rate (in per cent)	7.8	7.0	6.8	6.8
EMI	₹45,987	₹44,013	₹43,527	₹43,527
Interest	₹2,674,047	₹2,366,080	₹2,290,241	₹2,080,387
EMI Saving	–	1,974	2,460	0
Refinance Costs	–	₹5,000	₹25,000	₹25,000
Interest Savings after Costs	–	₹302,967	₹358,806	₹568,660
Net Monthly Savings	–	₹1,942	₹2,300	₹3,645

Pre-Pay or Invest?

If you have cash lying around, should you use it to pre-pay your loan or invest it for higher returns? This is a puzzling question in personal finance. There are many answers to it. Each is tied to a different situation. The broad question is this: how do you decide what is the best use for your surplus money?

Firstly, let us understand the matter of solvency. If your assets are greater than your liabilities, you are solvent. For example, you might have a home loan of ₹30 lakh, but your savings are ₹50 lakh. In the event of an emergency, such as a job loss, you have the capacity to end your loan with a single payment. This position of financial strength should encourage you to focus more on investment than pre-payment. There is another way to look at solvency. Even if your liabilities exceed your assets, if you can keep servicing your liabilities every month, you are solvent.

If your liabilities are big, you should focus on loan payments. High-interest loans, such as credit card debt, and large loans, such as home loans, should be repaid on priority.

My chats with bankers, friends and family members with mortgages revealed to me that home loans often get paid off in less than half their tenures. The pay-or-invest deliberations are not a big part of the average homeowner's decision process. They want to get out of debt fast.

But consider the pros and cons. For example, for a ₹50 lakh loan taken at 7 per cent for 20 years, if you pre-pay a single EMI (₹38,765) right at the start of the loan, your loan tenure reduces by three months and your interest by ₹1.15 lakh. But if you invest the same money in an index fund returning 12 per cent for 20 years, you would save ₹3.73 lakh. So why is the pre-payment better?

What 'better' is depends on what you want to achieve. You could focus on either debt payments or investments, or strike a balance between the two. We saw earlier in this chapter that the sweet spot for home loan pre-payment is 5 per cent of the loan balance once a year. You could go slower or faster on the basis of your situation or need. But looking at consumer behaviour, it can be argued that people want to be debt-free. It is a critical milestone for them on the path to Serenity. And so the appropriate amount of pre-payment should be done to achieve this objective.

Secondly, understand your priorities. Having adequate savings through an emergency fund, health and life insurance, and long-term investments are major priorities. If these needs have not been met, you should first focus on them. Once these needs are met, shift your focus to loan payments, while balancing it with your need to invest and be solvent.

Thirdly, do not be enamoured by tax deductions provided by your home loan. Pre-pay if your interest is high. This is especially important in the early stages of your loan. Your EMIs are money going out. They are the opposite of tax-saving investments such as PF, where the money remains with you. If you have spent ₹2 lakh a year on loan interest, and if you are in the 30 per cent tax slab, you have not saved 30 per cent of ₹2 lakh as a tax deduction. You have spent ₹2 lakh. The tax deduction is merely a balm to salve the outflow.

Fourthly, if you have limited liquidity but still want to pre-pay, you could simply increase your EMI by the small margin of a few thousand rupees. This acts as micro pre-payment. It also keeps your savings free for investment. Investing strengthens your finances. The micro pre-payments accelerate your debt payment. This way, you can focus on both investing and pre-paying. This is better than opting only for one.

Lastly, consider how you have planned for your life and finances. If you have, for example, retirement coming up, then pre-pay. You can even pre-close the loan. You do not need to take the liability to retirement.

Nominations and Handovers

> *I should get one of those signs that says,*
> *'One of these days, I'm gonna get organezized.'*
> *You mean 'organized'?*
> *Organezized. Organezized. It's a joke.*
>
> —Travis Bickle to Betsy in *Taxi Driver*

Serenity is also about knowing that our loved ones will be safe after us. Part of that process involves appointing nominees for your financial accounts. You also need to keep your family members informed about what you have signed them up for.

In August 2021, it was pointed out in Parliament that there are 8.13 crore unclaimed bank accounts in various commercial banks in India.[23] These accounts contained ₹24,356 crore.[24] A staggering 82 per cent of this money lay in 6.7 crore accounts with government banks, such as State Bank of India.

Furthermore, it was pointed out that unclaimed deposits with life insurance companies had ballooned to ₹24,586 crore by December 2020.[25] Out of this, 94 per cent belonged to unclaimed life insurance policies. It was also reported in 2019 that ₹26,497 crore lay unclaimed in dormant EPF accounts.[26]

This was money invested by people hoping for better futures. This money should have gone back to their families. The money could have helped pay for someone's loan, a child's college or a parent's cataract operation. Instead, it sits unclaimed in various accounts. In the worst-case scenario, it is not even accumulating interest.

There are three parts to this problem. The first is not appointing nominees to these accounts. In many of the above cases, the account holders may have passed away. Had they left nominees to their accounts, the nominees could have claimed the asset. Anyone can be a nominee—a family member or even a friend. They can authenticate their identities with the bank or insurance company. They can fill out some forms and claim the proceeds from the account. This is the easy part.

Secondly, if the accounts are not nominated, the nominees are faced with a world of bureaucratic pain. Without nomination, if the account holder has passed away, their family will have to produce proofs of identity, the death certificate and a legal heir certificate. A legal heir can be a spouse, children, parents or siblings of the account holder.

To get a legal heir certificate, one must apply with the local tehsildar or district civil court. The certificate could take weeks or months to be created. Till then, the process of claiming the account remains pending.

The worst is the third part of the problem: that the family does not know of these accounts at all. Often, financial services providers, such as banks, insurance providers and MF houses, contact the holders of dormant accounts only to find they died a long time ago.

The family members up to this point are in dark about the existence of these accounts. They have no clue about the account number or a passbook. They may not know where the insurance policy bond is kept. They do not know how much money there is in the account. The service provider may refuse to divulge any sensitive information about the account to the family. There is an impasse. The money gets stuck. Even if the family is going through a crisis due to the account holder's death, they may not be able to access the funds without wading through the bureaucracy.

As you work your way towards the apex of the 5S Pyramid, you should start streamlining your financial accounts. For starters, nominate everything properly.

The accounts should be updated and active. They should be linked to a working cell phone number and email address. They should be linked to your most current correspondence address. Aadhaar, where required, should be linked. The KYC should be updated as required.

Surplus bank accounts should ideally be closed. You can cut down on the clutter. By closing these accounts, you can reduce costs of account operation, such as debit card charges and minimum balance requirements. This way, you will also be removing blind spots—accounts you do not track—from being exploited by unscrupulous elements such as fraudsters.

Coming back to nominations, you can have one or multiple nominees for your accounts. You can even decide what per centage of an asset each nominee will receive. This can save your family from a lot of hassle in case of your untimely death.

Appointing nominees is especially important for high-value savings and investment accounts. It is most critical for government-run services such as PF where the documentation process can be cumbersome.

Some of your wealth may be tied to locker accounts, where you have stored gold and other precious items. Know about the locker usage rules and inform your family, too, so that they do not get locked out in your absence. If you are the single holder of this account, your nominee should be able to withdraw the locker's contents after submitting a death claim. For a joint account, the surviving account holder can access the locker only if it is in the 'either or survivor' mode. Without it, the locker may be sealed and a death claim may be required to access its contents. Therefore, you may want to check with your bank to understand how your locker can be operated by your dependents after your death.

If you believe that your family members can simply access your debit card or netbanking and withdraw the funds they need, you are wrong. Doing so would get them into trouble. It is a violation of terms for any person barring joint holders to use your bank account in any manner. Doing so can invite legal scrutiny. Also, there might be multiple heirs to your assets. Any one of them can initiate legal proceedings against the other accusing them of making an unauthorized dip into your funds.

Keep your family informed about what lays in store for them. Your next of kin—be it your spouse, parents or children—should know how to access funds, insurance policies and investments, should you not be present to do so yourself.

It is very important to share your financial information with your spouse. I mean everything: assets, insurance and debt. I learnt this when someone I had worked with professionally in another company died in a terrible accident. He was survived by a wife and a young child. They did not know anything about the details of his bank accounts. They were also in the dark about their loans, insurance and MFs.

Though insurance is full of technicalities and jargon, you must educate yourself as well as your family members about your coverage. They may need to make a claim on your policy in your absence.

My latest project on insurance is to set up an Electronic Insurance Account (EIA) and load all my policies—health, life and car—into it. I have given the login details to my wife. She is my nominee and beneficiary in all policies. If something happened to me, she would be able to access all my updated policies with a single login.

I also carbon copy my wife on all income tax filings. These capture my assets and liabilities.

Lastly, sort out your property affairs. Your assets need to pass in a debt-free manner, rid of any legal liabilities.

Sell the plot you will not build a house on. Dispose of the apartment you had bought for your non-resident child, who is not returning to India anymore. Above all, ensure your papers are in order and a trusted person can access them when the need arises.

The Need for a Will

Did you know that your nominees do not necessarily get to keep the asset you nominated them for? The nominee's job is to receive the asset after your death. However, the asset will pass to legal heirs as per the laws of succession. These laws vary from one religion to another.

The nominee, of course, can be a legal heir. But herein lies room for trouble. Your legal heirs may be embroiled in a dispute. When that happens, your assets may not be put to the use you had intended. This is trouble you will not be around to fix. You need to think of a solution beforehand.

While you might have reached the apex of the 5S Pyramid, for your family to be able to reach that level, you need to untangle the knotty ends of your financial affairs. One of the ways to minimize conflict is to draw up a will.

It is a document that states how you wish for your assets and liabilities to be managed and distributed following your death. At the heart of it, will-writing is not complicated. You, the testator, can take stock of your assets and liabilities. You can prepare a will by hand on an ordinary piece of paper.

Ensure you pack in as much personal details as possible into your will. This may keep ambiguities, misinterpretations and conflicts at bay. You may find a lawyer or an online service to help you with this.

The will must be signed by two witnesses who have seen you draw it up. The witnesses cannot be beneficiaries to the will. It is a good idea to get it registered, so that its validity cannot be challenged. Additionally, you can prepare a video recording of you reading out the will. These can reduce of dispute.

A will can be amended any number of times. You can put it away for safekeeping. The last will drawn up will be the one that can be upheld legally.

A will needs an executor—a trustworthy person you have chosen. The executor's role is ensuring your will is adhered to: your assets are given to your chosen heirs, your estate is liquidated and your affairs are brought to their intended ends.

If you have minor children, you will need to appoint a legal guardian for them until they turn 18. When fighting against unpleasant setbacks in the form of a protracted pandemic, a will makes a lot of sense. It becomes the safety net for your loved ones. It provides them a cushion against their loss and gives them the much-needed financial security in trying times.

Where a will is not drawn, the religious laws of succession come into play. Here, the law gets complex. Where the stakes are high, involve a lawyer. Your loved ones are counting on you.

A Systematic Kindness Plan

> *The greatness of a man is not in how much*
> *wealth he acquires, but in his integrity and his*
> *ability to affect those around him positively.*

—Bob Marley, singer

Thank you for reading till the end of this book. We are about to call it a wrap. It has taken over two years of intense work—some of it through the pains of the pandemic—to put this book together. If these lessons from the wild helped you defog the complexities of personal finance and sharpen your financial literacy, its job is done.

Over time, it has become increasingly easy to manage money. The tools and the knowledge are available online. Some of the financial mistakes that I made will not carry on to my daughter's generation.

Raniya, born in 2018, already has a bank account. I did not have one till I had started working. Her minor savings bank account with IndusInd Bank has her mother as the major. When a kith or kin gives her money, we put it into her account. Then we immediately buy an index MF for her. We intend to forget about it till she is an adult.

The only catch is that she will get full ownership of the account after she turns 18. Then, we will have no control on how she manages her money. At this age, she loves princesses and castles. The hope is she does not go out and buy one.

Recently, I have started working on giving back. I have come across good causes via professional and personal networks. I want to get Raniya involved and dedicate some of her time working for these causes. It feels good to give back and I want to keep increasing the amount that I give back every year.

I would like to end this chapter by drawing attention to the wider society around us. At any given point, it has problems begging for solutions.

The future belongs to India. The country has found its feet. As the CEO of a digital company, it particularly pleases me to see the wave of digitization creating world-class solutions for problems existing within every strata.

At the same time, we remain rooted in inequities and poverty. There is oppression on the basis of caste and creed. There is injustice and discrimination. It is our duty now to work towards solving these problems. We may not always be able to roll up our sleeves to get the job done, but we can at least aid those who do.

In this book, we have seen systematic savings, systematic investment, systematic pre-payment and systematic income. Now, I would like to propose a systematic kindness plan (SKP). The idea is very simple. In every place in this country, we have charities and volunteer groups working to solve local or national issues. The issues are diverse: feeding school kids, rehabilitating victims of abuse, raising funds for cancer care or sheltering street animals. The list goes on.

There is always a cause for which we can offer our support. At any given point of time, there are ongoing fundraisers to help such causes. We can step up as volunteers and provide our time, labour and whatever expertise we possess. We can also be financers and put our money to work for these causes.

Through SKP, we can find causes close to our heart. As individuals who have reached the apex of the 5S Pyramid, we should finance such causes. We must try to make sure that the problems that affect us deeply, as of today, are wiped out from this country.

Charitable organizations are typically registered entities with bank accounts. They are perennially looking to raise funds. Implementing an SKP, let us pledge to transfer a small amount to their accounts every month through netbanking or a payment app.

Environmental, social and governance issues are rapidly gaining prominence. Sides are being chosen. People are putting their money where their mouths are. By systematically financing causes, you will be investing for a better future. You can start with just one cause or extend support to many. Contribute to these causes regularly, just as you would contribute to a MF investment.

If you have been wondering about a possible financial angle to this, yes there is. Under Section 80G of the Income Tax Act[27], donating to qualified charities gets you tax deductions. These deductions can be 50 or 100 per cent of the donated amount, without or without limits.

Giving back through SKP can become part of your legacy—one of Serenity for yourself, your loved ones and even the society around you.

Between that and saving like a bee, securing yourself like an iron beetle, savouring life like a bowerbird, strengthening it like a beaver and enjoying the serenity of a long, healthy life like a bowhead whale, may you find financial fulfilment.

SELF-ASSESSMENT

ARE YOU THE ULTIMATE WEALTH WARRIOR?

Chapter 1—Savings Self-Assessment

Give yourself five points each time you respond with a 'yes' to the following pointers. Go step by step, adding up your points.

1. You save at least 10 per cent of your income before you spend it.
2. Give yourself five more points if you save 20 per cent.
3. Give yourself five more points if you save 30 per cent or more.
4. You have created an emergency fund worth three times your current monthly income.
5. Give yourself five more points if the fund is four to six times your current monthly income.
6. You understood how your interest income is taxed.
7. You have split your savings in bank, deposits or liquid funds for better returns and lower taxation.
8. You have checked that your bank is safe, well-capitalized and capable of paying back your deposit.
9. You have created a monthly budget.
10. You have automated your bill payments on netbanking or a payment app.

Total Save Score: ___/50

Chapter 2—Secure Self-Assessment

Give yourself five points for each task completed.

1. You have employer or group-provided health insurance.
2. You have boosted your health coverage by buying your own health policy.
3. Your personal health policy coverage is at least 50 per cent of your current annual income.
4. Give yourself another five points if it is over 100 per cent of your current annual income.
5. You have purchased a super top-up policy or critical illness policy to boost your health coverage.
6. All your dependent family members, such as parents, spouse and children have health insurance.
7. Every family member has health coverage of at least 50 per cent of your annual income.
8. You have bought term coverage.
9. The term coverage is at least 10 times your annual income.
10. Give yourself another five points if the term coverage is at least 20 times your income.
11. You have read and understood the terms and conditions, exclusions and waiting periods of your life and health policy.
12. You have made all declarations correctly, while filing your health and life insurance application forms.
13. You have not mixed life insurance with investment.
14. If you have a personal vehicle, you have purchased third party insurance.
15. You have home insurance for either structure, contents, fire, burglary, natural calamity.

Total Secure Score: ___/75

Chapter 3—Savour Self-Assessment

Give yourself five points for each task completed.

1. You pay your credit card bills and EMIs on time.
2. You have not had a late payment in the last 12 months.
3. You have not had a late payment ever.
4. You know your credit score.
5. You check your credit score regularly.
6. Your credit score is over 700.
7. Give yourself five more points if your score is over 750.
8. Give yourself five more points if your score is over 800.
9. Give yourself five more points if your score is over 850.
10. You are aware of your credit card rewards.
11. You are using credit card rewards to cut down expenses.
12. You can pay your dues without borrowing for them.
13. You can remain under 30 per cent of your credit card spending limits.
14. You pay your credit card dues in full every month.
15. You understand the difference between wants and needs.

Total Savour Score: ___/75

Chapter 4—Strengthen Self-Assessment

Give yourself five points for each task completed.

1. Your investments have clearly defined goals.
2. You have taken stock of your tax-deductible expenses.
3. You have optimized your 80C tax-saving investments for returns, risks and liquidity.
4. You know exactly when you need to liquidate any investment.
5. You understand the power of compounding.

6. You have calculated the right degree of risk for your investments.
7. Your long-term investments are performing at least as well as Nifty50 and Sensex.
8. Your long-term investments are performing better than Nifty50 and Sensex.
9. You have optimized commissions for better returns.
10. You have optimized your gold allocation.
11. You are investing in gold bonds, ETFs or mutual funds.
12. You are saving for home ownership.
13. Give yourself five points if you already own a home.
14. Your interest rate is optimal for your loan, income source and credit score.
15. Give yourself five points if you have paid off your home loan.

Total Strengthen Score: ___/75

Chapter 5—Serenity Self-Assessment

Give yourself five points for each task completed.

1. You have reviewed your savings, insurance coverage and investments needs at least once in the last year.
2. You have worked on an asset allocation plan for better risk-reward management.
3. You have a retirement age in mind.
4. You have calculated your retirement fund requirement.
5. Your current savings are on track to reach your retirement fund goal on time.
6. You have an idea about how you are going to draw a pension in retirement.
7. Your financial data is secure.
8. You have safely disposed of printed documents such as bank statements.

9. You have changed the passwords of your most sensitive accounts at least once in the last 12 months.
10. You file your tax returns on time.
11. You understand which tax regime works best for you.
12. You have a plan to pay off your current loans before time.
13. You have pre-paid a loan.
14. You have pre-closed a loan.
15. All your financial accounts are nominated.
16. Your next of kin how to access your accounts in case you were incapacitated or dead.
17. You have started working on a will.
18. You have a will.
19. You have donated to charitable causes in the last 12 months.
20. You optimize your donations for tax deductions.

Total Serenity Score: ___/100

The Ultimate Wealth Warrior Scorecard

Total Save Score: ___/50
Total Secure Score: ___/75
Total Savour Score: ___/75
Total Strengthen Score: ___/75
Total Serenity Score: ___/100
Total Score: ___/375

What's your score?

0–125:	It seems like you are an Early Jobber. You have made a good start to your financial life, but you have a long way to go to Serenity.
130–275:	You are probably a Moneymooner. Your financial life is shaping up well. You may want to refine your decisions for better results and accelerate your journey to Serenity.

280–345:   All hail the mighty Wealth Warrior! You have seen many ups and downs, and you have come a long way. You may be a few steps away from Serenity, so keep going.

350 and above: You have aced this test and you are the Ultimate Wealth Warrior. The bee, the beetle, the bowerbird, the beaver and the bowhead smile upon you. May your Serenity be everlasting.

ACKNOWLEDGEMENTS

The book is a compilation of our collective ideas and learnings at BankBazaar over the last decade. We have learnt from our experiences, involving each other and our millions of customers. Many special people have been involved in the compilation of this book. Thanks are due to them for their innovative ideas and their passion for helping consumers make the right financial decisions.

Navneeta, for driving our early conversations with publishers and helping us land a book contract. Nanda, for ensuring the manuscript stayed true to our cause of helping people make better financial decisions.

Abitha, for helping us compile the first draft and some of whose ideas we have retained in the final draft. Prince, for driving ideas such as the 5S Pyramid explained in the book.

Hemant, for being my co-author and keeping us on the straight and narrow to get the manuscript out the door. Dibakar at Rupa, for being our patient editor while deadlines whooshed past us during the pandemic.

Financial news editors—there have been many overs the years—who encouraged me to express myself in their newspapers, websites and TV channels. Your support has given us the confidence to produce this book.

Reha and Raniya, for letting me do what I do. Rati and Arjun, for putting us on this wild, amazing ride running BankBazaar. Dr Rekha and Jai, my parents who have shown us the way and supported the BankBazaar journey.

To the team at BankBazaar, thanks for making this possible with your hard work. Our mission is to create financial literacy and offer high-quality choices. God willing, the best is yet to come, so let us enjoy the journey.

NOTES

Introduction

1. Ethiraj, Govindraj, '97% Indians Poorer Post-Covid; Steady Fall in Salaried Jobs: Mahesh Vyas', *Business Standard*, 29 May 2021, https://bit.ly/3OTiMpp. Accessed on 2 August 2022.
2. 'COVID-19 to Plunge Global Economy into Worst Recession Since World War II', The World Bank, 8 June 2020, https://bit.ly/3Q9OnnJ. Accessed on 2 August 2022.
3. Kochhar, Rakesh, 'In the Pandemic, India's Middle Class Shrinks and Poverty Spreads While China Sees Smaller Changes', Pew Research Center, 18 March 2021, https://pewrsr.ch/3boHn7H. Accessed on 2 August 2022.
4. Ibid.
5. Kedrosky, Davis, 'The Long Decline of Global Interest Rates', *Berkeley Economic Review*, 30 March 2020, https://bit.ly/3OTju63. Accessed on 2 August 2022.
6. Maslow, A.H., 'A Theory of Human Motivation', *Psychological Review*, Vol. 50, No. 4, 1943, pp. 370–96, https://bit.ly/2IvvaLv. Accessed on 2 August 2022.
7. Ibid.
8. Ibid.
9. Ibid.
10. Ibid.
11. Ibid.
12. '76% Indians Not Financially Literate, Says S&P Survey', *Financial Express*, 15 December 2015, https://bit.ly/3bvwC3k. Accessed on 2 August 2022.

13. Klapper, Leora, Annamaria Lusardi and Peter van Oudheusden, 'Financial Literacy around the World: Insights from the Standard and Poor's Ratings Services Global Financial Literacy Survey', https://bit.ly/3SxsIHr. Accessed on 5 October 2022.

14. 'Only 27% Indians Are Financially Literate: Sebi's Garg', *Financial Express*, 24 November 2020, https://bit.ly/3vyLncE. Accessed on 2 August 2022.

Chapter I: Savings and the Building Blocks of Your Financial Life

1. '80% Adult Indians Now Have Bank Accounts', *Financial Express*, 21 April 2018, https://bit.ly/3RGrbOP. Accessed on 31 August 2022.

2. 'Number of Adult Indians with Bank Accounts Rises to 80%', *The Economic Times*, 20 April 2018, https://bit.ly/3RWelMD. Accessed on 19 September 2022.

3. RBI Bulletin June 2020, Reserve Bank of India, https://bit.ly/3C4PMYL. Accessed on 16 August 2022.

4. Ibid.

5. Rao, Nivedita, 'Who Is Paying for India's Healthcare?', *The Wire*, 14 April 2018, https://bit.ly/2jsUpSQ. Accessed on 16 August 2022.

6. 'Gross NPA Ratio Improves to 9.1% as of September-End: RBI', *The Hindu*, 24 December 2019, https://bit.ly/3Ajb4Qb. Accessed on 16 August 2022.

7. 'Banks' Gross NPAs Ratio Falls to Six-Year Low in March: RBI', *Mint*, 30 June 2022, https://bit.ly/3cES46C. Accessed on 2 September 2022.

8. Iyer, Aparna, 'How Do Indian Banks Fare against Their Other Emerging Market Friends?', *Mint*, https://bit.ly/3TsP6CX. Accessed on 31 August 2022.

9. 'PMC's HDIL Loan at 73% of Total Loan Book, Says Ex-MD Thomas in Letter to RBI', *Mint*, 29 September 2019, https://bit.ly/3fpxatn. Accessed on 28 September 2022.

10. Rebello, Joel, 'RBI Doubles Withdrawal Limit for PMC Depositors', *The Economic Times*, 19 June 2020, https://bit.ly/3B4jlZD. Accessed on 2 September 2022.

11. 'Profile', Deposit Insurance and Credit Guarantee Corporation, https://bit.ly/3CcSV91. Accessed on 16 August 2022.

12. 'Cabinet Clears Amendment to DICGC Act;' Bank Depositors, to Get Coverage of up to Rs 5 Lakh', ETBFSI.com, 29 July 2021, https://bit.ly/3UMR54J. Accessed on 2 September 2022.

13. 'Main Claims Settled during the year 2020-21 (Till 31.05.2021)', Deposit Insurance and Credit Guarantee Corporation, https://bit.ly/3B4Vol0. Accessed on 2 September 2022.

14. Roy, Anup, 'Aadhaar, PAN Cards Mandatory for Opening Bank Accounts, Says RBI', *Business Standard*, 21 April 2018, https://bit.ly/3PzYAt2. Accessed on 16 August 2022.

15. 'Governor's Statement, May 5, 2021', Reserve Bank of India, https://bit.ly/3QsVJ6i. Accessed on 16 August 2022.

16. 'Quarterly Estimates of Households' Financial Assets and Liabilities', RBI Bulletin, June 2020, https://bit.ly/3QJQxL1. Accessed on 16 August 2022.

17. 'One Fish Pen', One Red Paperclip, https://bit.ly/3As0XcZ. Accessed on 17 August 2022.

18. 'One Red Paperclip', One Red Paperclip, https://bit.ly/2YmA7wt. Accessed on 19 September 2022.

19. 'One Instant Party', One Red Paperclip, https://bit.ly/3cVisJF. Accessed on 7 October 2022.

Chapter II: Secure: Protecting Yourself against Life's Vagaries

1. Bottomry | Maritime Law, Britannica, https://bit.ly/3SW4LdH. Accessed on 17 August 2022.

2. Sengupta, Rajit, 'Private Hospitals Grow More Expensive Even as Insurance Coverage Remain Low: NSSO', Down to Earth, 23 July 2020, https://bit.ly/3A2Esdh. Accessed on 17 August 2022.

3. Ibid.

4. Ibid.
5. 'India's Per Capita Income Remains Below Pre-Covid Level in 2021-22', *Business Standard*, 1 June 2022, https://bit.ly/3CZZdZZ. Accessed on 7 October 2022.
6. 'India's Per Capita Income Remains Below Pre-COVID-19 Level at Rs 91,481: Govt', *Business Today*, 31 May 2022, https://bit.ly/3Qu3pVH. Accessed on 17 August 2022.
7. Sengupta, Rajit, 'Private Hospitals Grow More Expensive Even as Insurance Coverage Remain Low: NSSO', Down to Earth, 23 July 2020, https://bit.ly/3A2Esdh. Accessed on 17 August 2022.
8. Ibid.
9. Ibid.
10. Sharma, Yogima Seth, 'Nearly 30% of Indian Population Don't Have Any Health Insurance: Survey', *The Economic Times*, 29 October 2021, https://bit.ly/3r6qDpR. Accessed on 26 September 2022.
11. Ibid.
12. Nizamuddin, Md, 'Today is National Cancer Awareness Day 2020: Crowdfunding Throws a Lifeline to Cancer-Hit', *The Hans India*, 7 November 2020, https://bit.ly/3QwWvze. Accessed on 17 August 2022.
13. Insurance Regulatory and Development Authority of India, Annual Report 2020–21, https://bit.ly/3psRfkg. Accessed on 18 August 2022.
14. Ibid.
15. Ibid.
16. Ibid.
17. Persistency of Life Insurance Policies (Based on Number of Policies), https://bit.ly/3K0BJph. Accessed on 18 August 2022.
18. Ibid.
19. Ibid.
20. 'Brief Write Up on Aam Aadmi Mohalla Clinic', Government of NCT of Delhi, https://bit.ly/3wc742D. Accessed on 18 August 2022.

21. 'Economic Survey 2021–22, Ministry of Finance, Government of India, https://bit.ly/33AiRb0. Accessed on 7 October 2022.
22. Ibid.
23. Ibid.
24. 'Current Health Expenditure (% of GDP) - India, China, United States, France', The World Bank, https://bit.ly/3x1Lez2. Accessed on 7 October 2022.
25. 'Domestic Private Health Expenditure (% of Current Health Expenditure)- India, China, United States, France', The World Bank, https://bit.ly/3QqzblI. Accessed on 7 October 2022.
26. 'Current Health Expenditure (% of GDP) - India, China, United States, France', The World Bank, https://bit.ly/3x1Lez2. Accessed on 7 October 2022.
27. Ibid.
28. Dubey, Jyotindra, 'Healthcare Inflation Is Increasing at Double the Rate of Overall Inflation', *India Today*, 5 July 2019, https://bit.ly/2FTIp8y. Accessed on 18 August 2022.
29. 'Reduce your Premiums by 20% – Zone Based Health Insurance', JagoInvestor, 7 October 2019, https://bit.ly/3Au6DmA. Accessed on 18 August 2022.
30. Conditions apply. Insurance premium varies as per factors like age, health, income, coverage size, riders, add-ons and other factors determined by regulatory authorities and insurance sellers.
31. 'Deductibles in a Health Insurance Plan', BankBazaar, https://bit.ly/3V0g1WL. Accessed on 7 October 2022.
32. Dubey, Navneet, 'Is Treatment for Mental Health Covered by Insurance Policies?' *Mint*, 12 August 2021, https://bit.ly/3K1J9IG. Accessed on 18 August 2022.
33. 'Insurance Regulatory and Development Authority (Protection of Policyholders' Interests) Regulations, 2002', Insurance Regulatory and Development Authority of India, 26 April 2002, https://bit.ly/3wdyuoK. Accessed on 18 August 2022.
34. 'Star Health and St. Judes to Provide Health and Accident Cover

to Young Cancer Survivors', The CSR Journal, 22 November 2021, https://bit.ly/3c6M1aD. Accessed on 18 August 2022.

35. Maiti, Meghna, 'IRDA Proposes 20% Cap on Insurance Agents' Commission', Outlook, 27 August 2022, https://bit.ly/3SYUD2p. Accessed on 1 November 2022.

36. 'Free-Look Period', Insurance Regulatory and Development Authority of India, https://bit.ly/3BRQjwA. Accessed on 19 September 2022.

37. Dhawan, Sunil, 'How the 3-Year Clause Impacts Life Insurance Claims', *The Economic Times*, 22 November 2018, https://bit.ly/3wgg9Y1. Accessed on 18 August 2022; 'Applicability of Provisions of Sec 45 of Insurance Act 1938 in Various Scenarios', 28 October 2015, https://bit.ly/3QWIQkz. Accessed on 18 August 2022.

38. 'Guidelines for Standardization of General Terms and Clauses in Health Insurance Policy Contracts', 11 June 2020, Insurance Regulatory and Development Authority of India, https://bit.ly/3duhQKS. Accessed on 18 August 2022.

Chapter III: Savour: Enjoying Your Money

1. Shaheed, G., 'On the Trail of the Bowerbird', *Frontline*, 1 March 2019, https://bit.ly/3fnxfgW. Accessed on 27 September 2022.

2. Bond, Casey, '5 Refreshing Lessons from Elizabeth Warren's Personal Finance Book', *Huffpost*, 24 April 2019, https://bit.ly/2Wi2krj. Accessed on 19 August 2022.

3. Clegg, Dai, 'MoSCoW Method', https://bit.ly/3CZgXEZ. Accessed on 7 October 2022.

4. 'What Is the Eisenhower Matrix?', Eisenhower, https://bit.ly/2wDTdCv. Accessed on 7 October 2022.

5. 'Compare and Apply Personal Loan Online', BankBazaar, https://bit.ly/3Cjt67j. Accessed on 20 August 2022.

6. Shetty, Mayur, '"Buy Now Pay Later Loans" to Disrupt Market', *The Times of India*, 21 September 2021, https://bit.ly/3TLLpbF. Accessed on 7 October 2021.

7. 'He Opened 20 Bank Accounts... (and Got 12 Million Point...)', Nas Daily, Facebook, 9 May 2021, https://bit.ly/3R0f7XY. Accessed on 20 August 2022.

8. 'Chris Hutchins: How I Travel the World for Free with Credit Card Points', Marriage, Kids and Money | YouTube, 4 November 2021, https://bit.ly/3PDF1ja. Accessed on 20 August 2022.

9. Leonhardt, Megan, 'This 34-Year-Old Just Hit over 10 Million Credit Card Points. Here's How He Does It', CNBC, 29 May 2019, https://cnb.cx/3QSPA30. Accessed on 20 August 2022.

10. 'Chris Hutchins: How I Travel the World', Marriage, Kids and Money | YouTube, 4 November 2021, https://bit.ly/3x1Os5J. Accessed on 7 October 2022.

11. Mikkelson, David, 'Black American Express Card', Snopes, 21 April 2011, https://bit.ly/3QWp9cW. Accessed on 20 August 2022.

12. 'Master Direction–Credit Card and Debit Card–Issuance and Conduct Directions, 2022', Reserve Bank of India, 21 April 2022, https://bit.ly/3tkOseH. Accessed on 20 August 2022.

13. 'EMI Calculator for Personal Loan', BankBazaar, https://bit.ly/3Kb6yaB. Accessed on 20 August 2022.

Chapter IV: Strengthen: Growing Your Money

1. 'Role of Keystone Species in an Ecosystem', *National Geographic*, https://bit.ly/3ycPpca. Accessed on 4 October 2022.

2. 'BankBazaar Aspiration Index 2021: India Craves for Community', BankBazaar, https://bit.ly/3SAZWpp. Accessed on 4 October 2022.

3. Shetty, Adhil, 'Why You Should Step Up Your SIPs Every Year'! BankBazaar, 27 September 2017, https://bit.ly/3T3ye5n. Accessed on 21 August 2022.

4. 'Tax Saving Schemes', BankBazaar, https://bit.ly/3wjbAwg. Accessed on 21 August 2022.

5. 'Section 80C Deductions', BankBazaar, https://bit.ly/3PE0atG. Accessed on 21 August 2022.

6. Jain, Balwant, 'Income Tax Rebate Under Section 87A for Income Up To ₹5 Lakh-Explained', *Mint*, 17 April 2021, https://bit.ly/3ClDfQL. Accessed on 21 August 2022.
7. 'Section 80GG', BankBazaar, https://bit.ly/3pv5gOt. Accessed on 21 August 2022.
8. 'Section 80E', BankBazaar, https://bit.ly/3wkmBgM. Accessed on 21 August 2022.
9. 'Section 80DD', BankBazaar, https://bit.ly/3Ae75En. Accessed on 21 August 2022.
10. 'Equity Linked Savings Scheme', BankBazaar, https://bit.ly/3ADhzhK. Accessed on 21 August 2022.
11. 'EPF-Employees' Provident Fund', BankBazaar, https://bit.ly/3T5HYfz. Accessed on 21 August 2022.
12. 'PPF-Public Provident Fund', BankBazaar, https://bit.ly/3BjLHxQ. Accessed on 15 September 2022.
13. Motiani, Preeti, 'EPF Contributions Exceeding Rs 2.5 lakh? You Will Now Have Two PF Accounts', *The Economic Times*, 4 September 2021 https://bit.ly/3QXTGHk. Accessed on 21 August 2022.
14. 'Tax Benefits on Home Loan', BankBazaar, https://bit.ly/3Aj5YDw. Accessed on 21 August 2022.
15. 'SSY - Sukanya Samriddhi Yojana', BankBazaar, https://bit.ly/3PCJgMd. Accessed on 23 August 2022.
16. 'SCSS-Senior Citizen Savings Scheme — SCSS', BankBazaar, https://bit.ly/3QYhYRj. Accessed on 21 August 2022.
17. 'Fund Performance', Association of Mutual Funds in India, https://bit.ly/3ACHera. Accessed on 21 August 2022.
18. 'Mutual Fund Rolling Returns versus Equity: ELSS Category', AdvisorKhoj, https://bit.ly/3AgeUcN. Accessed on 21 August 2022.
19. Lioudis, Nick, 'The Inverse Relationship between Interest Rates and Bond Prices', Investopedia, 16 May 2022, https://bit.ly/2RM0N7a. Accessed on 21 August 2022.
20. 'Infosys Bonus', *The Economic Times*, https://bit.ly/3ClrB8F.

Accessed on 21 August 2022.

21. Anand, Kshitij, and Neha Alawadhi, '25 Years Since Listing! 100 Infosys Shares Bought in 1993 Could Have Turned You into a Crorepati', MoneyControl, 20 June 2018, https://bit.ly/2l7t7m0. Accessed on 21 August 2022.

22. 'Infosys Dividend History', *The Economic Times*, https://bit.ly/3A4yybu. Accessed on 21 August 2022.

23. Reid, Jim, et al., *The Age of Disorder*, Deutsche Bank Research, 8 September 2020, https://bit.ly/3CncbRq. Accessed on 22 August 2022.

24. Ibid.

25. 'Average Investor Blown Away by Market Turmoil in 2018', Dalbar, https://bit.ly/2G1Rgpn. Accessed on 22 August 2022.

26. 'Circular', Securities and Exchange Board of India, 6 October 2017, https://bit.ly/3KaF3xU. Accessed on 22 August 2022.

27. Tully, Shawn, 'Meet the "Trillion Dollar Club": How 5 Companies Took over the S&P 500—and Likely Your Portfolio', *Fortune*, 13 November 2021, https://bit.ly/3wm5paz. Accessed on 22 August 2022.

28. 'Top Companies in India by Market Capitalization–BSE', MoneyControl, https://bit.ly/2m0Xpal. Accessed on 22 August 2022.

29. Kriplani, Jash, 'A 100 NFOs in 2021 and Counting: Why Are Mutual Funds Rolling out Too Many New Schemes?', MoneyControl, 18 November 2021, https://bit.ly/3ygzB89. Accessed on 22 august 2022.

30. 'SPIVA® India Scorecard | Summary', S&P Dow Jones Indices, https://bit.ly/3R1NkXq. Accessed on 22 August 2022.

31. Madia, Chirag, 'Large-Cap Equity Schemes Lagged Benchmark Returns', Rediff.com, 16 April 2021, https://bit.ly/3T6LRAU. Accessed on 22 August 2022.

32. 'SPIVA® India Scorecard | Summary', S&P Dow Jones Indices, https://bit.ly/3R1NkXq. Accessed on 22 August 2022.

33. Fernando, Jason, 'FAANG Stocks', Investopedia, 29 June 2022,

https://bit.ly/3ADQhbm. Accessed on 22 August 2022.

34. Dhawan, Sunil, 'India's First ETF Based on Nifty 50 Equal Weight Index Launched – Check how it differs', *Financial Express*, 19 October 2021, https://bit.ly/3KdkYqR. Accessed on 22 August 2022.

35. 'SPIVA® India Scorecard | Summary', S&P Dow Jones Indices, https://bit.ly/3R1NkXq. Accessed on 22 August 2022.

36. Ibid.

37. Chen, James, 'Alpha: What It Means in Investing, With Examples', 19 March 2022, Investopedia, https://bit.ly/2oPp52X. Accessed on 22 August 2022.

38. Finney, Denise, 'A Brief History of Credit Rating', Agencies, Investopedia, 31 January 2022, https://bit.ly/3C1COcM. Accessed on 15 September 2022.

39. Tretina, Kat and Benjamin Curry, 'Understanding Junk Bonds', *Forbes Advisor*, 21 October 2021, https://bit.ly/3PF1dtt. Accessed on 22 August 2022.

40. 'Cost Inflation Index Table', BankBazaar, https://bit.ly/3PEdiza. Accessed on 22 August 2022.

41. 'Negative Real Interest Rate: Why Interest on Bank Deposits of Some Senior Citizens Should Be Exempted from Tax', MoneyLife, 25 September 2021, https://bit.ly/3pDxXZz. Accessed on 22 August 2022.

42. 'All Debt Funds', Value Research, https://bit.ly/3AaXfmM. Accessed on 22 August 2022.

43. 'Dividend History', MoneyControl, https://bit.ly/3dGt673. Accessed on 22 August 2022.

44. 'Axis Bluechip Fund - Direct Plan – IDCW', MoneyControl, https://bit.ly/3tp69Kq. Accessed on 22 August 2022.

45. Ibid.

46. D'Souza, Deborah, 'Top 10 Countries with the Highest Demand for Gold Jewelry', Investopedia, 29 November 2021, https://bit.ly/3pB1AKU. Accessed on 22 August 2022.

47. 'India Spends Record $55.7 Billion on Gold Imports in 2021', *The*

Times of India, 4 January 2022, https://bit.ly/3wkFuQM. Accessed on 22 August 2022.

48. Mathew, George, 'In a Sign of Distress, Gold Loans Soar 77% in 12 Months up to July', *The Indian Express*, 3 September 2021, https://bit.ly/3dIouNQ. Accessed on 22 August 2022.

49. 'Gold Rates Historical Data for India', BankBazaar, https://bit.ly/2QU1N8j. Accessed on 22 August 2022.

50. Ibid.

51. 'Commodities: Gold', Value Research, https://bit.ly/3trzbJ2. Accessed on 7 October 2022.

52. 'All-India House Price Index (HPI) for Q4:2020-21', Reserve Bank of India, 21 June 2021, https://bit.ly/3AEdbzc. Accessed on 22 August 2022.

53. 'Institutionalising the Rental Housing Market in India-2019', Khaitan and Co. | Knight Frank, https://bit.ly/3AdBT8j. Accessed on 22 August 2022.

54. Aiyappa, Manu, 'Housing Rents Fall 10-15% in Karnataka; Many Tenants Yet to Return', *The Times of India*, 16 June 2021, https://bit.ly/3ADblPb. Accessed on 22 August 2022; 'Monthly Rentals in Co-Living Properties Down 10-25% Post Covid: Report', *Mint*, 24 December 2021, https://bit.ly/3AgO8ki. Accessed on 22 August 2022; Mujawar, Madeeha, 'COVID-19 Impact: Mumbai Rental Prices Fall By up to 25%', CNBC TV18, 4 June 2020, https://bit.ly/3KaVfzc. Accessed on 22 August 2022.

55. 'Institutionalising The Rental Housing Market in India-2019', Khaitan and Co. | Knight Frank, https://bit.ly/3AdBT8j. Accessed on 22 August 2022.

56. Shetty, Adhil, 'REITs Allow You to Own a Tiny Slice of Prime Commercial Real Estate', Money9, 3 July 2021, https://bit.ly/3AgIxub. Accessed on 22 August 2022.

57. 'Individual Housing Loans: Rationalisation of Risk-Weights and Loan to Value (LTV) Ratios', Reserve Bank of India, 7 June 2017, https://bit.ly/3QKQDl2. Accessed on 15 September 2022.

58. Ramakrishnan, L., 'Loans on the Till Roll', *The Indian Express*, 18

September 2011, https://bit.ly/3T9zpQG. Accessed on 22 August 2022.

59. Dubey, Navneet, 'RBI Relaxes LTV Rules to Make Home Loans Taken Till March 2022 Cheaper', *The Economic Times*, 9 October 2020, https://bit.ly/3AG2xIp. Accessed on 22 August 2022.

60. 'Documents Required for Home Loan', BankBazaar, https://bit.ly/3fUJlPm. Accessed on 22 August 2022.

61. 'Current RBI Bank Interest Rates 2022', BankBazaar, https://bit.ly/3TrMqEj. Accessed on 22 August 2022.

62. 'External Benchmark Based Lending', Reserve Bank of India, 4 September 2019, https://bit.ly/2k3rDfN. Accessed on 22 August 2022.

63. 'Ibid.

64. 'Since 2015, RBI Has Cut Rates by 150 Bps But Not Much Has Reached You', *The Economic Times*, 6 October 2016, https://bit.ly/3wmBaAj. Accessed on 22 August 2022.

65. Kaur, Avneet, 'Can Both Husband and Wife Claim Income Tax Deduction for Home Loan Repayment?', *Mint*, 19 September 2020, https://bit.ly/3dOpnUW. Accessed on 22 August 2022.

66. 'Loan EMI Calculator', BankBazaar, https://bit.ly/3wpDYwB. Accessed on 23 August 2022.

67. @MorningBrew, Twitter, 28 October 2021, 1.06 a.m., https://bit.ly/3wnKyni. Accessed on 23 August 2022.

68. Fox, Matthew, 'A Crypto Wallet Shows an Investor Made an $8,000 Shiba Inu Coin Purchase Last Year. Today, It Is Worth $5.7', Markets Insider, 29 October 2021, https://bit.ly/3c8wwiN. Accessed on 23 August 2022.

69. Shetty, Adhil, 'Crypto Currency Finds Validity', *The Telegraph*, 2 February 2022, https://bit.ly/3PIVzq0. Accessed on 23 August.

70. 'Taxing Crypto Doesn't Mean It Is Legalised: FM', *The Times of India*, 12 February 2022, https://bit.ly/3chJPNB. Accessed on 23 August 2022.

71. 'India's Own Digital Currency to be Introduced in Phased Manner, RBI Informs Innovation *Hub*', News18, 27 May 2022,

https://bit.ly/3xn7bZO. Accessed on 15 September 2022.

Chapter V: Serenity and the Apex

1. Robson, David, 'The Secrets of Living to 200 Years Old', BBC, 16 September 2015, https://bbc.in/3dDHrkC. Accessed on 23 August 2022.
2. 'Lie Expectancy at Birth (Years)', World Health Organization, https://bit.ly/3eGjIAO. Accessed on 15 Sepetmber 2022.
3. 'Life Expectancy (from Birth) in India from 1800 to 2020', Statista, https://bit.ly/3cb6QlB. Accessed on 23 August 2022.
4. 'Child Mortality Rate (Under Five Years Old) in India from 1880 to 2020', Statista, https://bit.ly/3QLIxJK. Accessed on 23 August 2022.
5. Engle, Jeremy, 'Would You Want to Live to 200?', *The New York Times*, 30 April 2020, https://nyti.ms/3ymaQrf. Accessed on 6 October 2022.
6. Stepler, Renee, 'World's Centenarian Population Projected to Grow Eightfold by 2050', Pew Research Center, 21 April 2016, https://pewrsr.ch/2vsqqkc. Accessed on 23 August 2022.
7. Ibid.
8. 'Age and Cancer', Cancer Research UK, https://bit.ly/3wnNyAl. Accessed on 23 August 2022.
9. Mitchell, Olivia S., 'Why Low Interest Rates Hurt Retirees', *Knowledge at Wharton*, 6 October 2020, https://whr.tn/3Aj6ZuX. Accessed on 23 August 2022.
10. 'Tax Benefits under NPS', Protean, https://bit.ly/3QPYIWM. Accessed on 23 August 2022.
11. 'Applicable Fees and Charges Levied on NPS Subscribers', National Pension System Trust, https://bit.ly/3TcrC4E. Accessed on 23 August 2022.
12. 'Investment Options under NPS', https://bit.ly/30aCVhz. Accessed on 23 August 2022.
13. 'Initiation of Online Exit Request by eNPS Subscriber and Verification & Authorization of Exit Request by POP', NSDL

Technology, Trust and Reach, https://bit.ly/3AHSUcg. Accessed on 23 August 2022.

14. 'No Annuity Rider, NPS Subscribers Get ₹5 Lakh Exit Option', *The Hindu*, 16 April 2021, https://bit.ly/3Clvvyp. Accessed on 23 August 2022.

15. 'More Indians Fall Prey to Online Fraud, Millennials Suffer the Most', *The Economic Times*, 25 July 2021, https://bit.ly/3QVYXze. Accessed on 23 August 2022.

16. Upadhyay, Ashok, '229 Banking Frauds a Day in 2020-21, Recovery Rate Below 1%, RBI Says in RT I Reply', *India Today* 15 December 2021, https://bit.ly/3KtfkkN. Accessed on 23 August 2022.

17. 'Top 200 Most Common Passwords', Nordpass, https://bit.ly/3QN4t7q. Accessed on 23 August 2022.

18. 'How Secure Is My Password?', Security.org, https://bit.ly/3R24VOP. Accessed on 23 August 2022.

19. '83% Organizations in India Saw Rise in Phishing Attacks During Pandemic', *Mint*, 20 September 2021, https://bit.ly/3R7YPwB. Accessed on 23 August 2022.

20. Bagchi, Sohini, 'How India Is Using AI/ML against Tax Evaders and Frauds', CXOToday.com, 18 August 2020, https://bit.ly/3AkbOo9. Accessed on 23 August 2022.

21. 'Interest on Tax Payable u/s 234A, 234B, 234C', TaxGuru, https://bit.ly/3TwGavc. Accessed on 23 August 2022; 'Interest Payable by the Taxpayer under the Income-Tax Act', Income Tax Department, https://bit.ly/3Cq2n9l. Accessed on 23 August 2022.

22. 'Tax Calculator', BankBazaar, https://bit.ly/3QQ6EHy. Accessed on 23 August 2022.

23. 'Bank-Wise Details of Unclaimed Deposits Reported to RBI', Imgur, https://bit.ly/3Uhvoue. Accessed on 19 September 2022.

24. 'Unclaimed Deposits', Ministry of Finance, Government of India, https://bit.ly/3KgmVmp. Accessed on 23 August 2022.

25. Ibid.

26. Zaidi, Babar, 'Rs 82,000 Crore Lying in Unclaimed Bank A/Cs,

Life Insurance, Mutual Funds, PF: How to Get Your Money Back', *The Economic Times*, 6 July 2021, https://bit.ly/3wnvxlk. Accessed on 23 August 2022.

27. 'Section 80G', BankBazaar, https://bit.ly/3R4XaI4. Accessed on 23 August 2022.

www.ingramcontent.com/pod-product-compliance
Lightning Source LLC
Chambersburg PA
CBHW021507210326
41599CB00012B/1160